DATE DUE

DEMCO 38-296

MUSIC IN CANADA

MUSIC RESEARCH AND INFORMATION GUIDES
VOLUME 20
GARLAND REFERENCE LIBRARY OF THE HUMANITIES
VOLUME 1823

MUSIC RESEARCH AND INFORMATION GUIDES

DANCE
An Annotated Bibliography,
1965-1982
by Fred Forbes

THE TRADITIONAL MUSIC
OF BRITAIN AND IRELAND
A Research and
Information Guide
by James Porter

BAROQUE MUSIC
A Research and
Information Guide
by John H. Baron

MUSIC AND WAR
A Research and
Information Guide
by Ben Arnold

TUDOR MUSIC
A Research and
Information Guide
by Richard Turbet

THE RECORDER
A Guide to Writings about
the Instrument for Players
and Researchers
by Richard Griscom
and David Lasocki

MUSIC IN CANADA
A Research and
Information Guide
by Carl Morey

Music in Canada
A Research and Information Guide

Carl Morey

Garland Publishing, Inc.
New York and London
1997

Library of Congress Cataloging-in-Publication Data

Morey, Carl.
    Music in Canada : a research and information guide / Carl Morey.
       p.   cm. — (Music research and information guides ; v. 20)
Garland reference library of the humanities ; v. 1823)
    Includes indexes.
    ISBN 0-8153-1603-8 (alk. paper)
    1. Music—Canada—History and criticism—Bibliography.   I. Title.
II. Series: Music research and information guides ; vol. 20.   III. Series:
Garland reference library of the humanities ; vol. 1823.
ML120.C2M67   1997
016.78'0971—dc20   96-29156
                                           CIP
                                         MN

Printed on acid-free, 250-year-life paper
Manufactured in the United States of America

Contents

Preface

In 1985, George Proctor began work on an annotated bibliography on music in Canada. Within a few months he suffered a heart attack and died shortly thereafter. His work was briefly taken up by his assistant, David Lenson, but for various reasons was eventually abandoned. Professor Proctor projected a bibliography with at least twice the number of entries as are contained in this present *Research and Information Guide*. My view, set out more fully in the *Introduction*, is that the list should be much more selective, but I am grateful to the Proctor family, and to Mr. Lenson, for making available to me much of the material on which Professor Proctor was working. The final compilation is entirely mine, but I acknowledge the usefulness of Professor Proctor's original concept and outlines in developing my own project.

Many people have offered me much assistance in the preparation of this work. Claude Beaudry (l'Université Laval), Marlene Wehrle (National Library of Canada), William Sgrazzutti (University of Calgary), and Kirsten Walsh (University of British Columbia), all welcomed me into their libraries and provided help and advice. Sandra Acker (Victoria) and Jana Lynn Wyber (Calgary) responded helpfully to my inquiries. Dale McIntosh generously provided a list of material relating to British Columbia. Suzanne Meyers Sawa and Kathleen McMorrow aided and abetted in many ways in the Faculty of Music library. Bruce Harding did much of the labour in developing the compilation, especially in sifting through periodicals. The entire manuscript was reviewed by Kathleen McMorrow and Elaine Keillor, both of whom offered many useful suggestions. Gordon Smith was especially helpful with the sections on Native and folk music, and both he and Professor Keillor directed me to possibilities that I would otherwise have missed. I was fortunate to receive a research grant through the Faculty of Music, University of Toronto, from the Social Sciences and Humanities Research Council of Canada.

Above all, I am grateful to those who have developed the collections of the University of Toronto libraries. There is relatively little that I have needed to consult that I have not found somewhere in this extraordinary system. In particular, Kathleen McMorrow, Music Librarian, and John Whitepost, of the University's Collection Development Department, have created a music collection in the Faculty of Music that is unsurpassed in Canada. It is difficult to imagine realizing this *Research and Information Guide* without the resources of my home university's libraries.

In spite of all this help and goodwill, I have persisted nonetheless in my errors and omissions, against which I have no defence, save the hope that among them might still be found some merit.

Carl Morey
Jean A. Chalmers Chair
Institute for Canadian Music
Faculty of Music, University of Toronto
March 1996

Introduction

Serious study of the history of musical life in Canada is hardly more than about forty years old. MacMillan's *Music in Canada* (1955; no.118) was a stocktaking of the musical situation in the post-war years, but there was also an attempt in some of the essays to provide historical background. Only with Kallmann's *A history of music in Canada: 1534-1914* (1960; no.111) was there a comprehensive study of musical life built on European models as it had developed from the arrival of Jacques Cartier to the beginning of the 20th century. To be sure, there had been numerous small studies, especially in French Canada, and a rare biography, such as Lapierre's *Calixa Lavallée, musicien national du Canada* (1937; no.529), but Kallmann's book marked a new attitude towards the very idea of the study of music in Canada, and it has served as the point of departure for much that has happened in the years following. The study of folk music and the music of Native Peoples has a somewhat different background. Ernest Gagnon and the Frenchman, Julien Tiersot, are among those who already showed an interest in these other "musics" in the 19th century, as did Marius Barbeau and Luc Lacourcière in the first half of the 20th century. To some extent because of interest by researchers from outside Canada, research and study of these repertoires developed sooner than did interest in European urban music, but they always stood outside the canon of historical study in the categories of folklore and anthropology. Only very recently have the many varied aspects of Canada's musical life begun to be regarded as integral units of society.

The listings in this *Guide* reflect the research activity that has developed especially from the 1970s onward, but an attempt has been made to include some of the material from the earlier part of the century, material that often is in itself of historical interest for its points of view and underlying ambitions. It is hardly surprising that there was no attempt to provide any bibliographical study of musical Canada before 1940, since so little had been published, and what had appeared tended to be hidden away in specialized periodicals and journals that often had nothing to do with music. The *Répertoire bibliographique* (no.37) published annually 1940-70 by the journal *Culture* was the first to provide a regular indexing of humanities periodicals in both French and English where musical items sometimes appeared, but this was of little help for items that had appeared before 1940. Jean MacMillan's modest "Music in Canada: a short bibliography" in the *Ontario Library Review* (1940; no.63) was the first attempt to draw together a coherent list of titles. Subsequent up-datings of MacMillan's work kept it relatively current, but significantly there was a burst of bibliographic activity in the 1970s that reflected not only the activity of the previous decade but also the interest in knowing about that activity as the basis for further research. Bibliographies appeared by LeGendre (1970; no.60), a group of graduate students (1970; no.53), Proctor (1970/1975; no.73) and Bradley (1976; no.50). Beginning in 1973 the *Canadian Folk Music Journal* published specialized bibliographies (1978, 1983) on folk music, including First Nations and Eskimo music (no.734). Since then the volume of research and the interest in documentary and bibliographic collection has multiplied, providing vastly greater scope for the present *Guide* and also demanding a selectivity that was hardly necessary in previous bibliographies.

In the preparation of *Music in Canada: A Research and Information Guide* there have been two operating principles that have determined the selection of material and its organization: to provide access to any subject related to music and musicians of Canada; and to provide significant titles of works on most Canadian musical topics. Rather than aspire to a complete bibliographical study, the number of entries of which would far exceed those in the present volume, this *Guide* provides a broad spectrum of specialized studies that include information on most topics of research, and that open pathways to further research.

The kinds of material that will be found within each of the general topic groupings will be, it is hoped, self-evident. No arrangement, however, can be sufficiently analytical in itself to direct the user to all the titles that might be useful, but the three indexes at the end of the volume provide, it is hoped, the cross-references that make possible the finding of items that fall outside the obvious listings.

Printed monographs and articles make up the greatest part of the listings with almost no exception. The exception is collections of folk or native music, some titles of which will be found in the appropriate chapters. The collecting of such music has been fundamental to ethnomusicological work in Canada, and, indeed, it is not always easy to distinguish between an anthology of music with commentary, and commentary that has extensive musical material. Otherwise, scores and collections of music are not included. Nor are there listings of sound or video recordings.

Somewhat more problematic is the question of the inclusion of electronic sources available through internet services. The resources of this relatively new system are already formidable, but they also change and develop quickly. It is also the case that much of the musical information available would not be included in a research guide if it were in print form and there seems little point in drawing attention to it simply because of its technological currency. Nevertheless, there are some important electronic addresses that should not be overlooked, and these are noted in the appropriate commentaries to individual sections.

Theses written for a university degree are another group that pose a problem. There are relatively few at the doctoral level dealing with music in Canada, although there are some significant ones. There are, however, a number at the master's level, many of which contribute modestly but with originality to the study of important aspects of musical life. In some cases they are virtually the only source of important information on limited topics. Their number precludes complete listings and it must be hoped that a full indexing of theses will soon be available at all levels in both Canada and abroad that treat of Canadian musical topics. There already exist three important lists, none of which, unfortunately, is available in published form. Marie-Thérèse Lefebvre, Professor of Musicology at l'Université de Montréal, has compiled a list of Canadian theses on historical and analytical topics related to Canadian music (but see no.59). A more exhaustive computer-based list has been compiled by Paul Green, now retired from the Faculty of Music at the University of Western Ontario. Professor

Green's list includes all Canadian theses on music, whatever their level or specific interest, as well as foreign theses that relate to Canada. Diane Peters, of the Library at Wilfred Laurier University (Waterloo, Ontario), is working on an annotated bibliography of theses on Canadian music and music education. Comprehensive indexes of theses in Canada and the United States will be found in no.35 and no.38 of this *Guide*.

In 1759 the British General Wolf defeated the French General Montcalm at the Battle of the Plains of Abraham just outside Québec City. Canada was subsequently lost to the French crown by the Treaty of Paris (1763) and became an English colony, but the French population sustained itself and flourished to the present, mainly in what is now the Province of Québec, but also in the Atlantic provinces, in Ontario, and in some centres across the western provinces. It will be immediately evident that the titles in this *Guide* reflect Canada's linguistic duality. A number of publications, especially if they originate in some department of government or government-sponsored organization, have a peculiarly Canadian feature in that they appear in both French and English versions bound together. Other items have bilingual titles but contain material in both French and English, not necessarily in translation. Still other items appear as separate publications, the one being a translation of the other. In this *Guide* where the material is in French, the title and publication information are given in French, without translation, although the accompanying notation is always in English. If a publication has both French and English titles, both are given in the main entry and are indexed separately in the title index. Where one volume is a translation of another, both volumes are entered as separate publications but with a single annotation.

The Revolutionary War of 1776 that resulted in the United States of America served to confirm the British Dominion to the north of the new republic, and the administrative divisions of the Canadian colony quickly took the main shape of what they are today. Lower and Upper Canada were to become Québec and Ontario at Confederation in 1867, and the group of maritime colonies became Nova Scotia, New Brunswick and Prince Edward Island. These latter three constitute what are commonly referred to as the Maritime Provinces, a term that does not include Newfoundland. Although logically a part of the maritime group,

Newfoundland is not customarily included because it remained a colony of Great Britain until 1949, when it entered the Canadian federation. As that part of the continent west of Ontario was added to the country, another generalized area of "Western Canada" came into existence, with a further refinement by separating British Columbia from the Prairie Provinces -- Manitoba, Saskatchewan and Alberta. The language distinction of Québec and the regional distinctions and terminology of the country at large are all reflected in the kinds of research that have been carried out in Canadian musical studies, and the terminology just outlined often appears in both titles and annotations. All the material in this *Guide* relates to that geographical area that is defined as "Canada" in 1995.

In the Introduction to his *A History of music in Canada* (no.111), Kallmann wrote that "the record is concerned more with social than with artistic aspects of music" and that "such a history must deal with the planting of seeds rather than the harvesting of the fruits" (p.1). In 1960 "music in Canada" generally meant music in the European tradition and the seeds that were being planted came from that tradition and would bear fruit, modified by local circumstances, but clearly derived from the Old World origins. In the 1990s the view is somewhat different. Native Peoples have regained a presence in all aspects of Canadian life, folk music is discovered to have greater power and longevity than was perhaps once realized, and "popular" music is acknowledged to have a force in everyday life that "art" music frequently lacks. Without engaging any of the aesthetic and even moral questions that surround these subjects, this *Guide* has tried to reflect the interest and activity that they have engendered and to provide access to them along with traditional subjects and areas of research.

Music in Canada

Reference

The first section contains standard reference works, both historical and bibliographical, that may include musical material but in which the subject areas are broad, and in which music is at most an incidental topic. They are, however, useful sources for background and related information for most musical topics. The second section contains only items in which music is the sole subject. By far the major musical reference book is the *Encyclopedia of music in Canada* (no.10-13), which will be found to be a useful starting point for almost any research project. A number of foreign musical reference works are cited as sources that contain dependable if modest entries on Canada, and which are likely to be found in general music collections. Where a reference work is devoted to a specific musical subject, that item will be found in the section appropriate to that subject. For example, works devoted to Canadian composers are included in the Individual Musicians section, notably Kallmann (no.370) and MacMillan/Beckwith (no.374). Works on jazz, such as Gilmore's *Who's who in jazz in Montréal* (no.807), will be found under Popular Music and Jazz.

Among several music-related web sites, perhaps one of the most useful is that of the Canadian Association of Music Libraries, Archives and Documentation Centres/Association canadienne des bibliothèques, archives et centres de documentation musicaux (CAML/ACBM): http://www.caml.yorku.ca/. It provides information about the Association as well as links to related sites.

1. General

1. *Canada: an encyclopedia of the country.* J. Castell Hopkins, ed. Toronto: Linscott, 1898-1900. 6 vols.

   The principal reference source for contemporary information on the social and economic life of Canada in the late 19th century. Musical articles are: "Musical progress in Canada," iv, 383, by F.H. Torrington (no.149); "Historical sketch of music in Canada," iv, 389, by S. Frances Harrison (no.106); and three brief "notes by the editor": "Canadian songs and compositions," iv, 394; "Music in Québec City," iv, 410; "Madam Albani-Gye," iv, 411.

2. *The Canadian encyclopedia*, James H. Marsh, ed. Edmonton: Hurtig Publishing Ltd. 1988 (2nd. edition), 4 vols. ISBN 0-88830-326-2 (set).

   There are some entries relating to music and musicians, but the chief value is in the wide coverage of social, economic, geographic, cultural and historical aspects of Canada.

3. *Creative Canada. A biographical dictionary of twentieth-century creative and performing artists.* Toronto: University of Toronto Press , in association with McPherson Library, University of Victoria, 1971-72. 2 vols. xiv, 310/xiv, 306p. ISBN 0-8020-3262-1/0-8020-3285-0.

   The list is compiled on the basis of recognition in print and is entirely factual. Each volume is alphabetically complete, with a cumulative index in vol.2. There are curious imbalances in coverage, presumably reflecting the print basis for inclusion. Very few musicians are included, but other fields are well represented.

4. *Dictionary of Canadian Biography.* Toronto: University of Toronto Press, 1966-.

5. *Dictionnaire biographique du Canada.* Québec: Les Presses de l'Université Laval, 1965-.

   An on-going publication of the highest scholarly standards. Includes entries on important Canadians of all kinds from the earliest colonial period, among whom are some musicians. Entries are arranged alphabetically in each volume; each volume is defined by a period of time within which the deaths of the entrants occur. Volume 13 (1901-1913) appeared in 1993. Parallel publication in French and English.

6. Wallace, W. Stewart, ed. *Dictionary of Canadian Biography*. Toronto: MacMillan, 1926; revised and enlarged 1945; revised and enlarged as *The MacMillan dictionary of Canadian biography*, 1963; 4th edition 1977 by W.A. McKay.(ref F1005.D5) or 920.3 W19 ROBA

Some important musicians from the early part of the 20th century are included.

2. Musical

7. *Dictionary of Contemporary Music*. John Vinton, ed. New York: E.P. Dutton, 1971, 1972, 1974. xiv, 834 p.

The brief article on Canada by John Beckwith is a fine overview of the 1950s and 1960s. Short bibliography. The *Dictionary* contains a number of biographical entries for Canadian composers.

8. *Dictionnaire de la musique*. Marc Honegger, ed. 2 vols. Paris: Bordas, 1986 (nouvelle édition). xv/vii, 1371p. ISBN 2-04-015396-9.

A biographical dictionary that includes entries on a number of Canadian composers, with lists of works.

9. *Dictionnaire de la musique*. Marc Vignal, ed. Paris: Larousse, 1987. ii, 882p. ISBN 2-03-511306-1.

A very short but informative entry on Canada, which cites a large number of composers' names. A few biographical entries.

10. *Encyclopedia of Music in Canada*. Helmut Kallmann, Gilles Potvin and Kenneth Winters, eds. Toronto: University of Toronto Press, 1981. xxix, 1076p. ISBN 0-8020-5509-5.

11. *Encyclopédie de la musique au Canada*. Helmut Kallmann, Gilles Potvin and Kenneth Winters, eds. Montréal: Fides, 1983. xxxi, 1142p. ISBN 2-7621-1169-2.

12. *Encyclopedia of Music in Canada*. 2nd edition. Helmut Kallmann, and Gilles Potvin, eds.; Robin Elliott and Mark Miller, associate eds. Toronto: University of Toronto Press, 1992. xxxii, 1524 p. ISBN 0-8020-2881-0.

13. *Encyclopédie de la musique au Canada*, 2eme édition. Helmut Kallmann and Gilles Potvin, eds.; Mark Miller and Claire Versailles, associate eds. Montréal: Fides, 1993. lv, 3810p. ISBN 2-7621-1688-0.

By far the most important and authoritative reference work on music in Canada. The second edition is a significant expansion of the first edition, but a number of entries in the first edition were omitted in the second edition. All aspects of music are included, such as folk, ethnic, pop, jazz, classical, as well as biographical and regional subjects. An extensive index of names allows the locating of individuals, societies and organizations who do not have subject entries. Most entries have extensive and very useful bibliographies. While the French first edition includes a few details not in the first English edition, the French and English editions are in every significant way two linguistic versions of a single work, although illustrations sometimes vary between the two.

Kallmann discusses in some detail the background to the *Encyclopedia* and demonstrates its editorial policies and procedures in "The making of a one-country music encyclopedia," *Fontes Artis Musicae* 41/1 (1994): 3-19.

14. *Larousse de la musique*. Paris: Librairie Larousse, 1982. 2 vols. xv, 1803p. ISBN 2-03-511303-2.

The short entry on Canada -- slightly more than one column -- is directed mainly to composition and mentions many names, especially of those active from about 1945. No bibliography. There are a few biographical entries in the dictionary.

15. *Die Musik in Geschichte und Gegenwart*. Friedrich Blume, ed. Kassel: Bärenreiter-Verlag, 1949-1968. 14 vols. Supplementary volumes 1973, 1979, 1986 (Register).

The entry "Kanada" by Helmut Kallmann is a concise and thorough presentation of musical life up to the 1950s, limited only by the historical research then available. There is little attention given elsewhere in the encyclopedia to music in Canada. The second edition, the first volume of which appeared in 1994 (*Sachteil* I) is projected to have more extensive coverage of Canadian subjects.

16. *The New Grove dictionary of music and musicians.* Stanley Sadie, ed. London: MacMillan Publishers Limited, 1980. 20 vols. ISBN 0-333-23111-2.

There are entries on Canada and on all major cities, as well as individual entries for many Canadian musicians. Useful bibliographies follow each entry. The main entry "Canada" contains about twice as long a section on folk and native music as on the history of euro-related art music, with proportionate bibliographies.

17. *The New Grove dictionary of opera.* Stanley Sadie, ed. London: Macmillan Press Ltd., 1992. 4 vols. ISBN 0-935859-92-6.

There is a general entry on Canada as well as on major cities. Many individual entries on performers and composers.

18. *The New Harvard dictionary of music.* Don Michael Randel, ed. Cambridge, Massachusetts: Belknap Press of Harvard University Press, 1986. xxi, 942p. ISBN 0-674-61525-5.

A few historical points are sketched in and a short bibliography is provided for the compact entry, "Canada." Very limited usefulness.

Catalogues and Directories

The resources of libraries, organizations and professional groups appear in the following catalogues and directories. It is here that electronic resources can be particularly helpful for general searches of a subject as well as for the locating of specific titles. The catalogues of Canadian university libraries may be accessed on-line, and it is these libraries that contain the major music collections outside the National Library of Canada. The other non-university collection, and one noted several times in the following section, is that of the Canadian Music Centre. The Centre is a deposit library for its members, who are composers and who include virtually every Canadian composer of note. There are published catalogues (no.22, 24) but the entire collection may be accessed on-line at: http://www.ffa.ucalgary.ca/cmc/. The National Office in Toronto may be contacted at cmc@interlog.com. The regional offices may be reached at the following addresses: Maritime Provinces - cmc@mta.ca; Québec - cmc_que@cam.org; Ontario - cmc@interlog.com; Prairie Provinces - jcreid@acs. ucalgary.ca; British Columbia - cmc-bc@unixg.ubc.ca.

19. Association for Recorded Sound Collections. *A preliminary directory of sound recordings collections in the United States and Canada.* New York: New York Public Library, 1967. 157p.

    Only three and a half pages are given to Canada, and the information contained there is now very out of date. However, a number of private collectors are listed, information that is otherwise not easily available.

20. *Associations des organismes musicaux du Québec: répertoire 1992.* Montréal: Association des organismes du Québec, 1994. 96p.

A directory of ensembles of all kinds, festivals and music producers in Québec. There is a brief note, in French and English, on each organization with information on administration, personnel, recordings and repertoire.

21. Beaudry, Claude. "Catalogue des imprimés musicaux d'avant 1800 conservés à la bibliothèque de l'Université Laval." In *Musical Canada: words and music honouring Helmut Kallmann*, pp.29-49. J. Beckwith and F. Hall, eds. Toronto: University of Toronto Press, 1988. ISBN 0-8020-5759-4.

    This catalogue brings together all the titles of music published before 1800 now in the library of l'Université Laval after its separation from the library of the Séminaire de Québec in the 1960s. The interest of the collection lies at least in part in its reflection of music available - not printed - in Canada in the 17th and 18th centuries. Of 144 titles, nineteen are *unica*.

22. *Canadian choral music/Musique chorale canadienne*. Mitchell Kitz, ed. Toronto: Canadian Music Centre, 1993. [iv], 271p. ISBN 0-921519-16-8.

    A catalogue of choral music available from the libraries of the Canadian Music Centre. It is organized by ensemble, then by composer, with an index of names and titles. Each of the 2191 entries has a full descriptive note.

23. *Canadian music industry directory*. Toronto: RPM Music Publications, 1956, 1967, 1969, 1970, 1973, 1974, 1976, 1981.

    The *Directory* appeared as an issue of the magazine *RPM Music Weekly*. It is a source-book for the pop music industry in Canada with listings of all aspects of the business -- recording studios, radio stations, agencies, promoters, publishers, etc. -- as well as ancillary services such as photography and lighting. The 1973 and 1974 issues include names of winners of a Juno Award, the awards of the Canadian recording industry which began in 1964.

24. *Canadian orchestral music/Musique orchestrale canadienne*. Sam D. King, ed. Toronto: Canadian Music Centre, 1994. [v], 247p. ISBN 0-921519-19-2.

A catalogue of music for large instrumental ensembles, including vocal and instrumental ensembles, available in the libraries of the Canadian Music Centre. It is organized by ensemble, then by composer, with an index of names and titles. Each of the 2205 entries has a full descriptive note.

25. *Catalogue des partitions musicales publiées avant 1968.* vol. I. Montréal: Bibliothèque nationale du Québec, 1995. xx, 188p. ISBN 2-551-13317-3.

The first of a series of publications that will encompass about 5000 works, this volume includes 700 titles of pieces published in Québec, or outside Québec where there is a relationship through the composer, author, text, etc. Franco-Canadian and Franco-American works are also included.

26. *Directory of conductors in Canada/Annuaire des chefs d'orchestre au Canada.* Toronto: Association of Canadian Orchestras and the Ontario Federation of Symphony Orchestras, [1976]. 163p.

A promotional venture that lists eighty-six conductors active in Canada at the time, and five abroad. Short biographies and outline of activities.

27. *Directory of musical Canada.* Don Sedgwick, ed. Agincourt, Ont.: GLC Publishers, 1978; rev. 1981. vii, 363p. ISBN 0-88874-086-7.

Extensive listings of musical organizations of all kinds - administration, performance, libraries, media - with addresses and telephone numbers, in some cases broken down by province and city. Despite the fact that much information is out of date, much remains constant and the *Directory* can still be a useful guide.

28. *Music directory Canada.* 5th edition. Toronto: CM Books, 1990. 646p. ISBN 0-9691272-5-1

A directory of trade information covering virtually all aspects of the music business in Canada, including production companies, associations of all kinds, libraries, schools, competitions, promotional organizations, auditoriums, etc. Addresses, and brief annotations for each entry. The emphasis is on pop music, with erratic inclusion of classical materials. The addresses have a practical use, and the listings themselves provide a view of the extent and complexity of the business aspect of music. Updated issues of the *Directory* appeared in the 1980s.

Bibliographies and Lists

The items included in the first section are comprehensive bibliographies in which musical titles are at most only one category among many. They form, however, a vast resource for the identifying of titles on related subjects and materials of all kinds.

Several items in Part 2 are published by the Canadian Music Centre in co-operation with the Canadian Music Educators' Association. They are lists of compositions directed to educational use and derive from the Centre's John Adaskin Project, which has as its aim the development of a repertoire of music by Canadian composers written specifically for use in the schools. The repertoire lists of the Project may be accessed as Adaskin Online at: gopher@epas.utoronto.ca/academic disciplines in the humanities/music/.

1. General

29. *Bibliographie du Québec*. Québec: Bibliothèque nationale du Québec, 1968- . ISSN 0006-1441.

This *Bibliographie* includes all items published in Québec and acquired by legal deposit at the Bibliothèque national du Québec from 1968, as well as documents relative to Québec and published elsewhere. Publication is monthly, with an annual cumulative index as well as monthly indexes, each arranged by author/title/secondary subject and by subject. Main entries are listed within subject categories. Printed music and recordings are included.

30. *Bibliographie du Québec 1821-1967.* Québec: Bibliothèque nationale du Québec, 1980-. ISBN 2-551-03716-6 (édition complète).

A bibliography of items published in or relevant to Québec which appeared in the period 1821-1967. Each volume consists of two parts: a list of titles arranged alphabetically by subject heading; and a set of extensive cross-indexes. Every volume includes all categories and no attempt is made to issue material by chronological or other arrangement; volumes appear as work progresses.

31. *Canada, the reprinted record.* Ottawa: Canadian Institute for Historical Microreproductions/Institut canadien de microreproductions historiques. microfiche, ISBN 0-665-90295-6.

The CIHM/ICMH project is to make available in microform all publications before 1901 that were printed or published in Canada, that were by a Canadian author but printed or published outside Canada, or that have Canadian subject matter. Not only monographs are included, but also such items as catalogues, pamphlets, playbills and broadsides. The microfiche catalogue (ongoing) has seven indexes that accommodate extensive cross-indexing. An indispensable source of material for the period pre-1901. Many musical items.

The complete CIHM/ICMH database is available on-line at: http://www.nlc-bnc.ca/cihm/. The more than 70,000 titles can be searched by author, title, and/or keyword. See also no.915.

32. *Canadian books in print.* Toronto: University of Toronto Press, 1973- . ISSN 0315-1999.

The listings are compiled from information obtained from Canadian publishers, and represents the attempt "to include all titles bearing the imprint of Canadian publishers or originated by Canadian subsidiaries of international publishing firms." Predominantly English-language listings. Sheet music is not included, but volumes of music are. The "Author and Title Index" is issued quarterly, the "Subject Index" appears only annually. For French-language publications, see no.44.

33. *Canadian index*. Toronto: Micromedia Ltd.; 1986-92 as *Canadian magazine index*, ISSN 0829-8777; 1993- , ISSN 1192-4160.

A comprehensive indexing of a broad range of journals, magazines and newspapers, similar to no.34 below. Cross-indexed by names and subjects. Available online as the Canadian Business and Current Affairs (CBCA) database.

34. *Canadian periodical index*. Ottawa: Canadian Library Association, 1966-1986; Toronto: Info Globe, 1987-1994; Toronto: Gale Canada, 1995- . ISSN 0008-4719.

A comprehensive indexing of a broad range of journals, magazines and newspapers, similar to no.33 above, but with a somewhat different set of items indexed. Vol.1 begins with the year 1938. Available online as part of Globe Information Services's news package.

35. *Canadian theses/Thèses canadiennes*. Ottawa: National Library of Canada, 1973-1983 (print form), 1984- (microfiche). ISSN 0068-9874.

List of titles of both master and doctoral theses accepted at Canadian universities, as well as theses published outside Canada with Canadian authors or a Canadian association. Vol.1 covers theses for the period 1947-60.

36. *Canadiana*. Ottawa: National Library of Canada, 1953-.

The national bibliography, which is comprised of listings of titles of Canadian origin or of relevance to Canada since 1952, including printed music and books and, since 1970, sound recordings. There are eleven issues per year, with an annual cumulation of the parts and indexes. Beginning with *Canadiana 1973-1980*, there have been cumulations published in microfiche format, appearing since 1981 in five-year cycles (1981-85, 1986-90, etc.).

A description of the sources of bibliographic information on music and its control in *Canadiana* will be found in: Joan Colquhoun, "Bibliographic control of Canadian music materials," *Fontes Artis Musicae* 34/4 (1987): 255-259.

37. *Culture. Science profanes et sciences religieuses au Canada. Répertoire bibliographique.* Québec: 1940-70.

Issued quarterly as a separately paged part of the review, *Culture*, this was an index of Canadian periodicals, varying in number from about seventy-five to ninety, in both French and English. Items are listed under subject heading. There are no indexes, which makes cumulative or subject searching impossible, but it remains a fine source of periodical articles in the humanities.

38. *Dissertation abstracts international* (vol.30- ; vol.1-29 as *Dissertation abstracts*). Ann Arbor, Mich.: University Microfilms. ISSN 0419-4209.

Abstracts for doctoral dissertations submitted to University Microfilms International, primarily from US institutions, but also from most Canadian schools with graduate departments. Indexed by categories. Vol.1 begins with entries from 1938.

39. Froeschle, Hartmut and Lothar Zimmerman. "German Canadiana; a bibliography." *German-Canadian Yearbook* 11 (1990): 420p.

The entire issue of the *Yearbook* is given over to a bibliography, arranged by subject groupings. The music section (pp.258-263) contains only eighty-eight items but does include a number of journal and newspaper articles, often in German, about German-related musical activity in Canada.

40. Garigue, Philippe. *Bibliographie du Québec (1955-1965)* Montréal: Les Presses de l'Université de Montréal, 1967. 227p.

An extensive bibliography for most aspects of Québec society and history, this work completely ignores music, save for a few random references to folkmusic.

41. Goggio, Emilio, Beatrice Corrigan and Jack H. Parker, compilers. *A bibliography of Canadian cultural periodicals (English and*

French from colonial times to 1950) in Canadian libraries.
Toronto: University of Toronto,1955. [ii], 45p.

A selective list of approximately 450 journal titles. It gives
locations and issues available. Items are arranged alphabetically by
title, without further cross-indexing. Few items relate to music, but
the list is useful for related cultural material.

42. *Guide to reference materials for Canadian libraries.* Kirsti Nilsen,
    ed. Toronto: University of Toronto Press for the Faculty of Library
    and Information Science, 1992. 8th edition. xv, 596p. ISBN 0-
    8020-6004-8.

    Comprehensive in scope and international in coverage, this is
    a useful guide to resources for general reference work. There are
    few specifically Canadian musical references, but the publication
    is helpful in tracing related subject material in the humanities and
    social sciences.

43. *An index to Saturday Night: the first fifty years, 1887-1937.* Grace
    F. Heggie and Gordon R. Adshead, eds. Toronto: Micromedia
    Ltd., 1987. ix, 482p. ISBN 0-88892-002-4.

    Saturday Night's significant coverage of the arts included a
    great deal on music, which makes it a particularly rich source of
    information on Toronto, since it was a popular local weekly
    magazine. All signed articles are listed, as well as unsigned items
    of at least 200 words. Fully indexed.

44. *Les livres disponibles canadiens de langue française.* Outremont:
    Bibliodata, 1979-. ISSN 0708-4889.

    The lists are based on information gathered in collaboration
    from authors, publishers and distributors, and attempt to include all
    publications issued in Québec. There are three volumes: authors,
    titles, subjects. They appear four times a year in print and ten times
    per year in microfiche format. For English-language publications,
    see no.32.

45. *Ontario since 1867: a bibliography.* [Toronto]: Ministry of
    Colleges and Universities, Government of Ontario, 1973. 330p.

A basic bibliography grouped under economic, social, cultural and intellectual history, and government and politics. Very few musical entries, but useful for historical background.

2. Music and Musicians

46. Apfelstadt, Hilary. *Canadian music for women's voices.* Greensboro, N.C.: Spectrum Music Publishers, 1989. iv, 160p.

    This fully annotated list of works is based primarily on the holdings of the Canadian Music Centre. Works are listed by composers, with indexes for title, type and voicing.

47. Bergeron, Chantal, et al. *Répertoire bibliographique de texts de présentation générale et d'analyse d'oeuvres musicales canadiennes (1900-1980)/Canadian musical works 1900-1980:a bibliography of general and analytical sources.* Établi par Chantal Bergeron et al., sous la direction de Lucien Poirier. Ottawa: Canadian Association of Music Libraries, 1983. xiv, 96p. ISBN 0-9690583-2-2.

    A checklist of 1995 references to almost 1500 compositions in 82 sources, arranged alphabetically by composer, with an index of authors. This is indispensable for tracing critical and popular reception of compositions. For a note on the project of which this is the result, see Poirier, no.72.

48. BMI Canada Limited. *Orchestra music by Canadian composers.* Toronto: BMI Canada, n.d. [1962]. [27 leaves].

    A list of works by twenty-five composers, with instrumentation and a very brief biographical note. Limited to composers who were members of BMI Canada, a performance rights organization.

49. BMI Canada Limited. *Yes, there is Canadian music!/Oui, notre musique existe!* Don Mills, Ontario: BMI Canada, 1971 (8th edition).

A list of Canadian music licensed by BMI Canada that has been recorded. Most of the material is popular music, listed by title, with a separate section of "concert music" listed by composer. For each piece the record company is given but no other information. The first edition was issued in 1952. Subsequent editions and supplements were issued (1964, 1968) up to this 1971 edition. Monthly or bi-monthly supplements continued to be issued until April 1977.

50. Bradley, Ian L. *A selected bibliography of musical Canadiana* (revised edition). Agincourt, Ont.: GLC Publishers Limited, 1976. iii, 178p. ISBN 0-88874-050-4.

Approximately two thousand titles are listed under ten categories. There are no annotations and no indexes, which limits access to material. Nevertheless, it is a useful list, especially for periodical references and a list of theses.

51. Creelman, Gwendolyn, Esther Cook and Geraldine King, compilers. *Canadian music scores and recordings: a classified catalogue of the holdings of Mount Allison University libraries.* Sackville, NB: Mount Allison University, Ralph Packard Bell Library, 1976. 192p. ISBN 0-88828-000-9.

2662 items, representing an attempt by the Library to acquire all the available published scores and recordings of Canadian music, as of April 30, 1976. Entries are arranged numerically by Library of Congress classification number, with indexes for composer, performer, subject and title.

52. Denis, Jean-François, ed. *Résonance: Magnétothèque du groupe électroacoustique de Concordia/Concordia Electroacoustic Composers' Group tape collection.* Montréal: Concordia Electroacoustic Composers' Group, 1988. xii, 196. ISBN 0-88947-016-2.

The main part of this book is a catalogue of about 700 electroacoustic works held at Concordia University in Montréal, most of which are by Canadians. There are short biographical notes for 80 of the more than 250 composers listed, and a brief annotation to each composition. There is also a list of works performed by the Concordia Group 1982-88. Composer and title indexes.

53. Hall, Frederick A., Sharon Lea Hall, D. Bruce Minorgan, Kathryn Minorgan, Nadia Turbide, eds. "A basic bibliography of musical Canadiana." Toronto: Faculty of Music, University of Toronto, 1970. 38p.

Approximately 650 items arranged by categories without annotation. The work, which was in typescript, was not formally published and had limited distribution.

54. Hardy, Yvon. *Liste des ouvrages en musique publiés par les éditeurs québécois.* Québec: Bibliothèque, Université Laval, 1994. 225p.

This extraction from the computerized catalogue of l'Université Laval is a list of titles arranged by city of publication, publisher and year of publication. There are no indexes or annotations. Very limited interest.

55. Kallmann, Helmut. "The German contribution to music in Canada - a bibliography." *German-Canadian Yearbook 7* (1983): 228-33.

A selective but useful list of articles by and about German musicians in Canada, sometimes with brief annotations.

56. Keillor, Elaine. "A bibliography of items on music in Canada." Toronto: (Faculty of Music, University of Toronto), 1972. 89p.

A typescript list of 1214 items arranged chronologically by periodical, and cross-indexed by subject. The list is compiled from eight English-language journals published from 1883 to 1937.

57. ------ "Canadian items in *The Musical Courier*, 1880-1897" Ottawa: E. Keillor, 1979. 25p. Toronto: (Faculty of Music, University of Toronto), 1974. 25p.

A typescript list of 249 items arranged by subject. No annotations or indexes.

58. Lande, Lawrence. *A checklist of early music relating to Canada.* Montréal: McGill University, 1973. [v], 23p.

This list of 112 items in Lande's personal library includes 92 sheet-music prints. The remaining titles are a variety of manuscripts, books and pamphlets, including some Indian and Eskimo material. Each entry is fully annotated; several illustrations. Interesting, but of limited usefulness.

59. Lefebvre, Marie-Thérèse. "Répertoire des travaux universitaires sur la musique du Québec (1924-1984)." *Canadian University Music Review / Revue de musique des universités canadiennes* 6 (1985): 45-57.

An inventory of 140 studies and theses at the bachelor's, master's and doctoral levels on music and musicians of Québec. Universities outside Québec are included. Arranged chronologically (from 1924 to 1985, with a list of "in progress") and by author.

60. LeGendre, Victor. *Musique canadienne: bibliographie.* typescript. Cap Rouge, Que.: Bibliothèque, Séminaire Saint-Augustin, 1970. 28p.

Items appear sometimes by author and sometimes by subject in the same list. Mostly items in French. Perhaps most interesting for the extensive list of articles by Nazaire Levasseur in *La musique*, 1919-22.

61. *List of Canadian copyrights (musical compositions)* 1899? 32p. CIHM/ICMH microfiche series no. 05248.

Entries are listed by title, with author, date and number of entry, and the registrant (publisher). Almost all the entries are from the 1880s, up to December 31, 1888, with a few from the 1870s.

62. MacInnis, Peggy. *Guidelist of Canadian free bass accordion music suitable for student performers.* Toronto: Canadian Music Centre in co-operation with the Canadian Music Educators' Association, 1991. x, 92p. ISBN 0-921519-05-2.

Seventy-two works are listed and carefully annotated as a pedagogical guide. Although the repertoire is limited to "easy" and "medium" levels of difficulty, it provides a useful guide to contemporary accordion composition in Canada.

63. MacMillan, Jean Ross. "Music in Canada; a short bibliography." *Ontario Library Review* 24/4 (1940): 386-96.

A pioneer effort, although brief, to gather a bibliography of musical Canadiana. Folk-song collections and arrangements are included, as are teaching methods and song collections that originated in Canada but which do not address a Canadian subject. Limited usefulness. See also May, no.65.

64. Marco, Guy, Ann M. Garfield and Sharon Paugh Ferris. *Information on music: a handbook of reference sources in european languages. Volume II, the Americas.* Littleton, Colo.: Libraries Unlimited, 1977. 296p. ISBN 0-87287-141-X.

There is a general bibliography of two pages on North America, and twelve pages devoted specifically to Canada. The list is selective and brief, but fundamental. Useful annotations. See also Wehrle, no.82.

65. May, Lucille. "Music and Composers of Canada." *Ontario Library Review* 33/3 (August, 1949): 264-70.

In effect a supplement to MacMillan (no.63), this list does not include items published before 1940, except a selection of articles from periodicals in the Music Division of the Library of Congress, Washington, not listed in the earlier bibliography. Nevertheless, it is more useful than its predecessor for the inclusion of many articles in various periodicals, notably *The Canadian Review of Music and Art*. Almost all the items are biographical or related to composition or individual musicians. No music publications. English-language items only. See also Willamson, no.83.

66. Maxwell, Karen A. *A guide to solo Canadian trombone literature available through the Canadian Music Centre.* Toronto: Canadian Music Centre, 1985. 14p.

This pamphlet lists nine solo pieces by eight composers. Information for each work includes range, musical characteristics, and technical aspects.

67. McMillan, Barclay. "Tune-book imprints in Canada to 1867: a descriptive bibliography." *Papers of the Bibliographical Society of Canada* 16 (1977): 31-57.

There is a chronological list of titles from 1801 in all known editions and impressions, followed by a section of full bibliographical descriptions, with informative notes, for each item. Four facsimiles of title pages, and one of music with "shape" notes (Toronto 1848).

68. Morley, Glen. *The Glen Morley collection of historical Canadian music.* Ottawa: Kingsmere Concert Enterprises, 1984. ii, 19f.

A list of 365 pieces printed in Canada from 1832 to 1914 and written by Canadians. Items are arranged chronologically with title, composer, and type of piece (ballad, pianoforte, etc.) No index.

69. *Musical Canadiana, a subject index.* Ottawa: Canadian Library Association, 1967. v, 62p.

"A Preliminary Edition in which will be found listed by subject matter some 800 vocal and instrumental pieces of music published in or outside Canada up to 1921..." Title and, where known, composer and publication information are given. No indexes.

70. O'Neill, Patrick B., ed. *A checklist of Canadian copyright deposits in the British Museum, 1895-1923.* Halifax: School of Library and Information Studies, Dalhousie University, 1989. Vol. IV, Part 1: *Sheet music: A - P*, vii, 464p., ISBN 0-7703-9730-1; Vol. IV, Part 2: *Sheet music: Q - Z and indexes*, vii, pp.465-893, ISBN 0-7703-9736-0.

Fire and mishap conspired to destroy almost all copyright deposits in Canadian Parliamentary libraries for the period 1875-1923. Between 1895 and 1923, deposits were also made to the British Museum, and it is the music publications so deposited that are indexed in this publication. The 11,333 entries, arranged alphabetically by composer, include material of foreign origin published and copyrighted in Canada. Indexes of composers and lyricists, and of titles.

71. Peters, Diane. *Music in Canada: a bibliography of resources in W.L.U. Library.* Waterloo, Ont.: The Library, Wilfred Laurier University, 1991. [ii], 24p. ISBN 0-9218-2115-8.

Items are listed under categories, with an alphabetical list of titles. Although the number of entries is relatively small, the bibliography serves as a useful checklist of basic publications.

72. Poirier, Lucien. "Répertoire bibliographique de textes de présentation générale et d'analyse d'oeuvres musicales canadiennes (1900-1980): historique et présentation." *Les cahiers de l'ARMuQ* 6 (septembre 1985): 39-43. ISSN 0821-1817.

A description of the project, the criteria for selection, and the procedures that lead to the publication of no.47.

73. Proctor, George A. *Sources in Canadian music: a bibliography of bibliographies.* 2nd edition. Sackville: Publication in Music No. 4, Ralph Pickard Bell Library, Mount Allison University, 1979. iv, 36p. ISBN 0-88828-027-0.

This supersedes the first edition (1975) of Proctor's compilation. Only titles of works are listed that contain, but are not necessarily limited to, bibliographies or lists. Included are publications in which musical entries appear only in part, and foreign publications that contain Canadian references. Despite its brevity and date, this remains a useful reference.

74. Shand, Patricia Martin. *Canadian music: a selective guidelist for teachers.* Toronto: Canadian Music Centre, 1978. viii, 186p. ISBN 0-9690836-0-2. *Musique canadienne: oeuvres choisies à l'intention des professeurs*, Jean Patenaude, directeur de l'édition française. Toronto: Centre de Musique Canadienne, 1982. viii, 133p. ISBN 0-9690836-1-0.

This selected list of music for a variety of vocal and instrumental combinations was compiled as a guide for use in schools. For each composition there is a musical excerpt and a note that includes an assessment of difficulties. Although the French version appears to be a translation of the earlier English edition, and is identical in format, there is considerable difference between the two in the choice of music, especially for voice.

75. ------ *A guide to published Canadian violin music suitable for student performers.* Toronto: Canadian Music Centre in co-operation with the Canadian Music Educators' Association, 1993. viii, 101p. ISBN 0-921519-17-6.

This selective list of fifty-one titles, intended as a pedagogical guide, also provides a limited survey of violin writing, especially of music directed to younger players. Each entry is fully described from stylistic and technical points of view.

76. ------ *Guidelist of unpublished Canadian band music suitable for student performers.* Toronto: Canadian Music Centre in co-operation with the Canadian Music Educators' Association, 1987. xi, 76p. ISBN 0-921519-01-X.

Sixty-three works are listed in categories of difficulty for use in schools. For each title there is a note on stylistic and technical characteristics. Although pedagogical in intent, the list also provides a review of contemporary composition for band.

77. Sherwood, Gayle D. *Indexed guide to the Dorothy H. Farquharson Collection of Canadian sheet music.* Hamilton: William Ready Division of Archives and Research Collections, McMaster University, 1989. [ii], 425p.

A "guide to 1178 items of sheet music that are traceable to Canadian sources through composer, author, arranger, publisher, or other affiliation" in McMaster University Library (Hamilton, Ont.). The period covered is 1830-1979. Items are listed in alphabetical groups by composer, with full publication information. There are extensive cross-indexes.

78. Stubley, Eleanor Victoria. *A guide to solo french horn music by Canadian composers.* Toronto: Canadian Music Centre in co-operation with the Canadian Music Educators' Association, 1990. ix, 75p. ISBN 0-921519-06-0.

Forty-six works are listed for solo horn or with keyboard, tape, electronic or percussion accompaniment. For each entry there is a concise but informative note on the stylistic and technical aspects of the piece. While not exhaustive, the list provides a comprehensive view of contemporary composition for horn.

79. ------ *A guide to unpublished Canadian brass chamber music suitable for student performers.* Toronto: Canadian Music Educators' Association in co-operation with the Canadian Music Centre, 1989. x, 106p. ISBN 0-921519-02-8.

    This selective and graded list of forty-three titles, although directed to pedagogical use, provides a cross-section of contemporary brass writing. Each entry has a detailed note on style and technical considerations. Most of the material is in the Canadian Music Centre.

80. Walter, Cameron Kenneth. *A guide to unpublished Canadian jazz ensemble music suitable for student performers.* Toronto: Canadian Music Centre in co-operation with the Canadian Music Educators' Association, 1994. ix, 76p. ISBN 0-921519-20-6.

    This graded list of thirty-two compositions, intended as a guide for educational use, also provides an overview of jazz composition by seventeen musicians. Each entry is fully notated from stylistic and technical points of view.

81. Wehrle, Marlene. "Liste sélective: Canada." *Fontes Artis Musicae* 23/4 (1976): 206-08.

    As the title indicates, this is a selective list of both music and books about music published in Canada in the period 1973-76. A few items by Canadians published outside the country are also included.

82. ------ "Reference sources on Canadian Music: a supplement to Guy Marco *Information on music*, Volume II." *Fontes Artis Musicae* 41/1 (1994): 40-52.

    This addition to Marco (no.64) is selective and contains only major items of comprehensive interest. The format established by Marco is continued. Concisely annotated and very useful.

83. Williamson, Nancy J. "Canadian music and composers since 1949." *Ontario Library Review* 38/2 (May,1954): 118-122.

    A continuation of May, no.65. The list is short, but as with the previous lists, especially May's, it is useful for periodical items in a variety of journals, few of them specifically musical. English language titles only. Includes some music collections.

History and Criticism

The items in this section deal mainly with music and musicians which relate to the European classical tradition. In those items where other aspects of music in Canada may be treated along with that classical tradition, an indication is given in the annotation.

Part 1 provides titles of works that take a comprehensive view of their subject, and which are not primarily regional or analytical in focus. Part 2, *Local and Regional*, includes titles of studies clearly delimited by place, whether city, region, or province. Part 3, *Organizations and Institutions*, includes works centered on an organization, such as a performing ensemble or a school. A book on the Vancouver Symphony Orchestra (Becker, no.261) , for example, will be found in Part 3, not in Part 2. Where there may be uncertainty as to locations of certain studies, consultation of the subject index will help guide the reader to appropriate sections.

Part 4, *Analysis and Genre Studies*, includes works that cover a particular category of composition, or which deal with compositions by composers for whom there is no individual entry in the *Individual Musicians* chapter. In the case of a composer for whom there is an entry in the chapter *Individual Musicians*, then all studies relating to that composer are grouped together under that entry, even if they are analytical in nature.

As has been already noted in the Introduction, the seminal study of musical life in Canada is Kallmann's *A history of music in Canada 1534-1914* (no.111). Although he deals with some aspects of folk and Native music, Kallmann was chiefly concerned with the development of European musical styles in Canada. He did, however, establish the idea of the study of the growth of a musical society, rather than the historical study of an already established and sophisticated musical culture, as in the traditional studies of European music and musicians. The pattern was continued in the surveys by Ford (no.102) and McGee (no.125), as well as in specialized studies. A significant new direction is taken by Diamond and Witmer in *Canadian music: issues of hegemony and identity* (no.101). Both in selection of material and in the extensive introductory material, a network of approaches to Canadian musical studies is established that is more embracing and more eclectic in its references than in any previous work. The multidisciplinary material places music within a complex social context that is fundamentally Canadian in its references and distinct from European traditions, and forms a paradigm for future study of Canadian music, musicians, and musical society.

Publications of music are not included in this chapter but attention must be drawn to a unique series, *The Canadian musical heritage/Le patrimoine musical canadien* (ISBN 0-919883-00-1 - set). Principally anthologies of music, each volume contains extensive notes and introductory material, in French and English, which makes the series an important source of information as well as of the music itself. The volumes published up to 1996 are:

1. *Piano music I*. Elaine Keillor, ed. 1984

2. *Sacred choral music I*. Clifford Ford, ed. 1984

3. *Songs I to English texts*. Frederick Hall, ed. 1985

4. *Organ music I*. Lucien Poirier, ed. 1985

5. *Hymn tunes*. John Beckwith, ed. 1986

6. *Piano music II*. Elaine Keillor, ed. 1986

7. *Songs II to French texts*. Lucien Poirier, ed. 1987

8. *Music for orchestra I*. Helmut Kallmann, ed. 1990

9. *Sacred choral music II*. Clifford Ford, ed. 1988

10. *Opera and operetta excerpts I.* Dorith Cooper, ed. 1991

11. *Chamber music I: piano trios.* Robin Elliott, ed. 1989

12. *Songs III to French texts.* Lucien Poirier, ed. 1992

13. *Chamber music II: string quartets.* Robin Elliott, ed. 1992

14. *Songs IV to English texts.* Frederick Hall, ed. 1993

15. *Music for orchestra II.* Elaine Keillor, ed. 1994

16. *Music for orchestra III.* Elaine Keillor, ed. 1995

17. *Secular choral music.* Richard Johnston, ed. 1996

18. *Oratorio and cantata excerpts.* John Beckwith, ed. 1995.

For background to the series and the development of CMHS, and for relevant research projects, see Elaine Keillor, "Finding the sounds of Canada's musical past", *Fontes Artis Musicae* 41/1 (January-March 1994): 20-31.

1. General

84. Amtmann, Willy. *La musique au Québec 1600-1875.* Michelle Pharand, trans. Montréal: Les Éditions de l'Homme, 1976. 420p. ISBN 0-7759-0517-8.

85. ------ *Music in Canada 1600-1800.* [Montréal]: Habitex, 1975. 320p. ISBN 0-88912-020-X.

La musique au Québec 1600-1875 is essentially a translation of *Music in Canada 1600-1800*, despite the different geographical reference and different dates. In both cases the subject is confined to the French colonies and the region of present-day Québec. If the English version is slightly fuller in foot-note references, the French version has many illustrations, and an additional chapter on 19th century activity in Montréal and Québec City.

86. Asselin, André. *Panorama de la musique canadienne.* Paris: Editions de la Diaspora Française, 1962; 2nd edition 1968 (unpaginated) (32p.)

Historically interesting only as a limited, sometimes erroneous, view of music in Canada, intended for a French audience.

87. Bail Milot, Louise. "Une musique d'ici, avec des hommes et femmes venus d'ailleurs (L'Apport des musiciens immigrants à la musique canadienne)." In *Célébration*, pp.128-138. G. Ridout and T. Kenins, eds. Toronto: Canadian Music Centre/Centre de musique canadienne, 1984. ISBN 0-9690836-5-3.

Acknowledging the difficulties of treating the topic of immigrant musicians because of the vastness of the subject, the author concentrates primarily on those from abroad who were most influential after 1945. References to individuals are brief but comprehensive, and deal with composers, performers, educators, broadcasters, and musicologists.

88. Beaudet, Jean-Marie. "Composition." In *Music in Canada*, pp.55-63. Ernest MacMillan, ed. Toronto: University of Toronto Press, 1955.

The brevity of the essay suggests its point of interest, which is how little serious musical composition the author considered to exist in Canada by the 1950s. Many names are mentioned, but little information is provided.

89. Beckwith, John. "About Canadian music: the P.R. failure." *Musicanada* 21 (July-August, 1969): 4-7, 10-13.

In this classic and carefully researched review of many current foreign reference works, Beckwith excoriates them for ignorance of and mis-information about music in Canada. His exposé of indifference to Canadian achievement was a direct spur to greater indigenous activity in research, study and promotion.

90. ------ *Canadian music in the 1960s and 1970s: a chronicle.* Toronto: Canadian Music Centre, 1979. [30p.]

Written to accompany a concert given to celebrate the 20th anniversary of the Canadian Music Centre, this extended pamphlet nevertheless provides an excellent résumé of compositional activity during the first two decades of the Centre's existence

91. ------ *The Canadian musical repertoire.* Sackville, N.B.: Centre for Canadian Studies, Mount Allison University, 1993. 22p.

In this lecture given at Mount Allison University in 1992, Beckwith reflects on the idea of "repertoire", on the difficulties of developing one in the later 20th century, and on the particular application to Canada. While carefully annotated, the lecture is personal in tone and in its frame of reference.

92. ------ "Music in Canada." *The Musical Times* 111 (1970): 1214-16.

An abridgement of the article "Canada" in Vinton (no.7). Nevertheless, a useful brief survey through the 1960s.

93. Beckwith, John and Dorith R. Cooper, eds. *Hello out there! Canada's new music in the world, 1950-85.* Toronto: Institute for Canadian Music, 1988. v, 197p. CanMus Documents, 2. ISBN 0-7727-8551-1.

The proceedings of a conference at the University of Toronto in 1986. There are a number of short presentations, and transcripts of discussions, about all aspects of the dissemination of Canadian music outside Canada. Some of the papers are speculative, others provide a good deal of factual information. Taken overall, they provide much commentary on the reception of new Canadian music abroad, and by extension, the reception in general of contemporary music.

94. Beckwith, John and Frederick A. Hall, eds. *Musical Canada: words and music honouring Helmut Kallmann.* Toronto: University of Toronto Press, 1988. xiii, 369p. ISBN 0-8020-5759-4.

A collection of nineteen articles on diverse topics, and four short pieces of music by Clifford Ford, Richard Johnston, John Weinzweig and R. Murray Schafer. A chronological list of Kallmann's writings from 1949 to 1987 is in itself a veritable research guide to music in Canada. The articles are indexed individually in this *Research and Information Guide* and may be located collectively in the title index under *Musical Canada....*

95. BMI Canada Limited. *Canadian music at Carnegie Hall: a report.* [Toronto, 1953?]. [16p.]

A promotional brochure about a celebrated concert of Canadian music at Carnegie Hall in 1953 conducted by Stokowski. Reprints of articles and reviews related to the concert.

96. Bridle, Augustus. "Composers among us." In *Yearbook of the arts in Canada 1928-1929,* pp.135-140. Bertram Brooker, ed. Toronto: MacMillan Company of Canada, 1929.

Bridle's strained and affected style seems more important to him than his subject, but he has some interesting, and severe, things to say about the state of original composition in the late 1920s.

97. *Canadian arts consumer profile: report for classical music, opera and choral music.* Toronto: Decima Research, 1993. vi, 146p.

Based on data collected 1989-1992, this is a collection of analyses in tabular form of the markets and audiences for classical music. Included are such categories as audience profiles, attitudinal profiles, ticket prices, etc. There are geographical breakdowns by province, and by Vancouver, Toronto and Montréal.

98. Cselenyi, Ladislav. *Musical instruments in the Royal Ontario Museum.* Toronto: Royal Ontario Museum, 1971. 96p.

None of the instruments in the catalogue originated in Canada. Its significance lies in the fact that it records the interests of a notable Toronto piano manufacturer and dealer in rare violins, R. S. Williams, who gathered the collection of about 400 items in the later 19th century and presented it to the Royal Ontario Museum (Toronto) in 1913.

99. Desautels, Andrée. "The history of Canadian composition 1610-1967." In *Aspects of music in Canada*, pp.90-142. A. Walter,ed. Toronto. University of Toronto Press, 1969. ISBN 8020-1536-0.

This eccentric essay is refracted through much French/Québécois bias, and offers some disputable opinions. Nevertheless, it provides a good overview of composition, and refers to a number of significant works.

100. Diamond, Beverley. "Narratives in Canadian music history." In *Taking a stand: essays in honour of John Beckwith*, pp.273-305. Ed. T. McGee. Toronto: University of Toronto Press, 1995. ISBN 0-8020-0583-7. Published also in *Canadian music: issues of hegemony and identity*, pp.139-171. Beverley Diamond and Robert Witmer, eds. Toronto: Canadian Scholars' Press, 1994. ISBN 1-55130-031-1.

In this original and searching examination of three history texts by Kallmann (no.111), Ford (no.102) and McGee (no.125), Diamond examines the values and assumptions that underlie the writing of music history in Canada. For purposes of comparison, there is a short discussion of similar American histories.

101. Diamond, Beverley and Robert Witmer, eds. *Canadian music: issues of hegemony and identity*. Toronto: Canadian Scholars' Press, 1994. xi, 615p. ISBN 1-55130-031-1.

The twenty-nine essays, with four bridging essays by the authors, are mostly reprinted from earlier publications, although there are also some new items. They form a coherent group, however, in that they address a variety of aspects of musical life in Canada, viewed from a number of scholarly disciplines. In an important introductory essay, Diamond sets out the idea of music as identity, its place in the hegemonic structures of society, and how these relate particularly to Canada. All the essays examine facets of these general themes. The individual essays frequently have extensive and useful bibliographies.

102. Ford, Clifford. *Canada's music: an historical survey*. Agincourt, Ont.: GLC Publishers, 1982. viii, 278p. ISBN 888-740-549.

This broad survey of musical activity from colonial days to the 1970s draws on secondary material in a narrative that remains

more factual than interpretative. About half the book deals with the
20th century, which makes it a useful companion to Kallmann
(no.111).

103.Fricker, H. Cecil. "The development of the orchestra in Canada."
The Twentieth Century 1/9 (April 1933): 21-24; 1/10 (May 1933):
41-43; 1/11 (June 1933): 31-32; 1/12 (July, 1933): 43-44.

Each short article deals with a single orchestra in Toronto,
Montréal, Hamilton and Saskatoon. They contain only the most
cursory information and are interesting only as contemporary notes
on then current orchestras.

104.Gibbon, John Murray. "The Canadian lyric and music."
Proceedings and Transactions of the Royal Society of Canada
Series 3, Vol. 28, Sect. 2 (May 1934): 95-102.

In an unusual argument, the author suggests that Canadian
lyric poetry would benefit from being written to existing tunes. He
gives some examples of his own work, which are now more likely
to elicit smiles rather than emulation. Gibbon was an influential
figure, especially as the originator of important folk music festivals
for the Canadian Pacific Railway in the 1920s.

105.Hambraeus, Bengt. "Ny musik I Kanada." *Nutida Musik* 15/4
(1971/72): 40-43.

Directed to a Swedish audience that, especially in the early
1970s, would have little information about music in Canada, this
article provides a concise guide to current activity across the
country in composition.

106.Harrison, S. Frances. "Historical sketch of music in Canada." In
Canada: an encyclopedia of the country. vol. IV, pp.389-94. J.
Castell Hopkins, ed. Toronto: Linscott, 1898.

Mrs. Harrison was well-known as a writer on music under the
sobriquet "Seranus." Her historical outline is brief and touches
mostly on Toronto and Montréal, with mention of Hamilton and
Québec, but is useful for a 19th-century view of what was
important at the time.

107.Hatch, Peter and John Beckwith, eds. *The fifth stream*. Toronto: Institute for Canadian Music, 1991. iv, 126p. CanMus Documents, 6. ISBN 0-7727-8557-0

Proceedings of a conference held at Waterloo, Ontario, in May, 1989, a gathering of mostly young composers to hear and discuss recent music composed by Canadians. The report takes the form of sets of presentations by individuals, followed by a transcript of discussion. The subject matter is rarely technical, but is more generally philosophical or aesthetic.

108.Howell, Gordon Percy. "The development of music in Canada". PhD dissertation, University of Rochester, Eastman School of Music, 1959. xiv, 545p.

Although dependent on very limited secondary sources, the author was resourceful in developing an overview that can still be useful, especially for the later period. The first part, which covers material up to the 1950s, treats the subject geographically: the maritime provinces, Québec, Ontario, western provinces. The second part examines, with some analysis, the music of five composers: Willan, Champagne, Weinzweig, Papineau-Couture, Pentland.

109.Kallmann, Helmut. "Beethoven and Canada: a miscellany." *Les Cahiers canadiens de musique/The Canada Music Book* 2 (Printemps-été 1971): 107-17. reprinted in *German-Canadian* Yearbook 4 (1978): 286-94.

The author cites a number of events -- chiefly first performances -- that relate to Beethoven.

110.------ "The German contribution to music in Canada." *German-Canadian Yearbook* 2 (1975): 152-66.

A short but comprehensive survey of important German musicians who settled and worked in Canada from the late 18th century to the 1960s.

111.------ *A history of music in Canada 1534-1914*. Toronto: University of Toronto Press, 1960. xiv, 311p. Reprinted with some changes 1969. ISBN 8020-5089-1 (cloth)/8020-6102-8 (paper).

The first and still the basic history of music in Canada, despite the fact that subsequent research has augmented and sometimes corrected information in this book. The material is set out in chapters that reflect development through time but also by genre and geographically. The subject matter is mainly euro-centric art music, with almost no mention of folk music or native music. Index, and extensive bibliography, with a list of books with music published in Canada before 1850.

112. Keillor, Elaine. "The conservative tradition in Canadian music." In *Célébration*, pp.49-56. G. Ridout and T. Kenins, eds. Toronto: Canadian Music Centre/Centre de musique canadienne, 1984. ISBN 0-9690836-5-3.

Although even a definition of "conservative" is elusive, the concept nonetheless provides a background against which to view contemporary Canadian composition, primarily in the period from the mid-1950s to the 1980s.

113. Kirkconnell, Watson. "Music from the sidelines." *The Canadian Music Journal* 1/4 (Summer 1957): 19-26.

The author was a distinguished man of letters, not a musician, and these somewhat rambling reminiscences are interesting chiefly for an amateur's views of music in various Canadian towns and cities from early in the century to the 1940s.

114. Lapierre, Eugène. "Aspect national de la musique." *L'Action Nationale* 1/2 (février, 1933): 98-109.

This short essay is now interesting mostly for the author's plea, in 1933, that music be taken seriously in (French) Canada, including the recognition of a musical tradition and the conserving of musical records.

115. ------ *Un style canadien de musique.* Québec: École des sciences sociales, politiques et économiques de Laval, 1942. 34p.

A personal and decidedly nationalist view of music in Québec.

116. Lazarevich, Gordana. "Aspects of early arts patronage in Canada: from Rockefeller to Massey." In *Taking a stand: essays in honour*

of John Beckwith, pp.259-272. T. McGee, ed. Toronto: University of Toronto Press, 1995. ISBN 0-8020-0583-7.

Patronage of the arts during the period from 1918 to the founding of the Canada Council in 1957 is briefly reviewed. Mention is made of institutional sponsorship of music (Canadian Broadcasting Corporation, Canadian Pacific Railway), private donors, and the activities of American charitable foundations.

117. Logan, John Daniel. "Canadian Creative Composers." *Canadian Magazine* 41/5 (September, 1913): 486-94.

The article discusses four composers whom the author considers to be the first "native-born Canadian composers to undertake the systematic creation of fine music": Calixa Lavallée, Clarence Lucas, W.O. Forsyth, and Gena Branscombe. In addition to a biographical sketch, there is critical comment on their music. Logan is notable for his strong criticism (in 1913) of universities and conservatories who neglect the literary and musical history of Canada, at a time when such an idea had little acceptance.

118. MacMillan, Ernest, ed. *Music in Canada*. Toronto: University of Toronto Press, 1955. xii, 232p.

This collection of nineteen essays on a wide variety of topics was intended as a summary and, to some extent, a survey of musical activity in Canada from colonial times to the 1950s. Because relatively little research had been carried out at the time of preparation of this book, many of the essays make original contributions to historical study. MacMillan provides an "Introduction" that outlines the scope of the essays and the general picture of music in Canada by 1955. Helmut Kallmann provides a "Historical background" (pp.10-31) of musical growth up to the early 20th century. The remaining essays are listed individually in this *Research and Information Guide*, and may be located collectively by consulting the entry, *Music in Canada*, in the title index. See also Walter, no.150/151.

119. ------ "Orchestral and choral music in Canada." Music Teachers National Association *Proceedings* 40 (1946): 87-93.

A succinct statement of recent and current activity at the mid-1940s, chiefly in Vancouver, Toronto, and Montréal.

120.Mahon, A.Wylie. *Canadian hymns and hymn-writers.* St. Andrews-by-the-Sea, New Brunswick: n.p. [1908]. 56p.

For the period from 1827, the date of the dedication of St. Luke's in Halifax, to the end of the 19th century, the author presents eight short essays, each on the writer of hymn texts. There is no mention of composers or music.

121.Maniates, Maria Rika. "Musicology in Canada 1963-1979." *Acta Musicologica* 53/1 (1981): 1-14.

Comprehensive in intention, this article touches upon all aspects of musicology -- publication, research fields and support, individual contributions, libraries, programs. See also Roman, no.142.

122. Mazzoleni, Ettore. "Solo artists." In *Music in Canada*, pp.106-113. Ernest MacMillan, ed. Toronto: University of Toronto Press, 1955.

An insubstantial review of solo performers, perhaps most notable for singling out the pre-eminence of Glenn Gould before he became famous outside Canada.

123.McDowell, Louise. *Past and present: a Canadian musician's reminiscences.* Kirkland Lake, Ont.: [the author?], c. 1957.

Much of the book is given over to the author's recollections of her days as a music student in Leipzig around 1900. There are, however, some comments on her early studies in Toronto, and more particularly on Winnipeg, where she taught after her return from Europe.

124.McGee, Timothy J. "An Elegant band of music: music in Canada in the 18th-century." *International Journal of Canadian Studies/Revue internationale d'études canadiennes* 5 (1992): 25-37.

This is a concise review of late 18th-century musical activity, drawing on newspaper and diary reports.

125.------ *The Music of Canada*. New York, W.W. Norton, 1985. xii, 257p. ISBN 0-393-95376-9 [PBK]; ISBN 0-393-02279-X.

A comprehensive history of music in Canada from colonial days to 1984, including a chapter on Inuit and First Nations music. The book is oriented towards college and university use. There are very useful bibliographical and recordings lists, and a short anthology of thirteen compositions or excerpts.

126.McGee, Timothy J., ed. *Taking a stand: essays in honour of John Beckwith*. Toronto, University of Toronto Press, 1995. x, 313p. ISBN 0-8020-0583-7.

This collection of fifteen essays (and one poem by James Reaney) covers a range of topics on Canadian music that reflects Beckwith's own broad interests as composer and scholar. The short introductory essay by McGee (p.5-8) sketches, with a few over-generalizations, the many ways in which Beckwith participated in and influenced Canadian music and musical studies. The remaining articles are indexed individually in this *Research and Information Guide*, and may be located collectively in the title index under *Taking a stand: essays in honour of John Beckwith*.

127.McInnis, Campbell. "Music in Canada." In *Yearbook of the arts in Canada 1928-1929*, pp.113-121. Bertram Brooker, ed. Toronto: MacMillan Company of Canada, 1929.

The sketch is brief, but it does give a glimpse of activities and plans on the eve of the Depression.

128.McMillan, Barclay F.H. "Music in Canada 1791-1867: a travellers' perspective." MA dissertation, Carleton University (Ottawa), 1983. iv, 137f.

Among the many visitors to Canada in the 19th century, a number published books about their travels. This narrative account of music references in travel literature includes many excerpts and provides outsiders' views of musical aspects in the relatively new towns.

129.Morey, Carl. "Canada's first operatic ensemble." *Opera Canada* 11/3 (September 1970): 15, 75.

A short history of the Holman opera company, which established itself in Toronto in 1867, and after 1873 in London, Ontario.

130. "Musique et critique au Canada / Music and criticism in Canada." *Les Cahiers canadiens de musique/The Canada Music Book* (Automne/hiver 1973): 61-95.

This is a report of the meetings held by the Canadian Music Council in May, 1973. It consists of several short presentations on various aspects of musical criticism in Canada.

131. *Music in Canada, its resources and needs.* conference report. Canadian Music Council, 1966. [iii], 72p.

A review of musical life at the time of the conference, chiefly from the perspectives of patronage and of education.

132. Neel, Boyd. "Music in Canada." *Tempo* 38/winter (1955/56): 7-9.

Neel has more enthusiasm for than information about musical activity in Canada, but he does provide an impressionistic account of a time of great expansion and optimism. The English conductor had been in Canada for two years as Dean of Music at the University of Toronto.

133. Poirier, Lucien. "La fortune de deux oeuvres de Jean-Jacques Rousseau au Canada français entre 1790 et 1850." In *Musical Canada: words and music honouring Helmut Kallmann*, pp.60-70. J. Beckwith and F. Hall, eds. Toronto: University of Toronto Press, 1988. ISBN 0-8020-5759-4.

The similarities between Rousseau's *Le Devin du village* and Quesnel's *Colas et Colinette* are carefully examined. Rousseau's *Dictionnaire* appears to have been known in Québec at the end of the 18th century.

134. Potvin, Gilles. "Maurice Ravel au Canada." In *Musical Canada: words and music honouring Helmut Kallmann*, pp.149-63. J. Beckwith and F. Hall, eds. Toronto: University of Toronto Press, 1988. ISBN 0-8020-5759-4.

Ravel visited Vancouver, Toronto, and Montréal during his tour of 1928. Details of his programs and his reception in Canada are set out.

135.------ "Performers." In *Aspects of music in Canada*, pp.143-66. A. Walter,ed. Toronto. University of Toronto Press, 1969. ISBN 8020-1536-0.

With very little historical reference, this is mainly a report of the current (1960s) state of orchestras, opera companies, ensembles and soloists

136.Proctor, George A. "Canadian music from 1920 to 1945: the end of the beginning." *Studies in music from the University of Western Ontario* 9 (1984) 2-26.

A concise and extensively documented survey of attitudes to composition, including reactionary views of commentators, and the gradual changes that took place by the 1940s. There are several reproductions of concert programs.

137.----- *Canadian music of the twentieth century*. Toronto: University of Toronto Press, 1980. xxvi, 297p. ISBN 0-8020-5419-6.

About three-quarters of the book deals with music from 1950 to 1978. The author emphasizes repertoire and analysis rather than general historical information and interpretation. Some musical examples, but extensive lists of representative pieces, with publishing and recording information. Chronological table; extensive bibliography that is particularly useful for journal and periodical articles.

138.------"Recent trends in Canadian music." *Studies in music from the University of Western Ontario* 3 (1978): 1-6.

A very brief but informative survey of works composed 1968-1977, developed around types of composition and stylistic features.

139.Qureshi, Regula Burckhardt, et al. "From composer to audience: the production of 'serious' music in Canada." *Canadian University Music Review/Revue de musique des universités canadiennes* 9/2 (1989): 117-37.

Qureshi was moderator of a colloquy in 1985 on the nature and role of contemporary music making. She provides an introduction, followed by the statements of Alan Lessem, John Beckwith, Alfred Fisher and Barry Truax.

140. Ridout, Godfrey. "Fifty years of music in Canada? Good Lord, I was there for all of them!" In *The arts in Canada*, W.J Keith and B.-Z. Shek, eds. pp.116-34. Toronto: University of Toronto Press, 1980. ISBN 0-8020-2401-7(cloth)/0-8020-6425-6(pbk.).

The period 1930-1980 is recalled personally by Ridout more in anecdote than in historical detail. Useful for a sense of the period, especially in Toronto, but there is almost no documentation for the information set out.

141. Ridout, Godfrey, and Talivaldis Kenins, eds. *Célébration*. Toronto: Canadian Music Centre, 1984. 144p. ISBN 0-9690836-5-3.

Twelve essays, on various topics, in English or French to mark the twenty-fifth anniversary of the founding of the Canadian Music Centre. The articles are indexed individually in this *Research and Information Guide*, and may be located collectively in the title index under *Célébration*.

142. Roman, Zoltan. "Musicology in Canada 1980-1987." *Acta Musicologica* 60/3 (1988): 273-289.

A survey of research, publication, and related activity in all aspects of musicology in Canada. See also Maniates, no.120.

143. Rousseau, Marcelle. "The rise of music in Canada." MA dissertation, Columbia University, 1951. 137p.

Necessarily limited in background information because of the time at which it was written, this thesis nevertheless provides a general view of music up to about 1900. The bibliography lists primarily articles in books, periodicals and newspapers.

144. Schafer, R. Murray. *On Canadian music*. Bancroft, Ont.: Arcana Editions, 1984. xi, 105p.

A collection of thirteen essays, all of which were previously published. Some of the articles deal with Schafer's own music, but most of them are his views, often acerbic, stimulating, and idiosyncratic, on music in Canada and on the work of some admired colleagues. "Canadian culture: colonial culture" is reprinted in *Canadian music: issues of hegemony and identity*, pp.221-237. Beverley Diamond and Robert Witmer, eds. Toronto: Canadian Scholars' Press, 1994. ISBN 1-55130-031-1.

145. Schwandt, Eric. "*Musique spirituelle* (1718) Canada's first music theory manual." In *Musical Canada: words and music honouring Helmut Kallmann*, pp.50-59. J. Beckwith and F. Hall, eds. Toronto: University of Toronto Press, 1988. ISBN 0-8020-5759-4.

Written by a member of the order of Saint Augustine, the short work that is discussed here was intended to edify her religious sisters in Québec city. A complete transcription is given (in French) of *Musique spirituelle où l'on peut s'exercer sans voix*.

146. Sellick, Lester B. *Our musical heritage*. Hantsport, N.S.: Lancelot Press, 1984. 74p. ISBN 0-88999-255-X.

This rambling personal view of music in the Maritimes includes much irrelevant material and is undependable in its information. Not useful.

147. Smith, Gordon E. "Dualité dans l'historiographie musicale canadienne." *Les cahiers de l'ARMuQ* 13 (mai 1991): 29-37. ISSN 0821-1817.

The author examines the characteristic problems found in the historiography of Canadian music, deriving from the different points of view of anglophone and francophone historians. He uses the treatment of Ernest Gagnon as the reference point for a critical consideration of how anglophone writing on Québec music must develop a distinctive approach.

148. Spell, L. "Music in New France in the seventeenth century." *Canadian Historical Review* 8/2 (June, 1927): 119-131.

The material is drawn from *The Jesuit relations and allied documents* (Cleveland, 1896-1901), from which there is much quotation. There is also a comparison of the introduction of music in New France and New Spain.

149.Torrington, Frederick H. "Musical progress in Canada." In *Canada: an encyclopedia of the country.* Vol.IV, pp.383-386. J. Castell Hopkins, ed. Toronto: Linscott, 1898-1900.

The author had very little information on which to base a historical view, but he offers a personal account of current musical life, chiefly in Toronto, but also in Hamilton and Montréal.

150.Walter, Arnold, ed. *Aspects of music in Canada.* Toronto: University of Toronto Press, 1969. x, 336p. ISBN 8020 1536 0.

151.------ *Aspects de la musique au Canada.* Édition française dirigée par Gilles Potvin et Maryvonne Kendergi. Montréal: Centre de Psychologie et de Pédagogie, 1970. xv, 347p.

Seven essays which were intended to be a kind of review and stock-taking of music in Canada up to 1970. The essays range between the highly informative and the vaguely speculative. Kallmann's "Historical background" (pp.26-61) is an updated version of his essay in MacMillan (no.118), to which volume this publication serves as a sequel. The French edition contains a short but useful bibliography and a discography, both of which are lacking in the English edition. The articles of the English edition are indexed individually in this *Research and Information Guide* and may be located collectively in the title index under *Aspects of music in Canada.*

152.------ "Canadian composition." Music Teachers National Association *Proceedings* 40 (1946): 101-106.

Difficulties faced by contemporary composers are mentioned, and some idea of the current range of activity is conveyed. Several active (1940s) composers are mentioned.

153.Wright, Robert. "Music and Canadian studies." *Journal of Canadian Studies* 25/2 (Summer 1990): 160-169.

Written as a review of five biographies of Canadian musicians, this essay raises issues about the general lack both of music items in journals and of musical organizations devoted to Canadian studies. In large part, the author attributes the problem to one internal to Canadian musicology, which marginalizes or ignores popular music and consequently isolates critical musical study from the reality of Canadian musical culture.

154. *The year book of Canadian art 1913.* compiled by The Arts and Letters Club of Toronto. London and Toronto: J.M. Dent and Sons, n.d. x, 291p.

The book is a compilation of many short accounts of activity in the arts during the period 1912-1913. The music section (pp.61-148) consists of eleven brief essays that report on a variety of aspects of music across the country, although with an emphasis on Ontario and Québec.

2. Local and Regional

155. Baillie, Joan Parkhill. *Look at the record; an album of Toronto's lyric theatres, 1825-1984.* Oakville, Ont.: Mosaic Press, 1985. 298p. ISBN 0-88962-236-1.

With copious illustrations, the history of operatic performance in Toronto is recorded through the halls, theatres, auditoriums and even sports arenas where performances have taken place.

156. Barrière, Mireille. "Exposé d'une problématique de culture urbaine appliquée à l'étude du développement du théâtre lyrique à Montréal (1840-1913)." *Les cahiers de l'ARMuQ* 10 (juin 1988): 103-08. ISSN 0821-1817.

This model for the study of an aspect of urban culture defines the parameters of such a study, locates the subject socially and geographically, and proposes details to be considered. The article is exclusively a proposal, not an application.

157.------ "La société canadienne-française et le théâtre lyrique à
    Montréal entre 1840 et 1913." PhD diss., l'Université Laval, 1990.
    xv, 583f.

    This thesis is the realization of no.156. It records the social,
economic, and linguistic aspects of the Montréal lyric theatre up to
1913. There is a detailed survey of theatres, information on
patronage and financial backing, and on the influences
determining repertoire. A list of repertoire gives, among other
things, the language of presentation, but not the dates. The
controlling idea of the work is the dichotomy of the French and
English communities, the domination of the latter in the Montréal
theatre, and the emergence of a francophone influence.

158. Beckwith, John. "Composers in Toronto and Montreal." *University
     of Toronto Quarterly* 26/1 (October, 1956): 47-69.

    Eight composers are chosen as representative of the interest
and variety of composition in Canada in the 1950s. The discussion
of each composer's work is short but illuminating. There are some
musical examples, but the article is directed to a general, non-
professional reader. The composers are: Weinzweig, Somers,
Freedman, Kasemets, Joachim, Anhalt, Charpentier and Papineau-
Couture.

159. Bélanger, Nicole. "Le vécu musical d'un royaume: la musique au
     Saguenay-Lac-Saint-Jean." *Les cahiers de l'ARMuQ* 14 (mai
     1992): 14-27. ISSN 0821-1817.

    A cursory and uncritical assessment of musical experience in a
particular district (Saguenay-Lac-Saint-Jean) of Québec.

160. Belkin, Alan. "The new generation of composers in Quebec."
     *Canadian University Music Review / Revue de musique des
     universités canadiennes* 9/2 (1989): 22-35.

    Twenty-five composers who had lived in Québec for a
substantial length of time, who made their careers in the Province,
and who were not older than their forties, were interviewed as to
their background, training, approach to composition, and career.
The information was too divergent to be brought together in a

single format -- a book was originally intended -- but the article attempts to summarize the main findings and points of view.

161.Berg, Wesley. "Music in Edmonton, 1880-1905." *Canadian University Music Review/Revue de musique des universités canadiennes* 7 (1986): 141-70.

Isolation and a sparse population made the establishment of Edmonton's musical life difficult, as this article makes clear. Several individuals are cited for pioneering efforts, notably Vernon Barford. Photographs.

162.Blakeley, Phyllis R. "Music in Nova Scotia 1605-1867." *The Dalhousie Review* 31/2 (Summer, 1951): 94-101; 31/3 (Autumn, 1951): 223-230.

The groundwork is set out in this two-part sketch for the historical study of musical life in the province. While Halifax figures prominently, other communities are also surveyed, and most aspects of musical activity are touched on. The material is derived largely from newspapers and archival material, for the period 1749 to about 1850.

163.------ "The theatre and music in Halifax." *The Dalhousie Review* 29/1 (April, 1949): 8-20.

Much detail is given about both the spoken and musical theatre, as well as about some concert performances, in Halifax during the second half of the 19th century.

164.Bourassa, Dominique. "La contribution des bandes militaires Britanniques au developpement de la musique au Québec de la conquète à 1836." MMus dissertation, l'Université Laval, 1993. xii, 194f.

The arrival of British military bands after 1759 provided significant numbers of trained musicians who could both perform and teach. This dissertation draws extensively on newspapers as a source of information to trace the activities and influences of military bands in Québec up to the point where civilian bands also began to appear. Some information on the musical styles of marches is not strictly relevant, but otherwise there is a good deal of information on a little-investigated subject.

165. Bourassa-Trépanier, Juliette and Lucien Poirier. "L'Interprète au Québec selon la presse de 1764 à 1789." *Les cahiers de l'ARMuQ* 7 (mai 1988): 10-28. ISSN 0821-1817.

This is a synthesis, with commentary, of information found by a research team at l'Université Laval in a systematic investigation of the Québec press. See no.166.

166. ------ eds. *Répertoire des données musicales de la presse québécoise*. Tome I: Canada. Volume I: 1764-1799. Québec: Les Presses de l'Université Laval, 1990. xxi, 273p. ISBN 2-7637-7247-1 (v.1).

The first of a projected series of publications, this volume includes notices from newspapers in the cities of Montréal and Québec that relate to music in Canada. (Other volumes will include local notices about foreign events.) In a lengthy introduction, the period is dealt with comprehensively. Journal notices are arranged chronologically, gathered under the cities. Advertisements, notices, articles, letters are all included. Bibliography, general index as well as indexes of names, places and titles. See also Poirier, no.233.

167. Brault, Lucien. "Les instruments de musique dans les églises de la Nouvelle-France." *Société canadienne d'histoire de l'Église Catholique, Rapport* (1956-57): 91-101.

In reviewing the evidence for instruments in churches, up to the mid-18th century, the author quotes a number of sources which give this short article a particular interest.

168. Bridle, Augustus. "Two pères de musique." In *Sons of Canada: short studies of characteristic Canadians*. Toronto: J.M. Dent & Sons, 1916. pp.139-147.

F.H. Torrington and Guillaume Couture are each the subject of a biographical sketch. There is an outline of each man's contribution to music in Toronto and Montréal, with some astute observations on differences between the cities from a musical standpoint.

169.*Chapeau bas. Réminiscences de la vie théâtrale et musicale du Manitoba français.* Saint-Boniface: Éditions du Blé, première partie, 1980. 160p.; deuxième partie, 1985. xi, 161-266p. ISBN 0-920640-26-5.

The first part includes essays on religious and theatrical music in Saint-Boniface in the 19th and early 20th centuries. There is an extensive section on composer-conductor Marius Benoist (1896-1985), and an essay on musical/theatrical topics in the second part. Other items are on the spoken theatre.

170.Chartier, Émile. "La vie de l'esprit au Canada français; 9e étude: Les arts: architecture, peinture, sculpture, musique." *Mémoires de la Société Royale du Canada,* Série 3, Vol. 32, Sect. 1 (1938): 41-54.

The distinctive character of the arts of French Canada is rapidly and superficially sketched out. The section on music includes mention of a number of musicians, but finds the most activity in folklore.

171.Chatillon, Louis. "A la recherche de l'ancienne musique québécoise." *Vie Musicale* 9 (septembre, 1968): 10-14.

A brief and insubstantial appeal for research into the early musical life of Québec.

172.Chester, Russell E. "Music in Winnipeg 1900-1907." *Les Cahiers canadien de musique / The Canada Music Book* 8 (Printemps/été 1974): 109-15.

The author was born in Winnipeg in 1892 and left the city in 1907, so that his reminiscences are those of a young boy. Nevertheless, there are some personal glimpses of the city at the turn of the century.

173.Cooper, Dorith Rachel. "Opera in Montréal and Toronto: a study of performance traditions and repertoire 1783-1980." PhD dissertation, University of Toronto, 1983. xxx, 1399f.

This compendious study presents details relating to all aspects of opera in the two cities -- touring companies, local troups, training, local personalities. There are many lists of repertoire, often with cast and production details, and extensive excerpts from newspapers and other archival sources. The work concludes with historical and analytical commentary on five important works: *Torquil* (Harriss), *Deirdre* (Willan), *Night Blooming Cereus* (Beckwith), *Le magicien* (Vallerand), and *Louis Riel* (Somers).

174.Dixon, F.E. "Music in Toronto: as it was in the days that are gone forever." *Daily Mail and Empire* (Saturday, November 7, 1896): section 1, p.9.

Few dates are given, but these reminiscences go back to the 1840s when the author was a choirboy. The essay is unusual for the references to mid-19th-century Toronto musicians made by someone who knew them. Dixon was a violinist.

175.Draper, Norman. *Bands by the Bow: a history of band music in Calgary*. Calgary: Century Calgary Publications, 1975. 72p.

A survey of military and community bands in Calgary from 1875. Many photographs.

176.Dufresne, Jean. *Au carrefour des souvenirs <par> Marcel Valois* <pseud.>. Montréal: Beauchemin, 1965. 158p.

More reflective than informative, this set of reminiscences nevertheless conveys a sense of musical as well as other aspects of artistic life in Montréal during the first half of the 20th century, particularly in the 1930s and 1940s.

177.Duguay, Raoul. *Musiques du Kébèk*. Montréal: Éditions du Jour, 1971. 331p.

A set of essays and interviews by or about Istvan Anhalt, Walter Boudreau, Robert Charlebois, Gabriel Charpentier, Lucie Hirbour-Coron, Serge Garant, Maryvonne Kendergi, Michèle Lalonde, Pierre Leduc, Jean-Pierre Lefèbvre, Gilles Manny, Bruce Mather, Pierre Mercure, François Morel, Jean Papineau-Couture, Clermont Pépin, Jean Préfontaine, André Prévost, Jeanne Renaud, Françoise Riopelle, Jean Sauvageau, Pierre Saint-Jacques, Patrick Straram, Françoise Sullivan, Andrée Paul, Gilles Tremblay, Claude Vivier, Luc Racine Robert, and Raoul Duguay.

178.Elliott, Carleton. "Music in New Brunswick." In *Arts in New Brunswick*, pp. 191-201. Robert A. Tweedie, Fred Cogswell and W. Stewart MacNutt, eds. Fredericton: Brunswick Press, 1967.

Although brief, and part of a popular, celebratory publication, the essay touches on many facets of 19th and 20th century musical life in New Brunswick, and mentions many individuals who have played significant roles.

179.Émond, Vivianne. "La chronique musicale de LeVasseur: entre le réel et l'imaginaire." *Les cahiers de l'ARMuQ* 8 (mai 1987): 42-47. ISSN 0821-1817.

LeVasseur's "Musique et musiciens à Québec; souvenirs d'un amateur," appeared in forty-eight consecutive issues of *La Musique*, 1919-1922. Its unquestionable value as a history of music in New France, especially of the period with which LeVasseur had personal contact, is undermined by the author's frequent dependence on erroneous anecdote and imperfect recollection. Its importance is maintained in this article, but its shortcomings in documentation and dependability are also discussed. See no.180.

180.------ "'Musique et musiciens à Québec: souvenirs d'un amateur' de Nazaire LeVasseur (1848-1927): étude critique." MMus dissertation, l'Université Laval, 1986. vii, 203f.

The main purpose of the dissertation is to examine LeVasseur's work critically for error. In correcting LeVasseur, Émond provides useful accounts of many individuals and organizations. See no.179.

181.Evans, Chad. *Frontier theatre*. Victoria: Sono Nis Press, 1983. 326p. ISBN 0-919203-24-8.

There is extensive information on 19th-century spoken drama in what came to be British Columbia (Alaska and the Klondike). Musical information is difficult to extract from the main text (there is an index only of names and titles), but there is a short chapter on opera, pp.261-270.

182.Fenwick, G. Roy. "Some musical memories of Hamilton." *Wentworth Bygones* 6 (1965): 23-30.

The reminiscences are largely anecdotal. Some idea of musical life is conveyed from the 1920s and 1930s, especially about music in the schools, but references are often vague and there are few dates.

183. Gagné, Mireille. "Les jeunes compositeurs au Québec." In *Célébration*, pp.117-121. G. Ridout and T. Kenins, eds. Toronto: Canadian Music Centre/Centre de musique canadienne, 1984. ISBN 0-9690836-5-3.

The work of Québec composers who were between 30 and 40 years old in 1984 is briefly surveyed. Some attempt is made to convey the character of much of the music being composed, and to indicate who appear to be the important young composers of the moment.

184. Gagnon, Ernest. "La musique à Québec au temps de Mgr. de Laval." *La Nouvelle-France* 7/5 (mai, 1908): 207-13.

The essay, which is short and contains little information, is interesting primarily as one of the first essays by a distinguished musician on the musical history of French Canada.

185. Galaise, Sophie and Johanne Rivest. "Compositeurs québécois: chronique d'une décennie (1980-1990)." *Circuit* 1/1 (1990): 83-97.

Despite the title, this article is a general review of contemporary music in Québec in the 1980s, including teaching and performing as well as composing.

186. Gallat-Morin, Élisabeth. "Jean Girard: premier musicien professionnel de Montréal?" *Les cahiers de l'ARMuQ* 3 (juin 1984): 23-32. ISSN 0821-1817.

The author traces the life of Girard, a Sulpician, in France and after 1724 in Montréal, where he was one of the first fully trained musicians in the city.

187. Gallat-Morin, Élisabeth and Antoine Bouchard. *Témoins de la vie musicale en Nouvelle-France.* Québec: Ministère des Affaires culturelles, 1981. 74p. ISBN 2-550-04322-0.

The catalogue of an exhibition (the date and location are not given) associated with a symposium, "L'orgue à notre époque." There is an introduction, and annotations, in French and English for a wide variety of items that figured in the musical life of New France up to the end of the 18th century.

188.Garceau, Hélène. "L'opéra à Montréal en 1859." *Les cahiers de l'ARMuQ* 7 (mai 1988): 29-45. ISSN 0821-1817.

Derived largely from newspaper reports, this article surveys the operatic visitors , including Patti, Brignoli, and Parodi, who performed in Montréal in 1859.

189.Geoffrion, Diane. "La musique de salon au Québec: 1880-1915." *Les cahiers de l'ARMuQ* 3 (juin 1984): 33-36. ISSN 0821-1817.

A brief note that does no more than suggest an outline of the use and nature of salon music and how it might be studied.

190.George, Graham. "Music where the wind blows free." *The Canadian Music Journal* 6/3 (Spring 1962): 12-18.

This short and very personal ramble about music in the prairie Provinces derives from a 1960 trip by the author, and touches on interviews with John Waterhouse in Winnipeg and Lyell Gustin in Edmonton.

191.Godfrey, H.H., ed. *A souvenir of musical Toronto*. First edition, Toronto: 1897. Second edition, Toronto: 1898-99. 40p.

There are short notes on each of the principal music schools in Toronto, and brief biographies of all the important local musicians at the end of the 19th century.

192.Graham, Franklin. *Histrionic Montreal*. Montréal: J. Lovell, 1902. reissued New York: Benjamin Blom, 1969. 303, ivp.

There are notes on activities in individual theatres and short biographies of prominent players, with the information arranged chronologically, 1786-1900. There is a great deal of musical information scattered throughout the book, but it is difficult to locate. An index of names is helpful, but it is incomplete.

193.Grégoire, Carole. "L'orgue au Québec de la conquête à l'arrivée de Samuel Russell Warren d'après la presse québécoise de l'époque." MMus dissertation, Université Laval, 1990. iv, 83f.

The principal value of this work lies in the comprehensive presentation of information gathered from newspapers for the period 1764-1836. Instruments, builders and organists are treated, with moderate commentary on the quoted material.

194.------ "La situation de l'orgue au Québec entre 1764 et 1836 telle que présentée par la presse." *Canadian University Music Review/Revue de musique des universités canadiennes* 10/1 (1990): 1-11.

Derived from newspaper reports (see no.193), this summary sets out some basic information about the presence and construction of organs in Québec up to the arrival in Montréal in 1837 of the important builder, Samuel Warren.

195.Guertin, Marcelle, ed. *Musique contemporaine au Québec.* Montréal: Diffusion parallèle, 1984. 146p., audio-disc 33 1/3. (issue of *Dérives* 44/45 (1984) ISSN 0383-7521)

In a series of essays and interviews, many aspects of contemporary music (roughly the period 1960-1984) in Québec are examined, including composition in various genres, interpreters, and criticism. The contributors are: Carol Bergeron, Mireille Gagné, Serge Garant, Javier García Méndez, Michel Gonneville, François Guérin, Marcelle Guertin, Robert Léonard, Denise Monast, Gisèle Ricard, and Gilles Tremblay.

196.Hall, Frederick. "Hamilton, 1846-1946: a century of music." *Canadian Association of University Schools of Music Journal* 4/1-2 (Fall, 1974): 98-114.

Rather than offering a comprehensive sketch of Hamilton's musical life over the century, this essay concentrates on a number of names and events that figured in the city's early musical life.

197.------ "Musical life in eighteenth-century Halifax." *Canadian University Music Review/Revue de musique des universités canadiennes* 4 (1983): 278-307.

Almost from its founding in 1749, Halifax enjoyed an enterprising musical life. This survey of activity up to 1800 is drawn largely from newspaper reports and touches on music in the churches, the theatre and the halls and coffee-houses. List of opera performances 1791-1800.

198.------ "Musical life in Windsor: 1875-1901." *Les Cahiers canadiens de musique / The Canada Music Book* 6 (Printemps/Été 1973): 111-24.

Settled early in the 19th century, Windsor began to develop musical institutions only in the later part of the century. The author traces the foundations provided by the churches, the first music teaching, and performance organizations.

199.----- "Musical Yankees and Tories in Maritime settlements of eighteenth-century Canada." *American Music* 5/4 (Winter 1987): 391-402. Reprinted in *Canadian music: issues of hegemony and identity*, pp.447-458. Eds. Beverley Diamond and Robert Witmer. Toronto: Canadian Scholars' Press, 1994. ISBN 1-55130-031-1.

The British maritime colonies that became Nova Scotia and New Brunswick were much influenced by musicians who came from the colonies just to the south, especially from the mid-18th century and after the American War of Independence.

200.Hines, Frances Ruth. "Concert life in London, Ontario, 1870-1880". MMus dissertation, University of Western Ontario, 1977. vii, 88p.

Although mostly confined to the decade noted in the title, there is some information from before 1870. A general survey of local music making, visitors, and particularly the Holman opera troupe.

201.Hobday, Kathleen M. *Survey of the musical resources of the province of Ontario*. Toronto: Department of Education Research, Ontario College of Education, 1946. xxxvii, 288 p.

A survey made for the Department of Education of Ontario that sets out basic information about all organizations relating to music in the Province, mainly as were in operation in 1944-45. Education is not included although schools may be listed as part of community activity. Entries are organized by county. An exceptional musical profile of the Province at the end of World War II.

202. Huot, Cécile. "Musiciens belges au Québec." *Les Cahiers canadiens de musique / The Canada Music Book* 8 (Printemps/été 1974): 69-77.

From the later 18th-century Belgian musicians settled in Montréal, where they played important roles in the city's musical life. In this article the author notes these musicians and their contributions.

203. Kallmann, Helmut. "From the archives." *The Canadian Music Journal* 2/4 (Summer 1958): 45-52.

A few facsimiles of programs, reviews and other items relating to music in Victoria, Vancouver and New Westminster, B.C., in the 1860s and 1890s.

204. ------ "From the archives: the Montreal Gazette on music from 1786 to 1797." *The Canadian Music Journal* 6/3 (Spring 1962): 3-11.

This survey of musical items in *The Montreal Gazette,* which identifies numerous preformances and musicians, includes the reprinting of some of those items.

205. Keillor, Elaine. "Musical activity in Canada's new capital city in the 1870s." In *Musical Canada: words and music honouring Helmut Kallmann,* pp.115-33. J. Beckwith and F. Hall, eds. Toronto: University of Toronto Press, 1988. ISBN 0-8020-5759-4.

This richly detailed picture of musical Ottawa in the decade following Confederation is based on material taken from local newspapers of the period.

206. Kendergi, Maryvonne. "La musique des années cinquantes au Québec." *Studies in music from the University of Western Ontario* 9 (1984) 27-36.

A survey of the consolidation of music activity in Québec in the 1950s, which was a period of emerging nationalism, and the role played by Québec musicians.

207. Kennedy, Norman J. "The growth and development of music in Calgary (1875-1920)." MA dissertation, University of Alberta, 1952. 158p.

A general survey that touches on all aspects of musical activity. It is particularly valuable for information that was obtained from interviews with local musicians who were active early in the 20th century, a list of whom is included.

208. Lamarche, Jean-Marc. "Le théâtre au Québec de la Conquête à la fin du XVIIIe siècle: sa production et son répertoire d'après la presse québécoise de l'époque." *Les cahiers de l'ARMuQ* 11 (juin 1989): 27-35. ISSN 0821-1817.

This résumé of the findings of a research team at l'Université Laval deals with theatre (not necessarily musical) in Montréal and Québec city from 1764 to 1799.

209. Lande, Lawrence. *Beethoven and Québec.* Montréal: Redpath Library, McGill University, 1966. 17p.

This pamphlet records a curiosity, namely a canon *Freu Dich des Lebens* inscribed by Beethoven to the Québec musician Theodore Molt. A brief note on Molt; facsimile, photographs. In French and English.

210. Lasalle-Leduc, Annette. *La vie musicale au Canada français.* Québec: Ministère des Affaires culturelles, 1964. 103p.

The author traces the situation that she considers has led in twenty years from stagnation to the liveliness (by 1964) in the musical life of "l'État du Québec." A good review of all aspects of music in Québec in the 1950s.

211. Lefebvre, Marie-Thérèse."Les débuts du modernisme musical à Montréal." In *Célébration*, pp.73-79. G. Ridout and T. Kenins, eds. Toronto: Canadian Music Centre/Centre de musique canadienne, 1984. ISBN 0-9690836-5-3.

After a short survey of the years up to 1948, the author locates the beginning of modernism in Montréal in 1948-50, years in which a number of significant works appeared that broke with the past. Subsequent points of important development are found in 1954-55 and 1960-61.

212.------ "L'influence de John Cage au Québec: résistances et convergences." *Les cahiers de l'ARMuQ* 14 (mai 1992): 87-107. ISSN 0821-1817.

Cage visited Montréal in 1961, 1973 and 1989. In examining the local view of Cage, the author also speculates on the cultural fixation on France and the resistance to American influences by Québec musicians, and changes that took place in the 1960s and 1970s.

213.------ "La musique de Wagner au Québec au tournant du XXe siècle." *Canadian University Music Review/Revue de musique des universités canadiennes* 14 (juin 1994): 60-76.

The fascination with Wagner in the late 19th century extended to Québec where, compared to Europe, performances were relatively rare but nonetheless significant. This article concentrates on events in the period 1884-1914, with a survey of the presentations after 1938 by l'Orchestre Symphonique de Montréal.

214.------ "Place aux femmes-compositeurs du Québec." *Les cahiers de l'ARMuQ* 7 (mai 1988): 79-89.

As a result of a university research project, a list of 167 women composers in Québec was compiled. This report provides a general outline of the findings.

215.Loudon, J.S. "Reminiscences of chamber music in Toronto during the past forty years." *Canadian Journal of Music* 1/3 (July-August 1914): 47, 52-53.

Loudon was a violinist who settled in Toronto in 1871. He was an enthusiastic chamber musician, and he mentions many colleagues and others active in the city in the later 19th century.

216. Lugrin, N. De Bertrand. *The pioneer women of Vancouver Island 1843-1866.* Victoria: The Women's Canadian Club of Victoria, Vancouver Island, 1928. 312p.

Includes "Music and Drama of Long Ago", p.199-251, which contains glimpses rather than detailed information on musical life on the Island, mainly Victoria.

217. Magnan, Odile. "La musique à Québec de 1908 à 1918 d'après l'Action sociale et l'Action catholique." *Les cahiers de l'ARMuQ* 8 (mai, 1987): 48-50. ISSN 0821-1817.

A very brief survey, with a few quotations, of the treatment of music in a Montréal newspaper, 1908-18.

218. Malouin-Gélinas, France. "La vie musicale à Quebec 1840-1845." *Les Câhiers canadiens de musique / The Canada Music Book* 7 (Automne/hiver, 1973): 9-22.

This article is virtually identical to no.220, except for some illustrations, and for documentation on Charles Sauvageau.

219. ------ "La vie musicale à Québec de 1840 à 1845, telle que décrite par les journaux et revues de l'époque." MMus dissertation, l'Université de Montréal, 1975. xii, 229f.

The period studied follows the report of Lord Durham (1839) which recommended the assimilation of the French Canadians by the English. This study views the material in the context of the preservation of French society. The material, derived from newspapers in Québec City, is treated by subject, but there is also a chart of all concerts given in the period.

220. ------ "La vie musicale dans la ville de Québec de 1840 à 1845 à travers les journaux." *Canadian Association of University Schools of Music Journal* 3/1 (Fall 1973): 1-18.

Although there are numerous examples of writing about music in Québec journals included in the article, the author primarily gives an overview of the concert life that was the subject of the reviews, and comments on the style and philosophy of such writing at a period when there was a democratic mix of professional and amateur public music-making. Includes an extended review that is not in no.218.

221. McGee, Timothy J. "Music in Halifax, 1749-1799." *The Dalhousie Review* 49/3 (Autumn 1969): 377-87.

Based on newspapers and church records, this essay brings forward information about both sacred and secular music-making in Halifax during its first fifty years.

222. McIntosh, Robert Dale. *A documentary history of music in Victoria, British Columbia. Vol. I: 1850-1899.* Victoria: University of Victoria, 1981. xi, 304p.

A series of records, mostly drawn from newspapers. Reviews, notices and advertisements are arranged chronologically. There is a set of biographies arranged alphabetically, and a list of theatres and concert halls. A short "reminiscence" written by a local musician in 1918 is included. A later-discovered concluding section is printed in vol.II (no.223). Many photographs. Indexes.

223. ------ *A documentary history of music in Victoria. Vol.II: 1900-1950.* Victoria: Beach Holme Publishers, 1994. vii, 548p. ISBN 0-88878-358-2.

A continuation of no.222 in a similar format, with illustrations. The material is arranged chronologically, but within categories, such as choral groups, composition, festivals, education, etc. Biographical sketches, notes on theatres and halls. A section is devoted to Gertrude Huntley Green. Indexes. Although selective, the items cover a broad range of musical life in great detail.

224. ------ *History of music in British Columbia 1850-1950.* Victoria: Sono Nis Press, 1989. 296p. ISBN 0-919203-99-X.

This comprehensive and detailed study makes available a wealth of material not previously published. The book is organized around bands, choirs, orchestras, musical drama, education, festivals, and commercial and social aspects. There are important checklists for most of these subjects, an extensive bibliography, and indexes. Many photographs.

225.------ "Ships of the fleet: the Royal Navy and the development of music in British Columbia." In *Musical Canada: words and music honouring Helmut Kallmann*, pp.143-148. J. Beckwith and F. Hall, eds. Toronto: University of Toronto Press, 1988. ISBN 0-8020-5759-4.

The presence of the Royal Navy around Vancouver Island in the 19th century and the naval base at Esquimalt provided bands and individual musicians for the musical growth of the colony. Although brief, this article cites many examples of activity related to the naval presence.

226.Morey, Carl. "The beginnings of modernism in Toronto." In *Célébration*, pp.80-86. G. Ridout and T. Kenins, eds. Toronto: Canadian Music Centre/Centre de musique canadienne, 1984. ISBN 0-9690836-5-3.

Events are chronicled from the early 20th century to the 1960s to demonstrate the growth of a modernist sensibility in both musicians and the public in Toronto. The importance of visitors as well as of local musicians is considered.

227.------ "Music and modernism: Toronto 1920-1950." In *Regionalism and national identity*, pp.117-125. Reginald Berry and James Acheson, eds. Christchurch, New Zealand: Association for Canadian Studies in Australia and New Zealand, 1985. ISBN 0-473-00385-6.

The emergence of vigorous creative musical activity in Toronto in the late 1940s and 1950s is considered here as part of a tradition of contemporary music that had been laid down since the 1920s. Slender as that tradition was, it was the necessary basis for an evolving contemporary sensibility.

228.------ "Orchestras and orchestral repertoire in Toronto before 1914." In *Musical Canada: words and music honouring Helmut Kallmann*, pp.100-114. J. Beckwith and F. Hall, eds. Toronto: University of Toronto Press, 1988. ISBN 0-8020-5759-4.

A review of visiting orchestras and bands from the mid-19th century, and the formation of Toronto's first orchestras. The gradual addition of significant works to local experience is noted.

229. ------ "Pre-confederation opera in Toronto." *Opera Canada* 10/3 (September 1969): 13-15.

Some notable visitors are surveyed in this article. In the period up to 1867, many renowned singers visited Toronto, as did companies presenting concert versions and sometimes fully staged productions of opera

230. Paul, Hélène. "*Le Canada musical* (1917-24): miroir d'une ville, reflet de deux continents." *Les cahiers de l'ARMuQ* 13 (mai 1991): 48-65. ISSN 0821-1817.

Without connections to Canada west of Montréal, *Le Canada musical* turned to Europe and the United States for most of its news. The author argues that this contributed to the development of Montréal's perception of itself within a cultural axis with Paris and New York.

231. ------ "La vie musicale montréalaise en 1917-1918: grandeurs et vicissitudes." *Les cahiers de l'ARMuQ* 11 (septembre 1989): 36-48. ISSN 0821-1817.

Although torn by the disturbances surrounding military conscription, Montréal in 1917-18 supported much musical activity and saw also increasingly strong statements calling for recognition of the importance of Canadian (Francophone) music.

232. Pinson, Jean-Pierre. "Quel plain-chant pour la Nouvelle-France? L'exemple des Ursulines." *Canadian University Music Review/Revue de musique des universités canadiennes* 11/2 (1991): 7-32.

Based on sources in the Ursuline archives in Québec city and Trois-Rivières, this article examines the repertoire of plainchant and its use in New France in the 17th and 18th centuries. There is a descriptive list of sources, both manuscript and printed.

233. Poirier, Lucien. "Le projet de recherche 'Histoire de la musique au Québec (1764-1918) d'après la presse québécoise de l'époque': une présentation." *Les cahiers de l'ARMuQ* 8 (mai 1987): 9-14. ISSN 0821-1817.

A statement of the objectives and organization of a research project at l'Université Laval that resulted in the publication of no.166.

234.------ "Style canadien de musique: mirage et réalité." *Les cahiers de l'ARMuQ* 3 (juin 1984): 2-7. ISSN 0821-1817.

The question is examined as to whether the idea of "Canadian music" has in any way evolved from the 1930s. The author outlines a proposal for the study of Québec music and musical life, which he hypothesizes has a distinctive style. See also no.235.

235.------ "Les vues de quelques auteurs canadiens-français de la première moitié du XXe siècle sur le sujet du style musical au Canada: compte rendu et analyse." *Les cahiers de l'ARMuQ* 4 (novembre 1984): 6-32. ISSN 0821-1817.

In the earlier 20th century a large number of francophone musicians wrote about music, and among them many discussed the question of "national music". Their views on a national musical identity are surveyed here. This and the preceding article (no.234), in English translation, taken together form the chapter "A Canadian music style: illusion and reality," in *Canadian music: issues of hegemony and identity*, pp.239-268. Beverley Diamond and Robert Witmer, eds. Toronto: Canadian Scholars' Press, 1994. ISBN 1-55130-031-1.

236.Rhéaume, Claire. "La Création musicale chez les religieuses enseignantes de Montréal." *Les cahiers de l'ARMuQ* 10 (juin 1988): 34-40. ISSN 0821-1817.

This short essay draws attention to the existence of more than 700 works composed by the sisters in three religious orders of Montréal for religious or pedagogical use.

237.Robbins, Vivian M. *Musical Buxton*. North Buxton, Ont.: North Buxton Centennial Community Club, 1969. [iv], 44p.

North Buxton is one of those communities in south-western Ontario that originated in the later 19th century as the result of settlement by escaped slaves from the United States. The author, a local musician, surveys the musicians and musical groups that have figured so prominently in the life of the community.

238.Roberts, John. "Stravinsky and the CBC." *Les Cahiers canadiens de musique / The Canada Music Book* 4 (Printemps-été 1972): 33-56.

In the 1960s Stravinsky made a number of visits to Toronto for concerts and recordings. Much of this article deals with Stravinsky himself, but it also conveys much about his presence among Toronto musicians.

239.Saddlemyer, Ann. ed. *Early stages: theatre in Ontario 1800-1914.* Toronto: University of Toronto Press, 1990. xiii, 412p. ISBN 0-8020-2738-5 (cloth), 0-8020-6779-4 (paper).

Eight essays on various topics. Musical information appears in several contexts, but it is difficult to locate except through specific reference in the index. Useful bibliography, including theses.

240.Sale, David John. "Toronto's pre-Confederation music societies, 1845-1867." MA dissertation, University of Toronto, 1968. iv, 420f.

An introductory section reviews the various musical organizations operating in Toronto from 1845 to 1867. The chief value of the study is in the chronological listing of concerts (not necessarily only those given by societies), derived from newspaper reports and advertisements. Cross-indexed by performers and composers.

241.Salisbury, Dorothy E. "Music in British Columbia outside Vancouver." *The Canadian Music Journal* 2/4 (Summer 1958): 34-44.

Despite the brevity of the references to most communities other than Victoria, this conveys some historical background to musical activity in a large number of towns.

242.Schwandt, Erich. *The motet in New France.* Victoria, éditions Jeu editions, 1981. 27p.

The transcription of twenty representative motets, antiphones and canticles from the 17th and 18th centuries found in Québec archives, with a brief historical note.

243.------ "The motet in New France: some 17th and 18th century manuscripts in Québec." *Fontes Artis Musicae* 28/3 (1981): 194-219.

An inventory of manuscript compilations of motets and other figural music in the collections of l'Hôtel-Dieu and the Ursuline Convent of Québec. According to the author, the repertoire appears to date from about 1675 to 1740. Introduction, and thematic catalogue of 128 items, with index of first lines.

244.------ "Some 17th-century French unica in Canada: notes for RISM." *Fontes Artis Musicae* 27/3-4 (1980): 172-74.

Although intended as a contribution to the recovery of French polyphonic music of the 1640s, this short inventory also provides insight into the early musical history of Québec. .

245.Slemon, Peter. "Montreal's musical life under the union, with an emphasis on the terminal years, 1841 and 1867." McGill University, MMA dissertation, 1975. [iv], 189f.

Performances, often with programs, are listed chronologically 1841-1867. The listing is extensive but not exhaustive. Information is drawn from Montréal journals and newspapers, but also often from secondary sources.

246.Smiley, Marilynn J. "Across Lake Ontario: nineteenth-century concerts and connections." In *Taking a stand: essays in honour of John Beckwith*, pp.149-165. Ed. T. McGee. Toronto: University of Toronto Press, 1995. ISBN 0-8020-0583-7.

Oswego, New York, was on a major 19th-century transportation route that connected to Canada, especially to nearby Kingston. The author refers to many touring musicians who appeared in Oswego and in Canada, but she depends for Canadian information entirely on general histories. There is a list of Oswego organists, many of whom came from French Canada.

247.Smith, Dorothy Blakey. "Music in the furthest West a hundred years ago." *The Canadian Music Journal* 2/4 (Summer 1958): 3-14.

This account of music in Victoria concentrates on the 1850s and 1860s, with particular reference to Arthur Thomas Bushby and Matthew Begbie.

248.Spier, Susan. "The Dubois String Quartet 1910-1938: its role in Montréal music history." MA dissertation, Université de Montréal, 1985. vii,135f.

The history of the Quartet is described in considerable detail, including the background of the players. The principal interest lies in the table of programs performed at all the regular concerts of the Quartet, and the index of composers represented at those concerts.

249.------ "Le Quatuor Dubois: sa place dans la musique de chambre à Montréal (1910-1938)." *Les cahiers de l'ARMuQ* 8 (mai 1987): 97-102. ISSN 0821-1817.

A brief statement on the activities of the Dubois Quartet of Montréal, with almost no information about their repertoire. See no.248.

250.Staebler, H.L. "Random notes on music of nineteenth-century Berlin, Ontario." *Thirty-Seventh Annual Report of the Waterloo Historical Society* (1949): 14-18.

Personal recollections of miscellaneous musical events in Berlin, later Kitchener, with reference to visitors as well as local musicians.

251.Thompson, J.-Antonio. *Cinquante ans de la vie musicale à Trois-Rivières*. Trois-Rivières: Le Mauricien Médical, Éditions du Bien Public, 1970. 68p.

This recounting of the principal musical events in Trois-Rivières covers the period 1901-1951. Many names are mentioned, mostly to do with concert life rather than with schools or church. No index, no citations of sources.

252.Trowsdale, G. Campbell. "The furthest west: the beginnings of modernism in Vancouver." In *Célébration*, pp.87-98. G. Ridout and T. Kenins, eds. Toronto: Canadian Music Centre/Centre de musique canadienne, 1984. ISBN 0-9690836-5-3.

After a short introductory section on the years up to 1945, developments since that time through to the 1980s are reviewed comprehensively. Not only composition is considered, but also performance, education, and influential individuals.

253.Vachon, Monique, and Maurice Carrier. "Les retrouvailles de la France et du Canada en 1855." *Les cahiers de l'ARMuQ* 6 (septembre 1985): 14-21. ISSN 0821-1817.

The renewed interest in 1854 of Louis-Napoléon in French Canada, an extension of an alliance with England, was reflected in some popular songs.

254.Vallée, Marcelle. *La vie musicale à Ste-Anne-de-la- Pérade 1876-1943*. Sainte-Anne-de-la-Pérade, Québec: Editions du Bien Public, 1978. 41p.

A glimpse of musical life in a small Québec community, with mention of main figures, choirs and bands.

255.Vézina-Demers, Micheline. "Vie musicale québécoise, 1790-1794: tendances et influences." *Les cahiers de l'ARMuQ* 8 (mai 1987): 31-41. ISSN 0821-1817.

Based on newspaper reports, this article presents a view of musical life in Québec City, which at the end of the 18th century was much under English influence. The article is based on the author's more extensive "Aspects de la vie musicale à Québec de 1790 à 1794 d'après la presse québécoise de l'époque," MMus dissertation, l'Université Laval, 1985; v, 222f.

256.Walker, Carl Ian. *Pioneer Pipers of British Columbia*. Squamish, B.C.: Western Academy of Pipe Music, 1987. v, 286p. ISBN 0-9693035-0-5.

About 700 entries, almost all of them biographical, are arranged alphabetically and include pipers active in British Columbia up to the 1950s. Many photographs.

257.------ *Pipe Bands in British Columbia*. Squamish, B.C.: Western
     Academy of Pipe Music, 1992. x, 270p. ISBN 1-55056-162-6.

There are 188 entries, arranged alphabetically, of pipe bands
that have been active in British Columbia from colonial times to
the time of publication. Notes on their founding, history and
principal activities. Many photographs.

258. Wood, Christopher. "Memories of music in Toronto in the
     thirties." *Le Compositeur Canadien/The Canadian Composer* 65
     (December 1971): 12-17, 46.

The author was music critic for the Toronto journal, *Saturday
Night*. His recollections of people and events are not entirely
without interest, but they are random and somewhat patronizing.

259. Woodford, Paul. *"We love the place, O Lord"*. St. John's,
     Newfoundland: Creative Publishers, 1988. ix, 253 p. ISBN 0-
     920021-50-6.

Subtitled "A history of the written musical tradition of
Newfoundland and Labrador to 1949", this book specifically omits
discussion of folk-material in favour of a history of music in the
communities of Newfoundland from the earliest colonial period.
Popular, concert, religious, educational, and patriotic music and
performance are all treated. Extensive bibliography.

3. Organizations and Institutions

260. Barrière, Mireille. "L'Opéra français du Monument national
     (1902)." *Les cahiers de l'ARMuQ* 15 (mai 1994): 54-66. ISSN
     0821-1817.

The chance discovery of documents allowed the
reconstruction of the business aspects of a season of opera in 1902
at the Monument national, a Montréal theatre.

261. Becker, John. *Discord: the story of the Vancouver Symphony Orchestra.* Vancouver: Brighouse Press, 1989. 180p. ISBN 0-921304-03-

A history of the Orchestra, with about half the book devoted to the events that lead to its suspension in 1988 for financial reasons, and its recovery.

262. Beckwith, John. *Music at Toronto: a personal account.* Toronto: by the author, at the University of Toronto Press, 1995. 60p. (Institute for Canadian Music) ISBN 0-9699416-0-9.

The text derives from two lectures given by Beckwith to recognize the 75th anniversary in 1993 of the founding of the Faculty of Music, University of Toronto. He reviews the curricula, changing points of view, and the general history of the Faculty. Much of the material is based on personal reminiscence, since the author was associated with the Faculty as student and staff member for more than half of its seventy-five years.

263. ------ "Réalisations et projets de l'Institut de musique canadienne." *Les cahiers de l'ARMuQ* 10 (juin 1988): 74-81.

A report on the founding (1984), objectives and projects of the Institute for Canadian Music at the University of Toronto, of which Beckwith was the first director.

264. Blume, Helmut. "The founding of CAUSM: a personal recollection." *Canadian University Music Review/Revue de musique des universités canadiennes* 11/2 (1991): 1-6.

An address given by one of the founders of the Canadian Association of University Schools of Music about the setting up of the Association in 1963-64.

265. Brault, Diana Victoria. "A history of the Ontario Music Educators' Association (1919-74)." PhD dissertation, Eastman School of Music, University of Rochester, 1977. xv, 667f.

With references back to the establishment in 1861 of the Ontario Educational Association, the history of the organization of music educators is traced from 1919, when the Ontario Educational Association began consideration of a music section.

The history of development is chronicled through discussion of events and personalities at each annual meeting. There is also a chapter on the Music Branch of the provincial Department of Education. Documents, lists of members, extensive bibliography.

266.Campbell, Amy. *Brass roots: a history of the Nanaimo Concert Band.* Nanaimo, B.C.: by the author, 1989. 68p. ISBN 0-9694313-0-9.

There is a short historical note on the Band, which was founded in 1872, and some reminiscences, but most of the book consists of testimonials to the Band and many photographs, dating back to the 1880s.

267.*Canadian League of Composers/Ligue canadienne de compositeurs 30: 1951-1981.* Edward Kovarik, ed. Windsor (1981): 48p.

This souvenir program records events at the celebration of the League's 30th anniversary, held at Windsor, Ontario, and Detroit, Michigan, June 11-14, 1981. There are several illustrations, and short but useful essays on the history of the League, on composition in Canada, and on composers represented on the concert programs.

268.Chambers, Pam. *Sixty years of music making: the Vancouver Youth Symphony Orchestra 1930-1990.* Vancouver: [1990?]. 32p.

The growth of the orchestra is succinctly covered, mostly in terms of activities, supporters and conductors. Repertoire is rarely mentioned.

269.Couture, Simon. "Les origines du Conservatoire de musique du Québec." *Les cahiers de l'ARMuQ* 14 (mai 1992): 42-64. ISSN 0821-1817.

The Provincially supported Conservatoire was founded in 1942. In addition to an exposition of the origins and objectives of the institution, information is also provided about earlier attempts to establish conservatories.

270.*Decade, the first ten years of The Music Gallery.* [Victor Coleman, ed.] Toronto: Music Gallery Editions, 1985. 88p.

The Music Gallery opened in 1976 in Toronto as an artist-run centre for new and experimental music. Performances are cited, arranged chronologically by month. Some excerpts are reprinted from the quarterly *Musicworks*: Schafer on Ten Centuries Concerts; an interview about the World Soundscape Project; and "Music of the Inuit."

271.Dent, Gloria and Leonard Conolly, eds. *Guelph and its Spring Festival.* Guelph: Edward Johnson Music Foundation, 1992. 180p. ISBN 0-88955-295-9.

A set of essays deals with various aspects of the Guelph Spring Festival, which began in 1968. There is a list of commissioned works, and a list of performances up to the 1990 Festival. Some information on the history of the city.

272.Eatock, Colin. "Arraymusic: the first fifteen years." In *Three Studies.* Toronto: Institute for Canadian Music, 1989. pp.147-193. CanMus Documents, 4. ISBN 0-7727-8554-6.

The Toronto organization began performances in 1972, devoted to music by young Canadian composers. The author reviews the changing personnel and points of view, and summarizes the organization's activities. There is a list of programs, with repertoire and performers, for 1972-1986.

273.*Edmonton Symphony Orchestra comes of age.* Rothmans of Pall Mall Canada, [1973]. [27p].

This brochure provides a brief outline of the history of the present Edmonton orchestra from 1952 to 1973. There is some information about earlier attempts to establish an orchestra, but the chief interest of this modest publication is in the photographs.

274.Falardeau, Victor and Jean Parent. *La Musique du Royal 22e Régiment: 50 ans d'histoire (1922-1972).* Québec: Éditions Garneau, 1976. 243p. ISBN 0-7757-2354-1.

The Band of the Royal 22nd Regiment was formally established at The Citadel, Québec City, in 1922, but its predecessor dates back to 1899. Most of this book is devoted to photographs of the Band, but there is a chronology of important performances in the period 1922-1972 (the Band played public concerts, toured widely, and broadcast), a short history, and lists of personnel.

275. Gardner, David. *Twenty-one seasons of the Ottawa Symphony Orchestra*. Ottawa: Ottawa Symphony Orchestra, 1986. 219p. ISBN 0-9692423-0-1 (soft cover).

   This general account of the orchestra, including its revenues, covers the period 1966 to 1985, with an introduction about earlier orchestras. Lists of conductors, guests, orchestra members, Canadian works, complete repertoire.

276. Geiger-Torel, Herman. "Canada - an operatic desert?" *German-Canadian Yearbook* 2 (1975): 145-151. in German as "Kanada - eine Opernwüste?", pp.139-144.

   A short personal statement about the establishment in 1950 of what would become the Canadian Opera Company in Toronto, and the difficulties of maintaining a permanent company.

277. George, Graham. "Three Canadian concert-halls." *The Canadian Music Journal* 4/2 (Winter 1960): 4-13.

   Vancouver, Calgary and Edmonton opened new concert halls in the mid-1950s. Only a small amount of pertinent information is provided about them in this article.

278. Gordon, Tom. "Music in absentia: Bishop's Faculty of Music, 1886-1947." *Canadian University Music Review/Revue de musique des universités canadiennes* 11/2 (1991): 33-50.

   From 1886 to 1947, Bishop's University in Sherbrooke had a Faculty of Music more in name than action. This article recounts the tentative place of the Faculty in its early days with the University, and its association with Dominion College of Music in Montréal.

279. Goudge, Helen. *Look back in pride: a history of the Women's Musical Club of Toronto, 1897-98 to 1972-73*. Toronto: [The Women's Musical Club], 1972. [38p.].

Much information is provided about the participants in and the programs of the early presentations of the Club. There are lists of winners of the Clubs awards, and of artists who appeared in the period 1925-1973.

280. G Sharp Major (pseudonym). *Crescendo, a business man's romance in music*. Winnipeg: (printed by Bulman Bros., n.d.), 100p.

A history of the first nineteen years (1915-1934) of the Men's Musical Club of Winnipeg, which consisted mainly of a Male Voice Choir but which was also the sponsor of musical events and a competitive festival.

281. Henderson, V.L. "Acoustic considerations at the O'Keefe Centre." *The Canadian Music Journal* 4/4 (Summer 1960): 25-32.

The author drew up the acoustical design of a new multi-purpose auditorium in Toronto. This article suggests a success that the completed hall does not bear out.

282. "Interview. The League of Composers: how hard work paid off." *Le Compositeur Canadien/The* Canadian *Composer* 119 (March 1977): 4-10.

Harry Freedman, Louis Applebaum and Clermont Pépin discuss the accomplishments of the Canadian League of Composers and the current situation of the composer in Canada.

283. Jolliffe, Mary E. *The Welsman Memoranda*. [Toronto]: Northern Miner Press, 1971. 63p.

Frank Welsman was the first conductor of the Toronto Symphony Orchestra (1906-18). His years with the orchestra are surveyed with many excerpts from articles and reviews of the period.

284. Jones, Gaynor G. "The Fisher years: the Toronto Conservatory of Music, 1886-1913." In *Three Studies*, pp.59-145. Toronto: Institute for Canadian Music, 1989. CanMus Documents, 4. ISBN 0-7727-8554-6.

The complex business and social history of the Conservatory, from its founding in 1886 through the first decade of the 20th century, is set out in some detail as the background to its musical development. Rival institutions and personalities are also discussed.

285.Kallmann, Helmut. "The Canadian League of Composers in the 1950s: the heroic years." *Studies in music from the University of Western Ontario* 9 (1984): 37-54. Reprinted in *Célébration*, pp.99-107. G. Ridout and T. Kenins, eds. Toronto: Canadian Music Centre/Centre de musique canadienne, 1984. ISBN 0-9690836-5-3.

The founding of the League in 1951 is seen to reflect the organizing of composers abroad, the maturing of the arts in Canada, and a desire among Canadian artists to form associations for artistic and professional purposes. Each of these conditions is examined, with discussion of the League's activities in the 1950s and consequent influence. The reprint in *Célébration* is complete despite a note indicating that it is partial.

286.------ "First fifteen years of Canadian League of Composers." *Le Compositeur Canadien/The Canadian Composer* 7 (March 1966): 18, 36, 45.

A straightforward account of the League's founding and its activities in lobbying, presentation of concerts, and distribution of materials.

287.Kieser, Karen. "The Canadian Music Centre; a history"/"Le Centre de musique canadienne et son histoire." In *Célébration*, pp.7-26, 27-48. G. Ridout and T. Kenins, eds. Toronto: Canadian Music Centre/Centre de musique canadienne, 1984. ISBN 0-9690836-5-3.

The actions that lead up to the founding of the Centre in 1958 are set out before turning to the development and growth of the organization. There is a good deal of information about the various undertakings of the Centre, about its administrators up to 1984, and its members. The French title given above appears in the *Célébration* table of contents. In the text it is "Le Centre de musique canadienne: présent et passé."

288.Kilbourn, William. *Intimate grandeur: one hundred years at Massey Hall.* Toronto: Stoddart Publishing, 1993. xiii, 161p. ISBN 0-7737-2742-6.

Since its opening in 1894, Massey Hall was the principal concert hall certainly for Toronto and in a sense, for Canada. This careful history of the hall recounts much about its famous visitors, and its central importance as home to Toronto's major performing organizations.

289.King, Valerie Verity. *The History of CAMMAC: Canadian Amateur Musicians/Musiciens amateurs du Canada 1952-1982.* Ottawa: Golden Dog Press, 1984. vii, 121p. ISBN 0-919614-52-3.

This celebratory account of what became a national organization includes information about one of the founders, George Little, and the Otter Lake Music Centre.

290.Lagacé, Bernard. "La renaissance de l'orgue au Québec." *Les Cahiers canadiens de musique/The Canada Music Book* 1 (Printemps-été 1970): 55-58.

A note primarily on *Ars Organi*, an organization in Montréal that presented organ recitals, 1960-1973.

291.Larose, Anik. "Historique du choeur de la cathédrale de Montréal." *Les cahiers de l'ARMuQ* 14 (mai 1992): 65-86. ISSN 0821-1817.

The Choir of the Montréal Cathedral (1882-1952) developed a wide repertoire and contributed to concert activity outside the Cathedral, notably under its directors Guillaume Couture and Arthur Laurendeau.

292.Leeper, Muriel. *Sounds of music: 1931-1981.* Saskatoon: [Saskatoon Symphony Orchestra], 1981. 73p.

A history of the Saskatoon Symphony Orchestra from its founding in 1931, to 1981. Basic information about conductors and some soloists is given, but very little about repertoire or about personnel.

293.Lefebvre, Marie-Thérèse. "Histoire du Conservatoire national de musique : 1922-1950." *Les cahiers de l'ARMuQ* 3 (juin 1984): 37-51. ISSN 0821-1817.

The Conservatoire national de musique was founded in 1905 by Alphonse Lavallée-Smith. From 1921 it was affiliated with l'Université de Montréal as the source of instruction in music before the creation of a faculty of music in 1950. Among the notable figures who were involved were Eugène Lapierre, the director, and Claude Champagne.

294.Lower, Thelma Reid. "The Vancouver Bach Choir: a retrospect." *Les Cahiers canadiens de musique/The Canada Music Book* 4 (Printemps-été 1972): 91-100.

Less than the title implies, the article mentions some successes of the Choir (founded 1930) and quotes some newspaper reviews. There is little historical detail or critical appraisal.

295.Machan, Claire. *The first 40 years (1945-1985); the history of the Kitchener-Waterloo Symphony Orchestra.* Kitchener, Ont.: Ainsworth Press, [1986]. [iv], 77p.

A popular narrative account of the orchestra from its founding, touching on conductors, soloists, community support and notable steps in the orchestra's development. No lists or index.

296.MacMillan, Keith. "National organizations." In *Aspects of music in Canada*, pp.288-318. A. Walter, ed. Toronto. University of Toronto Press, 1969. ISBN 8020-1536-0.

A survey of government and private organizations that support and present music and musical study throughout Canada.

297.McCallum, Douglas John. *Vancouver's Orpheum: the life of a theatre.* Vancouver: City of Vancouver Social Planning Department, 1984. 40p.

History of the Orpheum Theatre, originally a vaudeville house, which became the home of the Vancouver Symphony Orchestra. Little musical information.

298. McLean, Maude. *A responsive chord: the story of the Toronto Mendelssohn Choir.* [Toronto: The Toronto Mendelssohn Choir, 1969], 63p.

The short history of the Choir is organized around each of its conductors. There are lists of administrators and choir members at the time of publication, and retrospective (1894-1969) lists of guest conductors and soloists, repertoire, and recordings.

299. Mirtle, Jack. *The Naden Band: a history.* Victoria: Jackstays Publishing, 1990. xlvi, 167p. ISBN 0-9694753-0-6.

HMCS Naden is part of the Canadian Forces Base at Esquimalt, near Victoria, B.C. Its distinguished band was formed in 1940. This account provides a general history of the Band, and a chronicle of its activities organized around its directors up to 1990.

300. Mitchell, Norah and Sheila Forster. *The Symphony Story.* Vancouver: Women's Committee of the Vancouver Symphony Orchestra, 1971. 9 leaves.

A short history of the VSO. There is very little detailed information, but there are occasional observations on the social and musical life of Vancouver, especially early in the century, that are interesting.

301. Napier, Ronald. "The Canadian Music Council: a brief history." In *Musical Canada: words and music honouring Helmut Kallmann*, pp.262-273. J. Beckwith and F. Hall, eds. Toronto: University of Toronto Press, 1988. ISBN 0-8020-5759-4.

A review of the background to and the activities of the Canadian Music Council from its founding in 1944 to 1986. The CMC sponsored conferences, lobbied with government, published reports and a journal, made awards, etc. It should not be confused with the Canada Council, the federal arts council.

302. Nicholson, Georges. *Charles Dutoit: le maître de l'orchestre.* Montréal: Les Éditions de l'Homme, 1986. 241p. ISBN 2-7619-0627-6.

Primarily a biography of Dutoit, this study devotes a substantial section to his tenure with l'Orchestre Symphonique de

Montréal. There is some useful information about the orchestra, especially of a business nature.

303.Payette-Juneau, Yvonne. *L'Orchestre philharmonique de Drummondville (1935-1950)*. Drummondville, Qué.: chez l'auteure, 1990. 99p.

The author developed her history of the Drummondville orchestra mainly through newspaper reports, and recounts the activities of a small community's musical activities. The orchestra had its own Chorale, and there are brief biographical notes on all the members of both organizations. The orchestra disbanded in 1950.

304.Peglar, Kenneth W. *Opera and the University of Toronto, 1946-1971*. Toronto: [Faculty of Music, University of Toronto, 1972], 40p.

The Opera School of the Royal Conservatory (later of the Faculty of Music) was the first such school in Canada. This booklet provides an outline of its development, short profiles of its founders, lists of students and of repertoire, and contains many photographs.

305.Pelletier, Wilfred. "Orchestras." In *Music in Canada*, pp.64-78. Ernest MacMillan, ed. Toronto: University of Toronto Press, 1955.

This very brief review of the state of orchestras by the 1950s includes short notes on thirty-three active orchestras, both professional and amateur.

306.Potts, Joseph E. "The Toronto Symphony Orchestra." *The Strad* 78/926 (1967/68): 88-90.

A short history of the orchestra and its conductors from 1906 to 1965. The comments regarding the relationship of the TSO to the CBC Symphony Orchestra are incorrect.

307.Potvin, Gilles. *Les cinquante premières années/The first fifty years: Orchestre Symphonique de Montréal*. Montréal: Alain Stanké, 1984. 199p. ISBN 2-7604-0234-7

A general account of the Montréal orchestra from its founding to 1984, organized around its principal conductors and mentioning prominent guests and notable performances. Lists of guest conductors and soloists, and administrative officers. No index. In French and English.

308.Quigley, Michael. "Cantatas, cadenzas, and conductors." *Wentworth Bygones* 14 (1984): 63-70.

The antecedents and history of the Hamilton Philharmonic Orchestra are outlined, from the mid-19th century up to 1984.

309.Racine, Anne. *L'orchestre symphonique de Sherbrooke: cinquante ans d'histoire 1939-1989.* Sherbrooke: [author?], [1989?]. 142p.

Although an amateur ensemble, the Sherbrooke orchestra achieved initial distinction under its original conductor of thirty years, Sylvio Lacharité. This history provides a good deal of information about the development of the orchestra up to 1989, with lists of conductors and guests artists, but not of repertoire.

310.*Remembered moments: the Canadian Opera Company 1950-1975.* [Toronto: The Canadian Opera Company, 1975?]. n.p.

Despite the ambiguity of its publication origin, this 162-page publication provides a good survey of Canada's most successful opera company. Most of the book is given over to excellent photographs of productions, but there are also essays on the Company and its first director, Herman Geiger-Torel, and lists of repertoire with casts for all productions in Toronto and on tour.

311.Rice, Kelly S. "Joseph Gould and the Montreal Mendelssohn Choir." MA dissertation, McGill University, 1991. x, 219f.

There is some biographical information about Gould, but the primary concern is with the Mendelssohn Choir (1864-94), and Gould's position as founder and life-long conductor. It was virtually a closed anglophone organization, with a repertoire of part-songs and miscellaneous pieces. There is a catalogue of the Choir's library, now in McGill University.

312.Rosen, Robert J. "Canadian composers at Banff." In *Célébration*, pp.122-127. G. Ridout and T. Kenins, eds. Toronto: Canadian Music Centre/Centre de musique canadienne, 1984. ISBN 0-9690836-5-3.

Not a survey of composer activity at the Banff Centre, as the title implies, but a few personal reminiscences from the period 1978-1983.

313.*St. Lawrence Hall*. Toronto: Thomas Nelson & Sons (Canada), 1969. 186p.

The book consists of several essays by various authors, mostly about the renovation of the hall in the 1960s. However, when it opened in 1850 it was the principal meeting and concert room in Toronto, and some information is provided about the historical background and early days of the hall. Many illustrations.

314.Schaeffer, Myron S. "The Electronic Music Studio of the University of Toronto." *Journal of Music Theory* 7 (Spring, 1963): 73-81.

The author, who was director of the Studio, discusses in non-technical language, equipment devised at and unique to the University of Toronto Studio.

315.Schulman, Michael. "The Music Gallery: a place for some music alternatives." *Le Compositeur Canadien/The Canadian Composer* 158 (February 1981): 10-16.

The Music Gallery opened in Toronto in 1976 as a performance centre for avant garde music. This article is a survey of its activities in both performance and recording, and of some people associated with it in its first five years.

316.------ "Twentieth year for our Music Centre." *Le Compositeur Canadien/The Canadian Composer* 146 (December 1979): 16-22.

A survey of the activities of the Canadian Music Centre, without providing much detail.

317.Smith, Ocean G. *The Toronto Mendelssohn Choir: a history, 1894-1948*. Toronto: [Heintzman and Co., 1948], 24p.

This brief history of the choir is organized around the three conductors up to 1948 -- Vogt, Fricker and MacMillan. There is a short chronology of important events, and a list of orchestras that were associated with the Choir, but no list of repertoire.

318.*La vie musicale à Sherbrooke 1820-1989.* Andrée Désilets, ed. Sherbrooke: La Société d'histoire de Sherbrooke, 1989. 133p.

A brief but comprehensive survey of music in education, the church and society in Sherbrooke. Some lists of teachers and other musicians; carefully documented references to newspaper and archival sources, and personal interviews.

319.Wall, Geoffrey and Clare Mitchell. *The Kitchener-Waterloo Symphony Orchestra: community impact.* submitted to The Association of Canadian Orchestras and The Council for Business and the Arts in Canada, 1984. viii, 111p. ISBN 0-9691028-7-9

An examination of socio-economic and cultural aspects of the Kitchener-Waterloo Orchestra and its audience. No musical evaluations; many tables. One of a series of similar studies of Canadian orchestras by the same authors; see following items.

320.------ *The Lethbridge Symphony: community impact.* submitted to The Association of Canadian Orchestras and The Council for Business and the Arts, 1983. ix, 118p.

An examination of socio-economic and cultural aspects of the Lethbridge Symphony Orchestra and its audience. No musical evaluations; many tables.

321.------ *L'Orchestre symphonique de Québec: community impact.* submitted to The Association of Canadian Orchestras and The Council for Buisness and the Arts in Canada, 1984. vii, 102p.

A study of the orchestra as in no.319, 320, above.

4. Analysis, Works and Genre Studies

322. Adeney, Marcus. "Chamber music." In *Music in Canada*, pp.114-125. Ernest MacMillan, ed. Toronto: University of Toronto Press, 1955.

Brief though it is, this essay provides a fine survey of chamber music performance from the mid-19th century to the 1950s.

323. Beckwith, John. "Choral music in Montreal circa 1900: three composers." University of Toronto Quarterly 63/4 (summer 1994): 504-517.

A critical review, with several short musical examples, of the works and activities of Guillaume Couture, Charles A.E. Harriss and Alexis Contant in Montréal in the period 1890-1913.

324. ------ "Le *Lucas et Cécile* de Joseph Quesnel: quelques problèmes de restauration." *Les cahiers de l'ARMuQ* 13 (mai 1991): 10-28. ISSN 0821-1817.

Only the vocal part of *Lucas et Cécile* has survived. Beckwith discusses the problems that arose in his reconstruction of the score and his approach to solutions. Many musical examples. The restored version of the piece was published by Doberman-Yppan, Saint-Nicolas, Québec, 1992; ISBN 2-921204-103-7.

325. ------ "On compiling an anthology of Canadian hymn tunes." In *Sing out the glad news: hymn tunes in Canada*, pp.3-32. John Beckwith, ed. Toronto: Institute for Canadian Music, 1987.

The anthology referred to is Volume 5 of *The Canadian Musical Heritage* series (see p.30). The essay is a broad survey of the publication and composition of hymns in Canada, with many musical examples, and a checklist of publications with music, 1801-1939.

326.Beckwith, John, ed. *Sing out the glad news: hymn tunes in Canada.* Toronto: Institute for Canadian Music, 1987. 166p. CanMus Documents, 1. ISBN 0-7727-8550-3.

The proceedings of, and seven presentations at, a conference in Toronto, February 7 and 8, 1986. The articles are indexed individually in this *Research Guide* and may be located collectively in the title index under *Sing out the glad news....*

327.Beckwith, John. "Tunebooks and hymnals in Canada, 1801-1939." *American Music* 6/2 (Summer 1988): 193-234.

A chronolgocial checklist of sixty-one Canadian publications. The extensive descriptions and historical commentary give a fine overview of Canadian hymnody up to 1939. Many musical examples and reproductions.

328.Blum, Stephen. "The fuguing tune in British North America." In *Sing out the glad news: hymn tunes in Canada,* pp.119-148. John Beckwith, ed. Toronto: Institute for Canadian Music, 1987.

The fuguing tune is traced in its publication and performance in Canada, and in the relationship to similar material in the United States. There is a list of 170 fuguing tunes in ten Canadian tunebooks published 1816-1887.

329.Bouchard, Marie-Claire. "Le plain-chant au Québec au milieu du XIXe siècle: sa spécificité et le reflet du plain-chant en France." *Les cahiers de l'ARMuQ* 12 (avril 1990): 1-10. ISSN 0821-1817.

The interpretation and performance of plainchant was much debated in France during the 19th century. In Québec, similar disputes arose, in which Pierre-Minier Lagacé and Ernest Gagnon were notable participants, as European editions of chant were replaced by those published in Québec.

330.Brisson, Irène. "Le *Cérémonial des Évêques* face au *Livre d'orgue de Montréal.*" *Les cahiers de l'ARMuQ* 7 (mai 1988): 3-9. ISSN 0821-1817.

The author suggests that the *Livre d'orgue* (no. 333-335) reflects the *Cérémonial* (1662) which regulated the use of the organ during religious offices in France.

331.Elliott, Robert William Andrew (Robin). "The string quartet in Canada." PhD thesis, University of Toronto, 1990. vi, 351f.

This historical and analytical study is organized around four main points: Performance, the Conservative Tradition, Innovation and Modernism, and the Spirit of Compromise. Two lists -- one chronological from 1875, the other of undated works -- provide relevant information for about 350 works, including publication, première, recordings and literature. Extensive bibliography.

332.Émond, Vivianne. "Trois oeuvres musicales dites canadiennes." *Les cahiers de l'ARMuQ* 4 (novembre 1984): 46-62.

The concept of musical nationalism is tested and analyzed in three compositions by Claude Champagne, Léo-Pol Morin, and Rodolphe Mathieu.

333.Gallat-Morin, Élisabeth. "Le livre d'orgue de Montréal aperçu d'un manuscrit inédit." *Canadian University Music Review/Revue de musique des universités canadiennes* 2 (1981): 1-38.

This constitutes the first published report on a manuscript of 17th-century organ music of some 500 pages now known as *Le livre d'orgue de Montréal*. A descriptive overview of the manuscript is given, including information on its contents and organization.

334.------ "Un manuscrit de cantiques à Montréal (XVIIIe siècle)." *Canadian University Music Review/Revue de musique des universités canadiennes* 11/2 (1991): 68-93.

A manuscript collection of fifty-three *cantiques* -- religious songs, with text and melody -- represents a particular aspect of 18th-century life in Québec. The author considers the possible uses of the songs, their relation to other collections, and the often secular origins of the music. Lists of contents, and of collections containing some of the repertoire. Facsimiles.

335.------ *Un manuscrit de musique française classique; étude critique et historique: Le Livre d'orgue de Montréal*. Paris: Éditions aux amateurs de Livres; Montréal: Les Presses de l'Université de Montréal, 1988. xiv, 459p. ISBN 2-905053-54-3 (Paris), ISBN 2-760608-18-2 (Montréal).

The collection of 398 French organ pieces, now known as *Le Livre d'orgue de Montréal*, was brought to New France early in the 18th century and rediscovered in 1978. This exhaustive study of the MS examines historical associations as well as the musical contents. Thematic catalogue, bibliography, indexes. A facsimile edition, by Gallat-Morin, was issued -- Outremont, Qué.: Fondation Lionel-Goulx, 1981. xv, 544p. ISBN 2-9800070-0-5; reprinted 1988 by Éditions aux amateurs de Livres and Les Presses de l'Université de Montréal. Critical edition by Gallat-Morin and Kenneth Gilbert. St-Hyacinthe, Qué.: Les Éditions Jacques Ostiguy, 1985, 1987, 1988. 3 vols. See also Brisson, no.330.

336. Gillespie, John. "Contemporary piano music in the Americas: Canada." In *Five centuries of keyboard music*, pp. 387-92. Belmont, California: Wadsworth Publishing Company, Inc., 1965. reprinted, New York: Dover Publications, 1972. xiii, 463p. ISBN 0-486-22855-X.

Reference is made to a number of composers from the late 19th century to the 1950s, but the comments are brief, and the notes on contemporary composers betray limited familiarity.

337. Green, Rebecca. "Gaudeamus igitur: college singing and college songbooks in Canada." In *Three Studies*, pp.3-57. Toronto: Institute for Canadian Music, 1989. CanMus Documents, 4. ISBN 0-7727-8554-6.

From 1879 through the 1920s, over thirty college songbooks were published in Canada. In this article, the contents of these collections are examined, and the social and educational contexts in which they thrived. List of thirty-three publications.

338. Guérin, François. "Aperçu du genre electroacoustique au Québec." *Circuit* 4/1-2 (1993): 9-31.

A survey of the development of electroacoustic music in the Province. Mention is made of many names, the establishment of studios, notable works and events.

339. Hepner, Lee Alfred. "An analytical study of selected Canadian orchestral compositions at the mid-twentieth century." PhD dissertation, New York University, 1971. x, 141f.

The author attempts to discover consistent style features within the individuality of three composers. Three works are treated: Weinzweig -- *Symphonic ode*; Freedman -- *Images*; Somers -- *Passacaglia and fugue*.

340. Hubley, Katherine L. "Canadian quartet heritage." *The Strad* 104/11 (November, 1993): 1088-89, 1091, 1093.

This short article purports to be a survey of the string quartet in Canada, 1776-1993. Many quartets are mentioned, but overall the article is a muddle of error and misunderstanding.

341. Kallmann, Helmut. "The acceptance of O Canada." *Le Compositeur Canadien/The Canadian Composer* 8 (April 1966): 18-19, 38-41.

Kallmann traces the gradual acceptance of *O Canada* and the search for a national hymn that would be acceptable throughout the country. At the time of writing, the song was not yet the official National Anthem.

341a. ------ "From the archives: organs and organ players in Canada." *The Canadian Music Journal* 3/3 (Spring, 1959): 41-47.

The brevity of the report allows for little more than a few random but nonetheless illuminating pieces of information from the 17th to the late 19th centuries.

342. Keane, David. "The birth of electronic music in Canada." *Studies in music from the University of Western Ontario* 9 (1984): 55-78.

This highly informative survey deals mainly with the period up to about 1963. There is mention of many individuals, technical developments, and compositions of the period, and photographs of LeCaine's touch-sensitive organ and his "Sackbut".

343. ------ "Electroacoustic music in Canada: 1950-1984." In *Célébration*, pp.57-72. G. Ridout and T. Kenins, eds. Toronto: Canadian Music Centre/Centre de musique canadienne, 1984. ISBN 0-9690836-5-3.

All the important points of development are dealt with, as well as those individuals who were the major innovators. Many composers are mentioned, with quick glances at their work. There is a list of studios active in Canada in 1984, with the current directors.

344. Kemp, Walter. "Three masses by Maritime composers." In *Musical Canada: words and music honouring Helmut Kallmann*, pp.274-285. J. Beckwith and F. Hall, eds. Toronto: University of Toronto Press, 1988. ISBN 0-8020-5759-4.

    Mass settings by three composers -- Dennis Farrell, Walter Kemp, and Michael Parker -- are discussed as three ways in which they may play a role in modern Catholic liturgy.

345. Lamb, J. William. "Canadian Methodism's first tunebook: *Sacred Harmony*, 1838." In *Sing out the glad news: hymn tunes in Canada*, pp.91-118. John Beckwith, ed. Toronto: Institute for Canadian Music, 1987.

    While there is information about the contents and publication history of *Sacred Harmony*, much of the article is devoted to a survey of Methodist hymnody in the United States and Canada. Short bibliography.

346. Lapalme, Anne-Marie. "L'après Vatican II: législation de la musique religieuse dans les paroisses du Québec." *Les cahiers de l'ARMuQ* 12 (avril 1990): 11-17. ISSN 0821-1817.

    In this very brief survey of the musical situation following the decrees of Vatican II (published 1963), the author claims that some requirements have been poorly interpreted in Québec.

347. MacMillan, Ernest. "Choral music." In *Music in Canada*, pp.79-91. Ernest MacMillan, ed. Toronto: University of Toronto Press, 1955.

    This brief review deals more with organizations active in the 1950s than with music, but some repertoire is mentioned.

348. Mahon, A. Wylie. *Canadian hymns and hymn-writers*. St. Andrews-by-the-Sea: n.p. [1908]. 56p.

This modest book consists of eight short essays on 19th century writers of hymn texts. There is no mention of the music or of the composers of the hymns.

349. Maloney, S. Timothy. "Canadian wind ensemble literature." DMA dissertation, Eastman School of Music, University of Rochester: 1986. xvi, 351p.

There is a short historical introduction about band activity from colonial days, but the focus of the study is on wind ensemble music after about 1950, especially from the 1970s and 1980s. A survey of the modern repertoire is followed by analyses of seven representative works. There is an annotated catalogue of works.

350. Martel, Jules. "Church music I." In *Music in Canada*, pp.177-187. Ernest MacMillan, ed. Toronto: University of Toronto Press, 1955.

This essay deals only with Roman Catholic rite, and is a companion essay to Peaker (no.353). The principles of Church music are set out with reference to the *Motu Proprio*. The brief discussion that follows deals mostly with educational institutions and with choirs. There is a short list of publications issued in French Canada.

351. Mathieu, Rodolphe. *Parlons ... Musique*. Montréal: Editions Albert Lévesque, 1932. 194p.

The many short essays in this book are in the nature of *pensées* rather than the development of musical subjects. The collection is not Canadian in focus, but it is interesting for the fact that Mathieu introduces Canadian topics into his thoughts on such topics as folklore, nationalism, musical languages, and government support.

352. Owen, Stephanie Olive. "The piano concerto in Canada since 1955." PhD dissertation, Washington University (St. Louis), 1969. xv, 207p.

The period surveyed is 1955-1967, and only composers born in Canada were considered, with the result that the works of several prominent composers are omitted. There is a review of the piano music (not only concertos) of nine composers, and detailed analyses of concertos by Papineau-Couture, Beckwith and Weinzweig.

353. Peaker, Charles. "Church music II." In *Music in Canada*, pp.188-197. Ernest MacMillan, ed. Toronto: University of Toronto Press, 1955.

This essay deals only with Protestant churches, with a brief reference to synagogues, and is a companion essay to Martel (no.350). The survey of repertoire, standards of choral singing, and ritual practice is general but does give some sense of activity in the 1950s.

354. Pinson, Jean-Pierre. "Le plain-chant à Québec, des origines au milieu du XIXe siècle: pour une musicologie de l'interprétation." *Les cahiers de l'ARMuQ* 11 (septembre 1989): 3-13. ISSN 0821-1817.

The author argues that the study of plainchant as it developed in New France opens significant avenues of research in such areas as sources, transmission, and performance.

355. Poirier, Lucien. "La face cachée des manifestations musicales au Québec dans le dernier tiers du XVIIIe siècle." *Les cahiers de l'ARMuQ* 13 (mai 1991): 1-9. ISSN 0821-1817.

Briefly set out is the thesis that freemasonry was an effective agent in the organization and presentation of musical events in Québec in the latter third of the 18th century.

356. Proctor, George A. "Neo-classicism and neo-romanticism in Canadian music." *Studies in music from the University of Western Ontario* 1 (1976): 15-22.

The author finds that "neo-classicism" served as a stylistic reference for emerging Canadian composition in the 1940s, and that a neo-romantic style, especially evident in works with an extra-musical association, emerged around 1960.

357. Sabiston, Colin and Pearl McCarthy. "Opera and ballet." In *Music in Canada*, pp.92-105. Ernest MacMillan, ed. Toronto: University of Toronto Press, 1955.

The authors charitably take into account virtually all the slender theatrical musical activity in Canada in the mid-1950s, consider what level of interest may exist for increased performance, and look toward the future.

358. Schwandt, Erich. "Les vêpres en Nouvelle-France: musique et liturgie." *Les cahiers de l'ARMuQ* 3 (juin 1984): 8-22. ISSN 0821-1817.

Music retained in the Ursuline archives provides hints as to what might have been used at Vespers by the order in the 17th and 18th centuries. Five extended musical examples are appended.

359. Temperley, Nicholas. "Stephen Humbert's *Union Harmony*, 1816." In *Sing out the glad news: hymn tunes in Canada*, pp.57-89. John Beckwith, ed. Toronto: Institute for Canadian Music, 1987.

The second edition of *Union Harmony* is the earliest surviving Canadian book of hymn tunes. Temperley examines its contents in some detail, particularly as to the origins of the tunes, relationships to other collections, and intended use of the publication. Tables, musical examples, and a short bibliography.

360. ------ "Worship music in English-speaking North America, 1608-1820." In *Taking a stand: essays in honour of John Beckwith*, pp.166-184. Ed. T. McGee. Toronto: University of Toronto Press, 1995. ISBN 0-8020-0583-7.

The subject is the music actually performed in Protestant worship, rather than the music that survives in printed books that were largely intended for singing schools. Most of the article deals with the colonies that became the United States, but there is some information relative to Canada.

361. Vautour, Réal. "Trois quadrilles canadiens du 3e quart du XIXe siècle." *Les cahiers de l'ARMuQ* 4 (novembre 1984): 33-45. ISSN 0821-1817.

The quadrille had great popularity in France during the 18th and early 19th century. The author proposes that the continuation of the dance in French Canada in the 19th century assumed local characteristics, as exemplified in three quadrilles by Dessane, Gagnon, and Labelle.

362. Voyer, Simone. "La naissance du cotillon et du quadrille." *Les cahiers de l'ARMuQ* 8 (1987): 118-26. ISSN 0821-1817.

Most of this short article is given to a history of the cotillon and quadrille. Its relevant interest is in a short note on the earliest known manuscript (1819) in Canada that records a five-part quadrille.

363. Zuk, Ireneus. "The piano concerto in Canada (1900-1980): a bibliographic survey" DMA dissertation. Baltimore: Peabody Conservatory of Music, Peabody Institute of the Johns Hopkins University, 1985. xxxi, 429f.

This catalogue of 103 concertos by fifty-nine composers is intended to be comprehensive for the period covered. Each work is treated individually, listed by composer. There is a biographical outline of the composer, detailed information about the work (date, publisher, first performance, recording, etc.), critical comments from published articles, and a selected bibliography. There is no attempt to treat the subject comprehensively, but the catalogue is extremely useful for primary information.

Musicians -- Biographies and Individual Studies

One of the most notable deficiencies in Canadian musical studies is in extended studies of individual musicians. Even articles devoted to individuals are relatively few, and uneven in thoroughness and detail. It is apparent in the following list that some musicians are accorded a great deal of attention, and anyone at all familiar with Canadian music will think of some musicians who are not included at all, or very slightly. The decisions about what and whom to include were determined almost entirely by the availability of material; the presence or absence of entries for an individual does not represent a value judgement on that individual -- at least, not by the compiler of this *Guide*.

1. General - collections, dictionaries, etc.

364.Bradley, Ian L. *Twentieth century Canadian composers*. Vol. 1. Agincourt, Ont.: GLC Publishers, 1977. x, 222p. ISBN 0-88874-052-2; vol.2. Agincourt, Ont.: GLC Publishers, 1982. xii, 281p. ISBN 88874-053-0.

Intended for pedagogical purposes, each volume treats ten composers by presenting a short biographical essay, a concise bibliography, and a discussion of works. The works chosen were all available in recordings, and there are extensive musical examples. Because of the projected use in schools, the discussions are not technically complicated. If the comments are sometimes naive, the comprehensiveness of the volumes and the emphasis on musical material result in a useful survey.

365. Colgrass, Ulla. *For the love of music.* Toronto: Oxford University Press, 1988. viii, 200p. ISBN 0-19-540665-6.

This set of interviews provides a forum for often stimulating and revealing views by the individuals about themselves and about music, often about music in Canada. Of the twenty-two interviewees, thirteen are Canadian: Robert Aitken, Istvan Anhalt, James Campbell, Maureen Forrester, Rivka Golani, Glenn Gould, Anton Kuerti, Arthur Ozolins, R. Murray Schafer, Teresa Stratas, Jon Vickers, Edith Wiens, and the Orford Quartet.

366. *Composers of Atlantic Canada '81.* Halifax: Atlantic Canadian Composers' Association, 1981. 24p.

Twenty composers active in Nova Scotia, New Brunswick, Newfoundland, and Prince Edward Island are represented with short biographical notes, and lists of selected works.

367. *Directory of associate composers.* Carolyn Beatty, ed. Toronto: Canadian Music Centre/Centre de musique canadienne, 1989. n.p. ISBN 0-921519-08-7; 0-921519-09-5 (version française).

This directory of composers who were members of the Canadian Music Centre as of 1989 was issued in loose-leaf format, with a view to updating. Each individual is given one sheet (two pages), with a selected list of works, and a short entry which in most cases was written by the composer.

368. Forsyth, Wesley Octavius. "Canadian composers." *The Canadian Journal of Music* 2/2 (June, 1915): 20-21.

Forsyth makes very brief mention of about thirty composers, in almost every case composers of songs, anthems and occasional pieces of salon music. Useful mainly as a glimpse of what Canadian composition was seen to be in the early 20th century.

369. Gingras, Claude. *Musiciennes de chez nous.* Montréal: éditions de l'École Vincent-d'Indy, 1955. 103p.

Brief articles, in a popular vein, on nineteen women musicians active in Montréal in the early 1950s. Sometimes informative because of the currency of the notes, but birth dates are avoided.

370.Kallmann, Helmut. *Catalogue of Canadian composers.* Toronto: Canadian Broadcasting Corporation, 1952. reprinted 1972, Scholarly Press Inc., St. Clair Shores, Michigan, 254p. ISBN 0-403-01375-5.

Brief biographical information and lists of works for 356 Canadian composers, with a supplementary list of figures of lesser interest as composers. Bibliographies on composition and folk song. An earlier edition, compiled by J.J. Gagnier, was published in typescript (1947; 105f.). It was the basis for the much expanded version by Kallmann, but the first publication does include a few composers not listed in the 1952 edition.

371.Kasemets, Udo, ed. *Canavanguard: the music of the 1960s and after.* Toronto: BMI Canada, 1968. 112p.

Fourteen composers, of whom nine are Canadian, are included with a brief biography, personal statement, and list of works. There is a chronology of the avant garde in Canadian music, 1957-67.

372.Kivi, K. Linda. *Canadian women making music.* Toronto: Green Dragon Press, 1992. 134p. ISBN 0-9691955-8-3.

A survey, from the 19th century to the present, of women who have been prominent in music, both classical and popular, as performers and composers. No index, which makes it difficult to locate individuals, especially the many who are mentioned only in passing.

373.Lefebvre, Marie-Thérèse. *La création musicale des femmes au Québec.* Montréal: les éditions du remue-ménage, 1991. 148p. ISBN 2-89091-102-0.

There is a historical review of the period up to 1867, and a discussion of the musical education of women and the emergence of a group of scholars, composers and performers. There are short notes on twenty prominent women, and a list of works by Micheline Coulombe Saint-Marcoux. Notes to the main text are a source of much information, and there is an extensive bibliography.

374.MacMillan, Keith and John Beckwith, eds. *Contemporary Canadian Composers.* Toronto: Oxford University Press

(Canadian Branch), 1975. xxiv, 248p. ISBN 19-540244-8. *Compositeurs canadiens contemporains*, édition française dirigée par Louise Laplante. Montréal: Presses de l'Université du Québec, 1977. xxviii, 382p. ISBN 0-7770-0205-1.

Biographical entries with lists of works and brief bibliographies for 144 composers in the English-language edition. The French edition includes an additional sixteen names, original texts that were translated for the English edition, and updating of information to January, 1977.

375. McCready, Louise G. *Famous musicians: Canadian portraits*. Toronto: Clarke, Irwin & Co., 1957, reprinted 1971. xi, 140p. ISBN 0-7720-0502-8.

Four essays in simple, somewhat naive style, on Edward Johnson, Ernest MacMillan, Wilfred Pelletier and Healey Willan.

376. Napier, Ronald. *A guide to Canada's composers*. Willowdale, Ontario: The Avondale Press, 1973. 50p. ISBN 0-9690452-1-2. 2nd edition, 1976. 56p. ISBN 0-9690452-5-5.

A brief and selective list which gives the most basic information, including principal publishers and performance rights affiliation, for each composer. The second edition is updated and includes fifty-three new composer entries.

377. *Reference sources for information on Canadian composers*. Toronto: Canadian Music Centre, 1970. 11p.

Despite its brevity and datedness, this list still offers some useful suggestions for locating information in encyclopedias, periodicals and books.

378. Soeurs de Sainte-Anne. *Dictionnaire biographique des musiciens canadiens*. Lachine: Soeurs de Sainte-Anne, 1935. 301p.

Only musicians associated with Québec are included. Information is variable in detail, and sometimes in accuracy, but the work is especially useful for Québec musical life in the late 19th and early 20th centuries.

379. Such, Peter. *Soundprints: contemporary composers.* Toronto: Clarke, Irwin & Co., 1972. [vii], 171p. ISBN 0-7720-0564-8.

Essays on seven composers, with a list of compositions for each, arranged by genre. The composers are John Beckwith, Norma Beecroft, Walter Buczynski, Murray Schafer, Harry Somers, and John Weinzweig. The author, who is a writer, confines his interest to biographical material, not musical.

380. *Thirty-four biographies of Canadian composers/Trente-quatre biographies de compositeurs canadiens.* Montréal: Canadian Broadcasting Corporation, International Service. 1964. [v], 110p. Reprint, St. Clair Shores, Michigan: Scholarly Press, 1972.

These brief biographies originated as notes for internal use in the CBC International Service. The text is in French and English. Each entry includes a list of works. The composers included are: Adaskin, Anhalt, Applebaum, Archer, Beckwith, Blackburn, Brott, Champagne, Coulthard, Davidson, Dela, Fiala, Fleming, Freedman, Garant, Joachim, Jones, MacMillan, Matton, Mercure, Morawetz, Morel, Papineau-Couture, Pentland, Pépin, Perrault, Rathburn, Ridout, Somers, Symonds, Turner, Walter, Weinzweig, Willan.

381. Toomey, Kathleen M., and Stephen C. Willis, eds. Musicians in Canada: a bio-bibliographical finding list/Musiciens au Canada: index bio-bibliographique Ottawa: Canadian Association of Music Libraries, 1981. xiv, 185p. ISBN 0-9690583-1-4.

An earlier edition (*Bio-Bibliographical finding list of Canadian musicians and those who have contributed to music in Canada.* Ottawa: Canadian Library Association, 1961. v, 53p.) is superseded by this much expanded edition. Biographical information for close to 4000 individuals is located in 218 sources. Individuals are listed alphabetically and indexed by categories in which they contributed.

2. Monographs and Articles

Harry Adaskin

382. Adaskin, Harry. *A fiddler's world: memoirs to 1938.* Vancouver: November House, 1977. 293p. ISBN 0-920156-02-0(v.1).

383. Adaskin, Harry. *A fiddler's choice: memoirs 1938 to 1980.* Vancouver: November House, 1982. 187p. ISBN 0-920156-06-1.

While much of the material in the two memoirs is reminiscences and musings on music and people outside Canada, Adaskin's involvement in so many important aspects of Canadian music as performer and teacher make these books often valuable records of such things as his early life in Toronto, the first years of the Hart House Quartet, and the University of British Columbia. No indexes.

Murray Adaskin (see also Frances James)

384. Schulman, Michael. "Murray Adaskin: 75 years of music." *Le Compositeur Canadien/The Canadian Composer* 164 (October 1981): 4-10.

The article consists almost entirely of short but informative statements by Adaskin himself about his training, experiences, and views on music.

Lucio Agostini

385. McNamara, Helen. "Lucio Agostini: amazing productivity, enthusiasm." *Le Compositeur Canadien/The Canadian Composer* 92 (June 1974): 4-8.

Basic biographical information is contained in the article, but much of its interest lies in the comments by Agostini on his work as a composer of incidental music for radio and films.

Pierrette Alarie

386. Maheu, Renée. *Pierrette Alarie, Léopold Simoneau: deux voix, un art.* Éditions Libre Expression, 1988. 377p. ISBN 2-89111-348-9.

The text deals mainly with the extensive careers of the two subjects. Included are discographies, lists of repertoire, and a detailed list of the principal engagements of the singers throughout their careers.

Emma Albani

387. Albani, Emma. *Forty Years of Song.* London: Mills & Boon, 1911. 285p.

A highly personal autobiography dealing mainly with Albani's triumphs and her associations with great musicians. In a French translation with annotations by Gilles Potvin as *Mémoires d'Emma Albani.* Montréal: 1972.

388. Charbonneau, Hélène. *L'Albani, sa carrière artistique et triomphale.* Montréal: Imprimerie Jacques-Cartier, 1938. 171p.

The professional life of Albani is treated conventionally, but the book is especially useful for the annotations and references for her early years in Chambly/Montréal.

389. Clément, Marie-Blanche. "Albani." *Le Bulletin des Recherches Historiques* 55/10, 11, 12 (octobre-novembre-décembre 1949): 199-210.

There is some detailed information about Albani's family. Much of the biographical material comes from a manuscript and newspaper clippings of "M. Sénécal."

390. Gour, Romain. "Albani (Emma Lajeunesse) reine du chant (1847-1930)." *Qui?* 1/1 (Printemps 1949): 3-20.

A short but nevertheless comprehensive account of Albani's life and career.

391.MacDonald, Cheryl. *Emma Albani: victorian diva.* Toronto: Dundurn Press, 1984. 205p. ISBN 0-919670-75-X (bound), 0-919670-74-1 (pbk.).

A straightforward and detailed account of Albani's life and career. List of operatic and oratorio roles, compiled by Gilles Potvin.

392.Potvin, Gilles. "Emma Albani (1847-1930)." *Les cahiers de l'ARMuQ* 7 (mai 1988): 46-64.

A biographical memoir of uncertain origin on Albani is reproduced here without editorial emendation or comment. It describes her life up to the age of 15. Appended are two articles by Gustave Smith, one from 1862 in which he criticizes the treating of Albani as a prodigy with plans to go to Europe; the other from 1889 in which he praises her after a concert in Ottawa.

Istvan Anhalt

393.Anhalt, Istvan. "The making of 'Cento'." *Les Cahiers canadiens de musique/The Canada Music Book* 1 (Printemps-été 1970): 81-89.

In non-technical ways, the composer outlines his development of the text and recorded materials of *Cento*, with some remarks on the live choral part.

394.------ *"Thisness*: marks and remarks." In *Musical Canada: words and music honouring Helmut Kallmann*, pp.211-231. J. Beckwith and F. Hall, eds. Toronto: University of Toronto Press, 1988. ISBN 0-8020-5759-4.

The composer describes, rather than analyses, his new "monodrama cycle," *Thisness*. The texts of the ten sections are given.

395.Gillmor, Alan M. "Echoes of time and the river." In *Taking a stand: essays in honour of John Beckwith*, pp.15-44. Ed. T.

McGee. Toronto: University of Toronto Press, 1995. ISBN 0-8020-0583-7.

The essay leads to a discussion of Anhalt's orchestral piece, *Simulacrum* (1987), but the greater part of the essay is a searching and sometimes personal examination of the biographical and artistic forces that underlie Anhalt's music. Without being in any way technically analytical, the author has much to say about the nature of the music.

396.Smith, Gordon E. "'Deep themes, not so hidden' in the music of István Anhalt." *Queen's Quarterly* 98/1 (Spring 1991): 99-119.

Although brief, this article deftly surveys Anhalt's work, especially his pieces for voice. The author attempts to identify underlying themes that run through much of Anhalt's music and that relate to his personal experiences and philosophy.

Louis Applebaum

397.Flohil, Richard and Michael Schulman. "Interview! From NFB and Hollywood to arts administrator." 87 (January 1974): 10-18.

The interview is confined almost entirely to questions, and Applebaum's replies, about composing for films, and about problems of arts administration and subsidy, particularly in relation to the Ontario Arts Council.

Violet Archer

398.Dalen, Brenda. "The composer's voice: 'what women can do'". *Canadian University Music Review/Revue de musicque des universités canadiennes* 16/1 (1995): 14-40.

Based extensively on an interview from 1994, this article deals mainly with Archer's early years as a student in Montréal, and her studies with Bartok and with Hindemith. The apparently unedited transcripts convey a degree of ingenuousness.

399.Hartig, Linda. *Violet Archer: a bio-bibliography.* Westport, CT: Greenwood Press, 1991. ix, 153p. (Bio-bibliographies in music, no.41. ISSN 0742-6968.) ISBN 0-313-26408-2.

A biographical essay is followed by a list of works that is organized in seven genre categories and indexed by title. There is a discography and an extensive annotated bibliography that includes many reviews and journal notices.

400. Proctor, George. "Notes on Violet Archer." In *Musical Canada: words and music honouring Helmut Kallmann*, pp.188-202. J. Beckwith and F. Hall, eds. Toronto: University of Toronto Press, 1988. ISBN 0-8020-5759-4.

When he died in 1985, Proctor was writing a study of Violet Archer. His rough notes were made following conversations with Archer in 1984 and are presented without significant editorial change. They range over many aspects of the composer's life and include a "biographical checklist."

401. Whittle, James. "Violet Archer's formative years: a bibliographical catalogue of her compositions, 1932-43." *Canadian University Music Review/Revue de musique des universités canadiennes* 16/1 (1995): 145-195.

The record of Archer's output before 1960, and especially for the 1930s and 1940s, is incomplete and sometimes inaccurate. This catalogue of her early compositions includes sixty-three entries, for which extensive historical and musical information is given about each work.

Michael Conway Baker

402. Baragon, Ellen. "Vancouver film composer says his art is `bloody hard work'." *Le Compositeur Canadien/The Canadian Composer* 228 (March 1988): 18-22.

Although not presented as an interview, the article consists largely of direct comments by Baker on his own work and his attitudes to composition. There is some biographical information.

Gerald Bales

403. Phillips, Edward R. "Neo-tonality or neo-atonality?: *I waited patiently for the Lord* by Gerald Bales." *Canadian University Music Review/Revue de musique des universités canadiennes* 4 (1983): 308-29.

After a brief exposition of the main features of "set theory", the analytical method developed by Allan Forte, the author applies it to an anthem by Bales. The analysis reveals certain structures in the piece and demonstrates as well a particular application of set theory to music that has features both tonal and atonal.

Marius Barbeau

404. Cardin, Clarisse. "Bio-bibliographie de Marius Barbeau." *Les Archives de Folklore* 2 (1947): 17-96.

Following a short biographical essay, the bibliography is divided by manuscripts, books and pamphlets, and articles. There are 578 items by Barbeau and 177 items about him. Alphabetical index of titles.

405. Katz, Israel J. "Marius Barbeau 1883-1969." *Ethnomusicology* 14/1 (January 1970): 129-142.

The short biographical section of this obituary notice provides numerous insights into the development of Barbeau's interests. This is followed by a "Bibliography of ethnomusicological works" arranged chronologically from 1915 to 1965, with a list of unpublished manuscripts.

Vernon Barford

406. George, Graham. "Vernon Barford." *The Canadian Music Journal* 5/2 (Winter 1961): 4-12.

This short biographical sketch of Barford also provides glimpses of musical life in Edmonton, where he settled in 1900.

Milton Barnes

407. Schulman, Michael. "Is Milton Barnes Canada's most neglected composer?" *Le Compositeur Canadien/The Canadian Composer* 161 (May 1981): 4-10.

A good review of Barnes's career as composer and conductor, with some insight into his musical views and personality.

Jean-Marie Beaudet

408.Arthur, Gérard. "Jean-Marie Beaudet, 1908-1971." *Les Cahiers de musique/The Canada Music Book* 2 (Printemps-été 1971): 99-106.

This brief obituary notice (in French and English) notes Beaudet's services, particularly at Radio-Canada/CBC, the National Arts Centre and the Canadian Music Centre.

John Beckwith

409.Beckwith, John. "Notes on *Harp of David.*" *Canadian University Music Review/Revue de musique des universités canadiennes* 11/2 (1991): 122-35.

The composer's discussion and analysis of his six-part cycle of psalm settings for *a capella* chorus.

410.Beckwith, Lawrence. "John Beckwith's principal compositions and writings to 1994." In *Taking a stand: essays in honour of John Beckwith*, pp.306-313. T. McGee, ed. Toronto: University of Toronto Press, 1995. ISBN 0-8020-0583-7.

A list, without annotations, of musical and literary works by Beckwith, arranged chronologically within categories. Publications and recordings of the music are given, but not their dates.

411.Dixon, Gail. "Symmetry and synthesis in Beckwith's *Etudes* (1983)." In *Taking a stand: essays in honour of John Beckwith*, pp.70-93. T. McGee, ed. Toronto: University of Toronto Press, 1995. ISBN 0-8020-0583-7.

The pitch material for the *Etudes* "consists of eight distinct, but closely related, hexachordally all-combinatorial 12-tone sets." This material is examined in technical detail, both for its innate properties and for its specific application in each of the six studies.

412.Mayo, John. "Coming to terms with the past: Beckwith's *Keyboard Practice.*" In *Taking a stand: essays in honour of John Beckwith*, pp.94-109. T. McGee, ed. Toronto: University of Toronto Press, 1995. ISBN 0-8020-0583-7.

From questions about the understanding of music, Mayo arrives at an understanding of a particular work by Beckwith. While technical analysis plays a small part in interpreting the work, many other aspects are examined, including the origin of the piece, the historical/musical context, its referential materials, the manner of performance.

413.------ "Expectations and compacts in Beckwith-Reaney operas: a case study." *University of Toronto Quarterly* 60/2 (winter 1990-91): 305-318.

The article is about the complex relationships between a work and its audience, with reference points in ritual, realism and irony. In illustrating his critical viewpoint, the author elucidates three operas by Beckwith with texts by James Reaney.

Norma Beecroft

414.Winters, Kenneth. "A composer who doesn't wear music like a straightjacket." *Le Compositeur Canadien/The Canadian Composer* 64 (November 1971): 4-9.

There is some biographical information and a brief mention of several of Beecroft's principal compositions up to 1970.

415."Miss Norma Beecroft: well-travelled composer." *Le Compositeur Canadien/The Canadian Composer* 9 (May 1966): 4-5, 40-41, 45-46.

A short biographical note, mostly about her studies and the beginning of her career.

Maurice Blackburn

416.Blackburn, Maurice. "Maurice Blackburn." *Le Compositeur Canadien/The Canadian Composer* 38 (March 1969): 4-7.

In a short, general article, Blackburn provides a few insights into his film composition and his association with film-maker Norman MacLaren.

417.Cloutier, Louise. "Maurice Blackburn et la 'filmusique'." *Les cahiers de l'ARMuQ* 10 (juin 1988): 24-33. ISSN 0821-1817.

A short homage to Blackburn and his work at the National Film Board. An outline of terms of classification is given for the documentaries and animated films, about 200 in number, for which he composed.

Alexander Brott

418. Schulman, Michael. "Interview! Brott: a total musicia." *Le Compositeur Canadien/The Canadian Composer* 115 (November 1976): 10-17.

The article is entirely in a question/answer format, in which Brott talks bluntly about the current musical and political situation in Montréal, and about his career.

419. ------ "Our salute to a most distinguished composer-conductor." *Le Compositeur Canadien/The Canadian Composer* 149 (March 1980): 4-11.

Not an article but a detailed chronology of Brott's professional life up to 1980, with a discography and list of works.

Boris Brott

420. Graham, June. "Boris Brott." *Le Compositeur Canadien/The Canadian Composer* 51 (June 1970): 38-45.

There is some biographical material, but the article is primarily about Brott's work as the new conductor of the Hamilton Philharmonic Orchestra.

421. Schulman, Michael. "Interview: Boris Brott." *Le Compositeur Canadien/The Canadian Composer* 141 (June, 1979): 8-14.

Most of the interview is about orchestras, repertoire and audiences, especially in Hamilton (Ontario) and Wales, where Brott was then conducting.

Walter Buczynski

422. Schulman, Michael. "Walter Buczynski, a composer whose music reflects his life." *Le Compositeur Canadien/The Canadian Composer* 106 (December 1975): 10-15.

Much of this short article is given to comments by the composer on his set of pieces, *Zeroing In,* composed in the early 1970s, and his evolving style.

Howard Cable

423."Howard Cable, musician for all seasons." *Le Compositeur Canadien/The Canadian Composer* 27 (March 1968): 4-5, 44-45.

Cable's varied career, especially in the areas of band and popular music, is surveyed briefly but comprehensively.

Claude Champagne

424.Archer, Thomas. "Claude Champagne." *The Canadian Music Journal* 2/2 (1958): 3-10.

This biographical sketch mentions many associates of Champagne and events in his musical life, but includes no critical or analytical comments.

425.Bail-Milot, Louise. "L'oeuvre et les procédés de composition chez Claude Champagne." MA dissertation, l'Université de Paris, 1972. xx, 316f.

This study is useful more for comprehensiveness than for detail in the examination of the works and compositional techniques of Champagne. The bibliography contains many review and journal items about him.

426.Barriault, Jeannine and Maureen Nevins. "Hommage à Claude Champagne: le traitement de son fonds d'archives et la préparation d'une exposition." *Les cahiers de l'ARMuQ* 13 (mai 1991): 38-47. ISSN 0821-1817.

A list of the categories in the classification of the papers of Champagne in the National Library, Ottawa. Useful chiefly in conjunction with the collection. See Duchow, no.431.

427.Brassard, François. "Une date pour la musique canadienne." *La Revue de l'Université Laval* 5/8 (avril, 1951): 738-46.

Champagne's *Symphonie gaspésienne* is discussed in the context of its importance in the development of "la musique canadienne" (which should be understood as Québec music). There is a general description of the work, illustrated with twelve very short musical examples.

428.*Claude Champagne (1891-1965): composer, teacher, musician/compositeur, pédagogue, musicien.* Maureen Nevins, ed. Ottawa: National Library of Canada, 1990. 81p. ISBN 0-662-57811-2.

Catalogue of an exhibition held in Ottawa, 1990-91. There is a biographical chronology, but the interest lies in the information to be gleaned from items, and notes to the items, in the exhibition. Text in French and English; many illustrations.

429.Duchow, Marvin. "Inventory list of the compositions of Claude Champagne." *Canadian Association of University Schools of Music Journal* 2/2 (Fall, 1972): 67-82.

The 228 entries are divided into groups of scores and parts, then further divided by genre, and finally by manuscript/published categories. Only the most basic description of each work is given.

430.------ "A selective list of correspondents drawn from the personal documents of Claude Champagne." *Canadian Association of University Schools of Music Journal* 3/1 (Fall, 1973): 71-79.

A list of about 150 correspondents to whom Champagne wrote or from whom he received letters. For each name are given the number of letters sent and received and the years. There is no information as to the subject of any of the correspondence.

431.------ "A summary account and partial inventory of the Claude Champagne collection." *Canadian Association of University Schools of Music Journal* 4/1-2 (Fall, 1974): 11-20; 5/1 (Spring, 1975): 72-87.

The complete inventory list of the documents of Champagne (in the National Library, Ottawa) numbers about 3500 items. Whereas the excerpts published above (no.429, 430) contained some degree of detail, this is essentially an index of the categories of the collection, except for the inventory of recordings (Spring,

1975) where titles are given. "Recordings" includes discs and tapes of music by Champagne, but also other recordings, commercial and private, that he owned. See Barriault, no.426.

432. Walsh, Anne. "The life and works of Claude Adonai Champagne." PhD dissertation, The Catholic University of America (Washington, D.C.), 1972. xi, 183f.

There is a short biography and chapters on Champagne as teacher and composer. Extended analytical discussion is confined to *Symphonie gaspésienne*, *String Quartet in C major*, and *Altitude*.

Gabriel Charpentier

433. Campbell, Francean. "Gabriel Charpentier is Shakespeare's musical composer." *Le Compositeur Canadien/The Canadian Composer* 54 (November 1970): 4-7.

Other than mention of some of his many works, this article provides little information, but does include an illustration of the chart that Charpentier devised for planning his theatrical incidental music.

434. Schulman, Michael. "From Gregorian chants to music for theatre and opera." *Le Compositeur Canadien/The Canadian Composer* 114 (October 1976): 4-9, 42.

A general overview of Charpentier's career as television producer and composer.

Gustav Ciamaga

435. Schulman, Michael. "Gustav Ciamaga: an important figure in electronic music today." *Le Compositeur Canadien/The Canadian Composer* 109 (March 1976): 22-27.

Very general in content, this article offers some glimpse of Ciamaga's interests and personality but very little about his music.

James Paton Clarke

436.Kallmann, Helmut. "James Paton Clarke -- Canada's first Mus. Bac." *Les Cahiers canadiens de musique/The Canada Music Book* 1 (Printemps-été 1970): 41-53.

The first carefully researched and documented biographical study of Clarke, one of Toronto's most important 19th-century musicians. There is a list of Clarke's compositions.

Alexis Contant

437.Contant, Jean-Yves. "Un pionnier de la musique canadienne." *Vie Musicale* 7 (1967): 23-29.

A straightforward biographical account of Contant, with brief musical examples from his *Trio* for piano, violin and violoncello.

438.Gour, Romain. "Alexis Contant: pianiste-compositeur (1858-1918)." *Qui?* 5/2 (Décembre 1953): 25-40.

Contant had been largely forgotten when this biographical sketch appeared, the main purpose of which was to encourage general recognition and the performance of his works. There is a reproduction of the first page of the first part of *Caïn.*

439.Willis, Stephen C. *Alexis Contant: catalogue.* Ottawa: Minister of Supply and Services Canada, 1982. v, 87/91p. ISBN 0-660-51891-0.

This catalogue of works, based on the Contant Papers in the National Library of Canada, is a chronological listing of all works composed or worked on by Contant, printed and manuscript, completed and unfinished, surviving or lost. Descriptive details of each work are given, as well as additional historical and publication information where known. The list of sound recordings includes not only the few commercial recordings but also extensive archival sources. The catalogue is in French and English versions, bound in one volume.

Jean Coulthard

440.Duke, David Gordon. "The orchestral music of Jean Coulthard: a critical assessment." PhD dissertation, University of Victoria (B.C.), 1993. x, 238f.

There is an extended and detailed biographical introduction to the main body of the study, which is itself perhaps most interesting for the information about the genesis, performance and history of Coulthard's orchestral works. The treatment of the music is more descriptive than analytical, but comprehensive. Extensive bibliography.

441.Rowley, Vivienne Wilda. "The solo piano music of the Canadian composer Jean Coulthard." MusAD dissertation, Boston University, 1973. 163p.

An overview of the piano music 1917-1972 with harmonic and formal analysis based particularly on five major works. Complete list of works of all kinds up to 1972, often with notes about dedications and first performances.

Guillaume Couture

442.Gour, Romain. *Guillaume Couture, compositeur*. Montréal: Éditions Éoliennes, 1951. 24p.

This very brief survey provides a résumé of biographical information, especially about Couture's periods in Paris, but there is little about his activities in Montréal. No annotations or indications of sources. This is an exact reprint of *Qui?* 3/1 (septembre 1951), which was devoted to Couture.

443.Laurendeau, Arthur. "Musiciens d'autrefois: Guillaume Couture." *L'Action Nationale* 36/1 (septembre 1950): 19-34; 36/2 (octobre, 1950): 110-26.

While providing little information that is new, Laurendau knew Couture and speaks of him and his contemporaries with personal knowledge. There are some interesting assessments of Couture as musician and as a person.

444.Maheux, Arthur. "Guillaume Couture, musicien canadien-français (1851-1915)." *La Revue de l'Université Laval* 16/9 (mai 1962): 842-854; 16/10 (juin 1962): 937-951.

Between June 1873 and January 1877, Couture wrote 21 letters from Europe, almost all to the Abbé Verreau in Montréal.

These letters are reprinted in full here with a minimum of commentary. They give glimpses of Couture's personality, his concerns for music in Canada, and they correct some dates in regard to his activities in Paris.

445.Quenneville, Pierre. "Guillaume Couture (1851-1915): l'éducateur, le directeur artistique et le musicien d'église." PhD dissertation, Université de Montréal, 1988. xvi, 567, 364f. (3 vol.)

The most complete and detailed biographical study of Couture. Volume II (ff.422-567) lists documentary sources -- books, articles, reviews -- arranged by author, or chronologically for the many anonymous notices. Volume III contains an annotated chronology, a list of Couture's writings, programs which he directed in whole or in part, a catalogue of works, a survey of his students, and reproductions of the following scores: *Memorare*, op.1; *Rêverie*, op.2; *Quatuor-Fugue*, op.3; *Hymne national canadien-français*, op.4; *Tantum ergo*, excerpt from op.5; *O Salutaris*, excerpt from op.6; *Atala*, MS. The analytical arrangement of material facilitates the locating of information, but there is no cross-indexing.

446.------ "Guillaume Couture, le pédagogue." *Les cahiers de l'ARMuQ* 8 (mai 1987): 93-96. ISSN 0821-1817.

A brief review of Couture as a teacher, without adding anything new to the subject.

Helen Creighton

447.Creighton, Helen. *Helen Creighton; a life in folklore*. Toronto: McGraw-Hill Ryerson, 1975. 244p. ISBN 0-07-082241-7.

These personal reminiscences of a long and active life touch on many people and events outside folksong collecting and are often interesting for their reflection of social and musical life in the first half of the 20th century. No index.

448.------ "Looking back on a satisfying career." *Le Compositeur Canadien/The Canadian Composer* 120 (April 1977): 24-28.

An interview with Creighton, in which she talks about her early collecting activities. Slight in information, but the material has some personal interest.

449.Sircom, Hilary. *Helen Creighton.* Tantallon, N.S.: Four East Publications Ltd., 1993. 64p. ISBN 0-920427-37-5.

A short and uncritical biographical résumé derived in large part from Creighton's own book (no.447).

Octave Crémazie

450.Condemine, Odette. "Portrait d'Octave Crémazie." *Les cahiers de l'ARMuQ* 10 (juin 1988): 82-102. ISSN 0821-1817.

Crémazie was the author of the text of some much admired 19th century songs, notably by Antoine Dessane and Charles Wugk Sabatier.

Lionel Daunais

451.Rudel-Tessier, J. "In the footsteps of the troubadours." *Le Compositeur Canadien/The Canadian Composer* 3 (October 1965): 8-9, 42, 45.

A narrative interview with Daunais about his career as songwriter, singer, and impresario.

Victor Davies

452.Schulman, Michael. "Victor Davies: television and film experience help this composer create music that's `user-friendly'." *Le Compositeur Canadien/The Canadian Composer* 222 (July 1987): 4-11.

The article is a brief account of Davies' background and training, and particularly of his work in theatre and film.

Géza de Kresz

453.Kresz, Mária and Péter Király. *Géza de Kresz and Norah Drewett: their life and music on two continents.* Toronto: Canadian Stage and Arts Publication Ltd., 1989. 204p. ISBN 0-919952-32-1.

The book draws in large measure on materials which were collected by Norah Drewett and which are now in Budapest. Included are parts of an unpublished memoir by Drewett. The book is particularly useful for the periods the couple spent in Toronto, 1923-35 and 1947-60, as teachers and prominent performers. Many photographs.

Gordon Delamont

454."Interview. Gordon Delamont talks about teaching and music." *Le Compositeur Canadien/The Canadian Composer* 123 (September 1977): 16-23.

Delamont talks about his career as a performer, but primarily the interview deals with his attitudes towards teaching composition in a context of popular music.

Auguste Descarries

455.Descarries, Marcelle L. "Un musicien canadien à Paris 1921-1930." *Les Cahiers canadien de musique/The Canada Music Book* 8 (Printemps/été 1974): 95-107.

These reminiscences by Descarries' wife are mostly about their sojourn in France, but include also some references to Québec

Jean Deslauriers

456.Deslauriers, Nicole. *Si mon père m'était conté...*. Ottawa: ÉdiCompo, 1982. 349p. ISBN 2-89066-070-2.

It is not always clear what the basis is for the material in this affectionate biography of Deslauriers by his daughter. It is a reminiscence by the daughter, cast in the first person, apparently based at least in part on interviews. It appears to recount the main facts of Deslauriers' career. No lists or indexes.

Pauline Donalda

457. Brotman, Ruth C. *Pauline Donalda: the life and career of a Canadian prima donna.* Montréal: Eagle Publishing Co., 1975. xvii, 125p.

This admiring biography concentrates on Donalda's career as a singer, but there is also a chapter on the Opera Guild of Montreal, of which she was founder. There is a discography and note on her small number of recordings. A list of productions by the Opera Guild, 1942-1969, includes complete cast information.

Norah Drewett (see de Kresz)

Sophie-Carmen Eckhardt-Gramatté

458. Eckhardt, Ferdinand. *Music from within: a biography of the composer S.C. Eckhardt-Gramatté.* Winnipeg: University of Manitoba Press, 1985. 207p. ISBN 0-88755-136-X.

This personal but careful biography by the composer's husband is based on recollections and on family documents, although there are no annotations to the narrative. List of selected works and discography

459. Harry, Isobel. "S.C. Eckhardt-Gramatté's life story: adventures, crises and achievements." *Le Compositeur Canadien/The Canadian Composer* 178 (February 1983): 16-21, 32-33.

This short but detailed biographical note on Eckhardt-Gramatté's life and family background is based on the researches of her husband.

Alfred Fisher

460. Lewis, Christopher. "Thin partitions: remembrance and reflection in Alfred Fisher's *Zakhor: Remember.*" *Canadian University Music Review/Revue de musique des universités canadiennes* 13 (1993): 55-70.

The author comments on pertinent aspects of the composer's background, then addresses the cycle of six songs, *Zakhor: Remember.* The thorough technical analysis of the music is closely related to the text in the discussion of the poetic and structural aspects of the work.

Robert Fleming

461.Godsalve, William. "The aesthetic functionality of film music based on cooperation and counteraction of tensities, illustrated in film music of Robert Fleming." MA dissertation, University of Saskatchewan, 1981. xxiii, 346f.

Fleming, as a composer at the National Film Board, composed scores for over 250 films. This study is fundamentally concerned with questions about the use of music in film, and about half the dissertation is given to applying the author's hypotheses about film music to a single film, *Antonio*, with music by Fleming.

462.Keitges, Christine DeWit. "The vocal music of Robert Fleming (1921-1976*)*." DMA dissertation, Arizona State University, 1988. xi, 244f.

This is primarily a briefly annotated list of 101 solo vocal pieces, treated chronologically and indexed by title. There is no analytical commentary, except for a separate chapter that deals extensively with *The Confession Stone*.

Maureen Forrester

463.Forrester, Maureen. *Out of character: a memoir*. Toronto: McClelland and Stewart, 1986. 326p. ISBN 0-7710-3227-7.

An autobiography that is frank and very detailed about Forrester's personal life and career and the people around her. The book lacks an index, or such things as a chronology, list of repertoire, etc.

Malcolm Forsyth

464.Champagne, Jane. "Malcolm Forsyth: how to get high on your own music." *Le Compositeur Canadien/The Canadian Composer* 99 (March 1975): 14-21.

This general article is primarily interesting for the information on Forsyth's early development as a composer.

Wesley Octavius Forsyth

465. Keillor, Elaine. "Wesley Octavius Forsyth 1859-1937." *Les Cahiers canadiens de musique/The Canada Music Book* 7 (Automne/hiver 1973): 101-21.

Much detail is provided about the studies, appointments and travels of Forsyth, who was one of Toronto's most notable musicians in the first part of the 20th century. There is a discussion of his compositions, but little about what sustained his reputation as a teacher of piano. List of works.

Achille Fortier

466. Boulianne, Lucie. "Achille Fortier (1864-1939): espoirs et désillusions d'un compositeur au tournant du siècle." *Les cahiers de l'ARMuQ* 12 (avril 1990): 54-61. ISSN 0821-1817.

A biographical sketch of a musician who was thought by Léo-Pol Morin to be a composer of great promise. However, Fortier abandoned professional musical life to become a translator while continuing to compose. All his manuscripts were lost in a fire.

Harry Freedman

467. Dixon, Gail. "A composer takes stock." *Le Compositeur Canadien/The Canadian Composer* 176 (December 1982): 4-7, 33.

A very brief over-view of Freedman's work., this article is continued in no.468.

468. ------ "An allegiance to craftsmanship." *Le Compositeur Canadien/The Canadian* Composer 177 (January 1983): 16-21.

Continuing on from no.467, the author briefly indicates Freedman's style and musical procedures, with an example drawn from *Chalumeau*.

469. ------ "Cellular metamorphosis and structural compartmentalization in Harry Freedman's *Chalumeau*." *Studies in music from the University of Western Ontario* 6 (1981): 48-76.

A detailed analysis of the piece for clarinet and strings, *Chalumeau*. The author explicates the structural relationships that all refer to a single generative cell. Many musical examples.

470.------ "Harry Freedman: a survey." *Studies in music from the University of Western Ontario* 5 (1980): 122-144.

There is a biographical sketch, a survey of stylistic development, a discussion of style characteristics that includes mention of many works, and a list of compositions 1947-1980. Musical examples.

471.Schulman, Michael. "Interview! Harry Freedman: on being himself." *Le Compositeur Canadien/The Canadian Composer* 96 (December 1974): 4-11.

The article consists almost entirely of direct statements by Freedman, interesting for his views on his personal interests and on music as culture, but there is nothing about his own music.

Jean-Josaphat Gagnier

472.Bourbonnais, Gabrielle. *Inventaire sommaire du fonds J.-J. Gagnier.* Montréal: Bibliothèque nationale du Québec, 1989. 107p. ISBN 2-551-12138-8.

This catalogue lists, with full bibliographical information, Gagnier's works by category: compositions, arrangements, and literary works. There is an index of persons and organizations, and an index of titles and first lines.

Ernest Gagnon

473.Letondal, Arthur. "Ernest Gagon: écrivain et folklorist (1834-1915)." *Qui?* 2/4 (mars 1951): 65-80.

Although short on detail, this article effectively outlines the main features of Gagnon's life and activities, and includes a rather long anecdote about meeting Rossini.

474.Smith, Gordon E. "Ernest Gagnon (1834-1915): musician and pioneer folksong scholar." PhD dissertation, University of Toronto, 1989. v, 305f.

There is material on Gagnon's life and career, and on his writings and compositions, but the main subject is the *Chansons populaires du Canada.* French, religious and nationalist influences are examined, as well as the background to the collection of Gagnon's material. There are an inventory of compositions; classifications of the repertory in *Chansons populaires* according to type and modality; and a bibliography.

475.------ "Ernest Gagnon on nationalism and Canadian music: folk and native sources." *Canadian Folk Music Journal* 17 (1989): 32-39.

Nationalism is seen to influence not only Gagnon's direct interest in French-Canadian folksong, but also his view about how a national style of art music might derive from folk and native sources.

476.------ "Ernest Gagnon: sa carrière comme musicien d'Église." *Les cahiers de l'ARMuQ* 11 (septembre 1989): 14-26. ISSN 0821-1817.

Gagnon's importance as a church musician is examined, particularly his involvement in the controversies around plainchant performance.

477.------ "La genèse des *Chansons populaires du Canada* d'Ernest Gagnon." *Les cahiers de l'ARMuQ* 15 (mai 1994): 38-53. ISSN 0821-1817.

After briefly examining an important precedent, the author elucidates the complicated publishing history of Gagnon's *Chansons populaires* from 1865 to 1955. An English version of this article appears as "The genesis of Ernest Gagnon's *Chansons populaires du Canada*" in *Taking a stand: essays in honour of John Beckwith*, pp.221-237. T. McGee, ed. Toronto: University of Toronto Press, 1995. ISBN 0-8020-0583-7.

Serge Garant

478.Fleuret, Maurice. "Rencontre avec Serge Garant." *Les Cahiers canadiens de musique/The Canada Music Book* 9 (Automne/hiver 1974): 13-32.

In this interview, which took place publicly at the Canadian Cultural Centre in Paris, 30 May 1974, Garant spoke at length about his experiences in France, about his music, and about music in Canada, notably in Québec.

479. Guertin, Marcelle, comp. "In memoriam Serge Garant." *Canadian University Music Review/Revue de musique des universités canadiennes* 7 (1986): 1-31.

A number of statements from colleagues in homage to Garant at his death in 1986. Eulogistic rather than informative, they convey something of Garant's character, the range of his activity, and his importance to 20th century music, especially in Québec.

480. ------ "L'oeuvre de Serge Garant." *Canadian University Music Review/Revue de musique des universités canadiennes* 7 (1986): 36-45.

Essentially part of no.479, this list of works is extensive but not exhaustive. Discography.

481. Lefebvre, Marie-Thérèse. "Nouvelle approche de la conception du matériau sonore dans les oeuvres post-sérielles: une analyse du *Quintette* de Serge Garant." PhD dissertation, Université de Montréal, 1981. vi, 207, [44]f, audio cassette.

The main thrust of the dissertation is to develop a critical and analytical position to post-serial music that takes into account creation and perception of the work, as well as the intellectual and musical context in which it is created. The application of this discussion is in the analysis of Garant's *Quintette* for flute, oboe, cello, percussion and piano. There is a transcript of a brief conversation with Garant, and a facsimile of the autograph score. The dissertation submission includes a recording of the work conducted by the composer.

482. ------ "Une partition inédite de Serge Garant: *Cage d'oiseau*, version de 1958." *Les cahiers de l'ARMuQ* 12 (avril 1990): 75-87. ISSN 0821-1817.

Garant's *Cage d'oiseau* (1962) for voice and piano was preceded by another different piece on the same text for voice and instrumental ensemble. The author analyses the formal structure of the earlier piece and discusses Garant's search for an appropriate musical language, and the influence of Varèse on that search.

483.------ *Serge Garant et la révolution musicale au Québec*. Montréal: Louise Courteau, 1986. 239p. ISBN 2-89239-036-2.

About one third of the book is biographical, the remainder being extensive reprinting of Garant's many and wide-ranging articles on music, musicians and musical life. There is a list of works, and of broadcasts devoted to him. The bibliography is particularly useful for the inclusion of a great many references to reviews and articles in journals and newspapers.

Éva Gauthier

484. Turbide, Nadia. "Biographical study of Éva Gauthier (1885-1958) first French-Canadian singer of the avant-garde." PhD dissertation, Université de Montréal, 1986. x, 732p. (3 vol.)

The Ottawa-born singer pursued her career almost entirely abroad. She included four years in Java among her musical activities, and had outstanding success as a performer of new vocal music in the 1920s and 1930s. This thorough biographical study includes a list of Gauthier's concerts, reproductions of programs, repertoire, a discography, and a list of reviews and articles.

485.------ "Éva Gauthier (1885-1958): première cantatrice canadienne-française d'avant-garde." *Les cahiers de l'ARMuQ* 7 (mai 1988): 65-78. ISSN 0821-1817.

Gauthier, who lived all of her professional life in New York, was a major figure in the performance of contemporary song in the period 1917-1937. This article provides a summary of her activities. Based on no.484.

Jean Girard

486. Gallat-Morin, Élisabeth. *Jean Girard, musicien en Nouvelle-France, Bourges, 1696 - Montréal, 1765*. Québec: Les éditions du Septentrion, 1993. 351p. ISBN 2-921114-87-9.

Girard was a French Sulpician musician/cleric who moved to Montréal in 1724, and who likely brought the *Livre d'orgue de Montréal* (no.333-335). This biography reveals much about the social, educational, religious and musical life of Montréal in the mid-18th century.

Frédérick Glackemeyer

487. Kallmann, Helmut. "Frédérick Glackemeyer: des données nouvelles sur sa vie et son style musical." *Les cahiers de l'ARMuQ* 8 (mai 1987): 86-92. ISSN 0821-1817.

A note on the birth date of Glackemeyer and his move to New France; and a short discussion of stylistic similarities between Glackemeyer's music and Mozart's.

Glenn Gould

488. Angilette, Elizabeth. *Philosopher at the keyboard: Glenn Gould.* Metuchen, N.J.: Scarecrow Press, 1992. xi, 232p. ISBN 0-8108-2467-1.

The aim of this examination of Gould's writings is to provide a foundation for understanding them as a philosophy of music, and to reconcile apparent discrepancies in the ideas of a thinker whose mind is rooted in the creative process.

489. Canning, Nancy. *A Glenn Gould catalogue.* Westport, Conn.: Greenwood Press, 1992. xxxi, 230p. ISBN 0-313-27412-6.

There is a list of Gould's published writings and of his repertoire, but the catalogue is mainly devoted to an exhaustive indexing of his recordings. There are fully detailed entries for all extant recordings by Gould, including broadcast and private recordings. Programs held in the Archives of the Canadian Broadcasting Corporation are given with date of recording, and there is a list of titles in the Sony Catalogue at time of publication as well as in other commercial releases.

490. Cott, Jonathan. *Conversations with Glenn Gould.* Boston, Toronto: Little, Brown & Company, 1984. 160p. ISBN 0-316-15777-5. (*Entretiens avec Jonathan Cott*, Jacques Drillon, trans. Paris: Jean-Claude Lattès, 1983. 167p. ISBN 2-266-03548-7.) (*Telefongespräche mit Glenn Gould.* Berlin: Alexander Verlag, 1987. 155p. ISBN 3-923854-23-4)

The interviews first appeared in *Rolling Stone* magazine and in *Forever Young* (Random House/Rolling Stone Press) in 1974 and 1977. Discography, and lists of CBC tape collection, radio and television programs, as well as Gould's appearances in or connections with films.

491. Friedrich, Otto. *Glenn Gould: a life and variations*. Toronto: Lester & Orpen Dennys Limited, 1989. xviii, 441p. ISBN 0-88619-106-8.

This "official" biography, written at the request of the Gould Estate, is a highly detailed account of Gould's musical life, with extensive quotations from articles by and about Gould, and from personal interviews. The book conveys a sense of Gould's personality. List of concerts. Nancy Canning (see no.489) provides a discography, list of radio and television broadcasts, and a bibliography of Gould's published writings.

492. *Glenn Gould.* Ottawa: National Library of Canada, 1992. 2 vols. xiv, 318/xiv, 326. ISBN 0-660-57327-X(set).

This descriptive catalogue of the Glenn Gould papers in the National Library of Canada was compiled by Ruth Pincoe. The collection includes letters, programs, musical manuscripts, and many miscellaneous items and documents of a personal nature. There is also a list of materials held in other collections outside the Library, a bibliography that is especially useful for the extensive listing of newspaper and journal articles; a discography that includes commercial releases of performances that originated on radio or television; and an extensive index. Many photographs. Text in English and French.

493. Gould, Glenn. *The Glenn Gould reader*. Tim Page, ed. New York: Knopf, 1984. xvi, 476p. ISBN 0-394-54067-0.

Gould's extensive and wide-ranging writings, lectures and record liner notes are gathered into a comprehensive anthology.

494. ------ *Glenn Gould: selected letters*. edited and compiled by John P.L. Roberts and Ghyslaine Guertin. Toronto: Oxford University Press, 1992. xxiv, 260p. ISBN 0-19-540799-7. (*Lettres*. Annick

Duchâtel, trans. Paris: Christian Bourgois, 1992. 440p. ISBN 2-267-01076-3.)

This selection of just under 200 letters (from among 2000) touches on every aspect of Gould's interests and activities, from the trivial to the most serious. The selection of letters is not identical in the French and English editions; and the annotations tend to be fuller in the French edition.

495. Gould, Glenn, in conversation with John Jessop. "Radio as Music." *Les cahiers canadiens de musique/The Canada Music Book* 2 (Printemps-été 1971): 13-30.

In what is much more a monologue than a conversation, Gould talks expansively about the origins of his radio documentaries, his imaginative and technical realization of them, and about radio and broadcasting in general.

496. Guertin, Ghyslaine, comp. *Glenn Gould pluriel*. Verdun, Québec: Louise Courteau, 1988. [viii], 278p. ISBN 2-89239-063-X

A colloquium held in 1987 at l'Université du Québec à Montréal examined the many sides of Gould as a person, performer, thinker, writer, producer. Many of the sixteen papers from that colloquium, gathered in this collection, are more reflective, even philosophical, than analytical.

497. ------ "Nature et fonction de la relation de Glenn Gould à Arnold Schoenberg." *Les cahiers de l'ARMuQ* 13 (mai 1991): 66-77. ISSN 0821-1817.

Gould's relationship to Schoenberg is seen here as grounded in his own musical aesthetic founded on reason and the fundamental importance of structure, an aesthetic closely related to Schoenberg's.

498. Hagestedt, Jens. *Wie spielt Glenn Gould?: zu einer Theorie der Interpretation*. Munich: Peter Kirchheim Verlag, 1991. 207p. ISBN 3-87410-041-3.

With references to more than one hundred works, the author attempts to analyse Gould's technique and interpretation, based on recordings. Many musical examples.

499. Kallmann, Helmut. *Glenn Gould 1988*. Ottawa: National Library of Canada, 1988. 69p. ISBN 0-662-55756-5.

This catalogue of an exhibition held in Ottawa at the National Library in 1988 includes an essay on Gould a chronology, and a short bibliography. There is often interesting information included in the descriptions of the items. Text in French and English. Photographs.

500. Kazdin, Andrew. *Glenn Gould at work; creative lying*. New York: E.P. Dutton, 1989. 178, [40]p. ISBN 0-525-24817-X. (*Glenn Gould: ein Porträt*. Lexa Katrina von Nostitz, trans. Zurich: Schweizer Verlagshaus, 1990. 210p. ISBN 3-7263-6631-8.)

Kazdin was the producer for fifteen years of Gould's CBS recordings. He recounts experiences that are personal and anecdotal, and not always flattering to the pianist, but they are illuminating of Gould's personality, his approach to recording, and some of his musical ideas. Discography of CBS Masterworks recordings, including re-issues.

501. Matheis, Wera. *Glenn Gould: der Unheilige am Klavier*. Munich: Scaneg, 1987. 137p. ISBN 3-89235-801-X.

An uncritical but not uninteresting account of Gould and his activities. The bibliography includes many newspaper and journal articles. There is a discography, a filmography, and a list of radio documents.

502. McGreevy, John, ed. *Glenn Gould variations: by himself and his friends*. Toronto: Doubleday Canada Ltd., 1983. 319p. ISBN 0-385-18995-8.

These twenty-one short essays cover a number of topics both personal and musical. Some are original to the collection, others are republished.

503. Morey, Carl. "Editing Glenn Gould." *GlennGould* 1 (fall 1995): 21-23.

Gould composed a few original works in addition to his transcriptions of orchestral material. The author discusses editorial problems that had to be solved for the publication by B. Schott's Söhne of two sets of piano pieces and a bassoon sonata.

504. Payzant, Geoffrey. *Glenn Gould: music and mind*. Toronto: Van Nostrand Reinhold Ltd., 1978. xiii, 192p. ISBN 0-442-29802-1; Toronto: Key Porter Books, 1984, 1992. xiii, 192p. ISBN 1-55013-439-6. (*Glenn Gould: un homme du futur*. Laurence Minard and Th. Shipiatchev, trans. [Paris]: Librairie Arthème Fayard, c1983. *Glenn Gould: kirjoituksia musükista*. Hannu-Ilari Lampila, trans. Helsinki: Kustannusoakeyhtiö Otawa, 1988.)

This first book on Gould is less a biography than a study of Gould as thinker and philosopher, as discovered in his writings, broadcasts and performances. The author drew on his own skills as both philosopher (at the University of Toronto) and musician, and his own active experience of Gould, but without Gould's participation. The 1984 edition has an "afterword", and the 1992 edition has a new Preface.

505. ------ "The Glenn Gould outtakes." In *Musical Canada: words and music honouring Helmut Kallmann*, pp.298-313. J. Beckwith and F. Hall, eds. Toronto: University of Toronto Press, 1988. ISBN 0-8020-5759-4.

The "outtakes" are not from recordings but from Payzant's book on Gould. They are philosophical observations that were removed by the author from the final version of the book when it was determined that it would be issued by a "trade" publisher rather than an "academic" one.

506. Schneider, Michel. *Glenn Gould piano solo: aria et trente variations*. Paris: Éditions Gallimard, 1988. 204p. ISBN 2-07-071547-7. 2nd. edition, with four previously unpublished texts, 1994. 277p. ISBN 2-07-038841-7

This is a sort of poetic biography/analysis of Gould the man, but the author has a shaky grasp of Gould's Canadian context. It is built mainly on information drawn from other studies of Gould.

507. Stegemann, Michael. *Glenn Gould: Leben und Werk*. Munich: Piper, 1992. 524p. ISBN 3-492-03584-1.

A meticulous chronology of concerts, recordings and various personal events serves as the framework for a biographical/musical study that derives much of its material from excerpts from interviews and articles. Discography.

Lyell Gustin

508.Leeper, Muriel. *The Gustin influence.* Saskatoon: Leopard's Head Publishing Ltd, 1982. 111p.

An admiring study of Gustin and his position in Saskatchewan music. There are notes on his approach to teaching, and a list of his students. There are reflections of musical life in Saskatoon through Gustin's life-long residence there.

Irving Guttman

509.Watmough, David. *The unlikely pioneer: building opera from the Pacific through the Prairies.* Oakville, Ont.: Mosaic Press, 1986. 186p. ISBN 0-88962-8; 0-88962-285-X (pbk).

Written from an enthusiastic and uncritical personal viewpoint, this biography of opera stage director Irving Guttman also includes much information about the opera companies in Vancouver, Edmonton and Winnipeg. Lists are given of repertoire, with casts, for productions in those cities through the period 1960-1985, whether or not directed by Guttman.

Ida Halpern

510.Chen, Kenneth. "Ida Halpern: a post-colonial portrait of a Canadian pioneer ethnomusicologist." *Canadian University Music Review/Revue de musique des universités canadiennes* 16/1 (1995): 41-59.

The author provides biographical background, and a critical examination of Halpern's methodology. Her notable documentation of Native music of the Pacific northwest coast consists of about 500 songs, and was carried out largely during a period when Canadian law technically forbade the celebration, or even the study, of Native ceremonies. Extensive annotations provide references on many aspects of the article. List of Halpern's writings.

Charles A.E. Harriss

511. Turbide, Nadia M. "Charles Albert Edwin Harriss: the McGill years." MMA dissertation, McGill University, 1976. vii, 138f.

The study is mainly about Harriss's role in establishing the British system of musical education and examination in Canada during the period 1898-1907. There is also information about the founding of the McGill Conservatorium, and a catalogue of works by Harriss.

Hattie Rhue Hatchett

512. Stewardson, Richard George. "Hattie Rhue Hatchett (1863-1958): an interdisciplinary study of her life and music in North Buxton, Ontario." MA thesis, York University, 1994.xiv, 393p.

The thesis deals with the life and work of a Black musician in an Ontario town, touching on many aspects of Gospel music, racial and gender restrictions, and general relevant social matters in Canada and Ontario in the early part of the twentieth century.

John Hawkins

513. Mather, Bruce. "Le collage musical: 'Remembrances' de John Hawkins." *Les Cahiers canadiens de musique/The Canada Music Book* 3 (Automne/Hiver 1971): 99-102.

The author identifies the works that are referred to in *Remembrances* (1969), and shows the relationships that exist among the nine sections of the piece. Musical examples.

514. McLean, Don. "Of things past: John Hawkins's *Remembrances* (1969)." In *Taking a stand: essays in honour of John Beckwith*, pp.46-69. Ed. T. McGee. Toronto: University of Toronto Press, 1995. ISBN 0-8020-0583-7.

Working from the quotations that occur within the structure of *Remembrances*, the author examines in a detailed and highly technical graphic analysis, the relationships of those quotations and the pitch context of the work. Also touched on are such topics as timbre and notation.

515.Plawutsky, Eugene. "The music of John Hawkins." *Canadian Association of University Schools of Music Journal* 8/1 (Spring, 1978): 112-34.

This survey of the eleven pieces composed by Hawkins from 1966 to 1975 provides brief but pertinent technical analyses, and conveys something of the effectiveness of the music and of the composer's intentions. A bibliographical note cites articles on Hawkins and the references for his own notes.

Derek Holman

516.Schulman, Michael. "Derek Holman calls himself an all-round church musician." *Le Compositeur Canadien/The Canadian Composer* 147 (January 1980): 10-17.

Holman's wide-ranging career is succinctly surveyed, with mention of his posts and many of his compositions.

Elmer Iseler

517.Champagne, Jane. "Interview! Elmer Iseler: a force for choral music in Canada." *Le Compositeur Canadien/The Canadian Composer* 90 (April 1974): 8-17.

Iseler talks of the founding of the Festival Singers, of his direction of the Mendelssohn Choir, and of choral singing generally in Canada.

Frances James

518.Lazarevich, Gordana. *The musical world of Frances James and Murray Adaskin.* Toronto: University of Toronto Press, 1988. x, 331p. ISBN 0-8020-5738-1.

In addition to the biographical treatment of the subjects, there is much material relating to the many organizations and individuals with whom James and Adaskin were associated together and singly over long careers throughout Canada. The narrative ends with retirement in Victoria in the 1970s. Musical examples, list of works by Adaskin, premieres and early performances of Canadian works given by James, and catalogue of air-check discs (1945-54) recorded by James for CBC. Bibliography.

Frantz Jehin-Prume

519. Houle, Jacques-André. "Frantz Jehin-Prume (1839-99): son apport culturel au milieu québécois." *Les cahiers de l'ARMuQ* 12 (avril 1990): 48-53. ISSN 0821-1817.

New biographical details are brought forward concerning the early days of the violinist Jehin-Prume in Montréal, where he settled in 1865. His importance to musical development, especially as a teacher, is assessed.

Raoul Jobin

520. Maheu, Renée. *Raoul Jobin*. Paris: Pierre Belfond, 1983. 234p. ISBN 2-7144-1639-X.

A biography that includes a discography, a detailed chronological list of all important engagements, but no index.

Edward Johnson

521. Benson, Nathaniel A. "Edward Johnson." *The Canadian Music Journal* 2/3 (Spring 1958): 28-34.

This derivative sketch makes no new contribution to the biography or to the musical evaluation of Johnson.

522. Mercer, Ruby. *The Tenor of his time*. Toronto, Vancouver: Clarke, Irwin & Co., 1976. xv, 336p. ML420.J64M47. ISBN 0-7720-07365.

A detailed biography, more admiring than critical, by an author fully familiar with Johnson's operatic milieu. J.B. McPherson and W.R. Moran contribute a discography that contains "essential details of all known recordings featuring Edward Johnson as a singer".

Helmut Kallmann

523. Keer, Dawn L. "Helmut Kallmann: an account of his contributions to music librarianship and scholarship in Canada." Master of Library and Information Studies dissertation, University of Alberta, 1991. [vii], 141f.

There is a full biographical account as well as much information surrounding Kallmann's work as librarian and scholar. Information is carefully documented, but the work also draws extensively on interviews with Kallmann and with friends and associates. A bibliography of works, 1947-1990, augments and updates the list in *Musical Canada* (no.94).

Maryvonne Kendergi

524. Bail Milot, Louise, comp. "Musialogue: Maryvonne Kendergi." *Les cahiers de l'ARMuQ* 5 (1985).

The entire issue of *Les cahiers* is given over to an appreciation of Kendergi, who played so vigorous a role in many aspects of Québec music from her arrival in Canada in 1952. Biography, lists of broadcasts, publications, professional and teaching engagements.

Talivaldis Kenins

525. Kariks, Edgars. "Talivaldis Kenins: *Beatae voces tenebrae.*" unpublished typescript, University of Adelaide (South Australia), 1989. 2 vols. vi, 437f. 40 plates.

The first volume (pp.1-155, appendix) provides a detailed biography, valuable for the quotation from many journals and from conversations with the composer. The second volume is an overview, without technical analysis, of Kenins' music, with many examples. (The work was prepared as a PhD dissertation for the University of Adelaide, but the degree was not completed. There is a copy at the Canadian Music Centre, Toronto..)

526.Levitch, Gerald. "Talivaldis Kenins." *Le Compositeur Canadien/The Canadian Composer* 107 (January 1976): 10-15.

In an interview, Kenins talks generally about influences and his musical style.

Calixa Lavallée

527.Chartier, F. "Calixa Lavallée." *L'Action Nationale* 2/1 (septembre 1933): 60-71.

A short résumé of Lavallée's career, but emphasizing his devotion to Canada.

528.Lapierre, Eugène. "Calixa Lavallée, compositeur national, 1842-1891." *Qui?* 1/2 (septembre 1949): 33-48.

This biographical outline by Lavallée's biographer (no.529) includes a short discussion of the music of *O Canada*, and a copy of the first publication of the song.

529.------ *Calixa Lavallée, musicien national du Canada.* Montréal: Éditions Albert Lévesque, 1937. 215p. reprinted Montréal: Fides, 1950, 1966. 291p.

The first full study of Lavallée is dependent to a large extent on recollections and reminiscences. There is little documentation. The 1966 edition contains numerous illustrations, a chapter on the re-burial of Lavallée in 1933, and appendices that include a speech given in London in 1888, facsimiles of correspondence, a note on the singer Rosita del Vecchio, and a chronology. No index.

Hugh Le Caine

530.Young, Gayle. *The sackbut blues: Hugh Le Caine pioneer in electronic music.* Ottawa: National Museum of Science and Technology, 1989. xiv, 274p. ISBN 0-660-12006-2.

In form a biography, this study of Le Caine is at least equally a study of the development of electronic music in Canada in the 1950s and 1960s. The discussions of Le Caine's technical developments are in language that is understandable by an informed but non-specialized reader. Extensive bibliography of Le Caine's writings, and of other sources of information. Discography, index.

Gilles Lefebvre

531. Lefebvre, Gilles. *La musique d'une vie.* [Montréal]: Les Éditions Fides, 1993. 199p. ISBN 2-7621-1685-6.

These reminiscences are chiefly valuable for remarks on the founding of Jeunesses musicales du Canada and the music centre at Mount Orford. The author touches on the many musical posts he has had, but the tone is conversational rather than critical or scrupulously detailed. No index.

Arthur Letondal

532. Lafortune, Pierre-Paul. "Arthur Letondal." *Amérique française* 8/3 (1950): 51-57.

Although superficial, this short essay provides a sense of Letondal's place as a teacher, and gives a glimpse of Montréal musical life in the first part of the 20th century.

Omer Létourneau

533. Huot, Cécile. *Entretiens avec Omer Létourneau.* Montréal, Les Éditions Quinze, 1979. 232p. ISBN 0-88565-176-6.

The text is derived from a series of interviews, posed as questions and answers. There is a good deal of information about musical life in Québec city in the first half of the 20th century. Lists of organizations with which Létourneau was associated, index of names.

Alexina Louie

534. Bégay, Diane. "Contemporary music in Canada: Alexina Louie." MMus dissertation, University of Ottawa, 1994. xvi, 188f.

About half the study if devoted to biographical material. The remaining section on the music surveys the composer's style and approaches, and deals more thoroughly with three representative works. Extensive bibliography and list of works.

535. Goulet, Colleen. "Alexina Louie: composition as a soul-searching voyage into the self." *Le Compositeur Canadien/The Canadian Composer* 193 (September 1984): 20-23.

   Of limited usefulness for information, but the article offers some views by the young composer on her approach to composition, with comments on *Songs of Paradise* and *O Magnum Mysterium*.

536. Schulman, Michael. "Exotic sounds, hypnotic rhythm from Vancouver's Alexina Louie." *Le Compositeur Canadien/The Canadian Composer* 150 (April 1980): 16-21, 32-33.

   Although written early in Louie's career, this article is a useful survey of her studies and her first extended compositions.

Clarence Lucas

537. "Clarence Lucas." *Musical Canada* 9/3 (July 1914): 63-65.

   The article is slight, but it has the interest of a contemporary account of Lucas's life and career up to 1914.

Sir Ernest MacMillan

538. *Le Compositeur Canadien/The Canadian Composer* 82 (July 1973).

   The entire issue of the magazine is devoted to a series of articles about virtually every facet of MacMillan's career, written by those closely associated with him. Frequently anecdotal, the articles convey much about the character of the man and of the musical community in which he worked.

539. MacKelcan, Fred R. "Sir Ernest MacMillan." *Queen's Quarterly* 43/4 (Winter, 1936-37): 408-14.

   While there is little significant information to be gathered from this article, it is a fine personal assessment of MacMillan's successes, written a few years after he became conductor of the Toronto Symphony Orchestra.

540. MacMillan, Sir Ernest. "The organ was my first love." *The Canadian Music Journal* 3/3 (Spring 1959): 15-25.

This reminiscence provides some insight into the early development of a brilliant young musician as well as into church music in Toronto in the early part of the 20th century.

541. MacMillan, Keith. "Ernest MacMillan: the Ruhleben years." In *Musical Canada: words and music honouring Helmut Kallmann*, pp.164-182. J. Beckwith and F. Hall, eds. Toronto: University of Toronto Press, 1988. ISBN 0-8020-5759-4.

This is an account of the internment of Ernest MacMillan in a German prison camp during the First World War, 1914-1918. His involvement in musical activities of the camp is described, as well as some of his fellow interns.

542. Schabas, Ezra. *Sir Ernest MacMillan: the importance of being Canadian.* Toronto: University of Toronto Press, 1994. xi, 374p. ISBN 0-8020-2849-7.

Because of MacMillan's central musical position in Toronto and in Canada generally, this important and thorough biography is often a source of information in terms wider than its subject. There are extensive notes and archival information, bibliography, lists of writings and compositions by MacMillan, a discography, and index.

543. Solway, Maurice. "Sir Ernest MacMillan vs. Reginald Stewart." *Le Compositeur Canadien/The Canadian Composer* 199 (March 1985): 14-21.

A reprinting from Solway's memoirs (no.592) about the supposed rivalry in Toronto between MacMillan and Stewart, the article is interesting for anecdotes about both men and about music in Toronto in the 1930s.

Bruce Mather

544.Evangelista, José. "Une analyse de 'Madrigal III' de Bruce Mather." *Les Cahiers canadiens de musique/Canada Music Book* 6 (Printemps/été 1973): 81-109.

The author considers *Madrigal III* to have special importance within the evolution of contemporary music in Canada, and to represent Mather's interest in utilizing anew traditional elements of composition. The analysis proceeds from an examination of the music itself, and not from a pre-conceived method. Extensive musical examples.

545.Schulman, Michael. "Bruce Mather: composing again." *Le Compositeur Canadien/The Canadian Composer* 124 (October 1977): 4-9.

A brief review of Mather's background and current activities. There are some insights into his musical interests and points of view.

André Mathieu

546.Rudel-Tessier, J. *André Mathieu, un génie.* Montréal: Éditions Héritage, 1976. 364p.

The biographical section contains a good deal of information but is written virtually in the style of a novel, with details and conversations that the author could not have known. The main interest is in the large number of reproductions of articles, reviews and programs related to Mathieu's short but notable career.

Rodolphe Mathieu

547.Bourassa-Trépanier, Juliette. "La langue musicale de Rodolphe Mathieu." *Les Cahiers canadiens de musique/The Canada Music Book* 5 (Automne/hiver 1972): 19-30.

Without engaging in technical analysis, the author reviews Mathieu's development as a composer up to about 1930, and the origins of his chromatic style.

548.------ "Rediscovering a forgotten composer." *Le Compositeur Canadien/The Canadian Composer* 79 (April 1973): 30-33.

The outline of Mathieu's work is very brief, but there is a list of scores available in the CBC Music Library and the Canadian Music Centre.

549.------ "Rodolphe Mathieu, musicien canadien (1890-1962)." DMus dissertation, l'Université Laval, 1972. xiii, 508f.

There is a short biographical note and a survey of Mathieu's literary work, but the main part of the dissertation is given to examinations of his compositions. For each work, there is a note which is descriptive and critical. The works are then considered comprehensively from stylistic points of view. Many musical examples, facsimiles, catalogue of works, index of names.

550.Trew, Johanne. "The Rodolphe Mathieu collection at the National Library of Canada: an annotated catalogue." McGill University, MA dissertation, 1987. x, 159f.

This catalogue describes Rodolphe Mathieu's personal papers and related items in the National Library collection identified as "The Mathieu Family Papers." Documents relating to other family members, including André, are included only if there is a connection with Rodolphe. No index, but material is divided into fifteen categories, which facilitates the locating of information.

Frank Stephen Meighen

551.Lamontagne, Charles-O. and Romain Gour. "Frank Stephen Meighen: dilettante et mécène (1870-1946)." *Qui?* 5/3 (mars 1954): 41-56.

Meighen was a Montréal businessman of great wealth at the turn of the 20th century. He was the founder and sole patron of the Montreal Opera Company, and this biographical account contains much information about the ambitious but short-lived Company. Lamontagne was an administrator of the Company.

Pierre Mercure

552.Chayer, Micheline. "Le fonds Pierre Mercure des archives nationales du Québec." MA dissertation, Université de Montréal, 1984. viii, 543f. (2 vol.)

Following some introductory material, there is a complete analytical catalogue of the papers of Pierre Mercure. Items are arranged by category (correspondence, programs, reviews, etc.) with a short descriptive note for each entry, followed by an alphabetical index.

Léo-Pol Morin

553. Villeneuve, Claire. "Léo-Pol Morin, musicographe." *Canadian Association of University Schools of Music Journal* 4/1-2 (Fall, 1974): 85-97.

This sketch of Morin as a severe but positive critic includes some background on him as a fine pianist. Chronology of his life, indication of his writings (he wrote almost 700 journal articles), and an outline of his pianistic repertoire. See no.554.

554. ------ "Léo-Pol Morin (1892-1941), musicographe." MMus dissertation, l'Université de Montréal, 1975. v, 250f.

The dissertation contains exhaustive lists of Morin's articles, essays, and concert criticisms, as well as references to him and to concerts at which he appeared or at which his works were played. Index of names. For a summary of the author's comprehensive examination of all facets of Morin's activities, see no.553.

Boyd Neel

555. Neel, Boyd. *My orchestras and other adventures: the memoirs of Boyd Neel*. J. David Finch, ed. Toronto: University of Toronto Press, 1985. [vi], 230p. ISBN 0-8020-5674-1

Although most of the memoirs relate to Neel's conducting career before moving to Canada, nevertheless they provide some insights into his years in Toronto, particularly with regard to the University of Toronto, where he was Dean of music. Some of the material is reprinted from earlier sources, notably Neel's *Story of an orchestra*. London: Vox Mundi, 1950.

Jean Papineau-Couture

556. Baillargeon, Pierre. "Jean Papineau-Couture." *Amérique française* 7/1 (1948): 75-77.

This brief interview offers only a few inconsequential opinions of the composer, and includes at least one error of fact and one misspelling.

557. Bail Milot, Louise. *Jean Papineau-Couture: la vie, la carrière et l'oeuvre.* (Cahiers du Québec. Collection musique: 87). Ville de Lasalle, Québec: Hurtubise HMH, 1986. 319p. ISBN 2-89045-799-0.

A thorough biographical section is followed by discussion of many works, grouped by four time periods. The detailed catalogue of works includes publishing and recording information. The most extensive study of the composer.

558. Beckwith, John. "Jean Papineau-Couture." *The Canadian Music Journal* 3/2 (Winter 1959): 4-20.

The author first presents Papineau-Couture in the context of Québec music, then without going into detailed analysis, provides a good overview of the technical and affective features of his music. Musical examples, and a list of works up to 1958.

559. Dixon, Gail. "The *Pièces concertantes* Nos. 1, 2, 3 and 4 of Jean Papineau-Couture." *Studies in music from the University of Western Ontario* 9 (1984): 93-123.

The four pieces (composed 1957-59) are each examined within the general framework of their representing solutions to distinctive structural procedures. Many charts and musical examples.

560. Papineau-Couture, Jean. "Regard sur près de cinquante années de création musicale." *Les cahiers de l'ARMuQ* 8 (mai 1987): 106-17. ISSN 0821-1817.

The composer's personal reminiscences over fifty years -- the text of an address given in May, 1986.

Kathleen Parlow

561.French, Maida Parlow. *Kathleen Parlow, a portrait*. Toronto: Ryerson Press, 1967. x, 167p.

The account of Parlow's career as soloist and teacher and of her later years in Toronto is personal in style, but careful in detail. There is no annotation, but it is clear that most of the information came from Parlow's papers, from the violinist herself, and from the author's personal knowledge.

562.Parlow, Kathleen. "Student days in Russia." *The Canadian Music Journal* 6/1 (Autumn 1961): 13-20.

Parlow recounts her experiences in Russia where she went in 1906 to study with Leopold Auer.

Frédéric Pelletier

563.Émond, Vivianne. "Frédéric Pelletier et la critique musicale à Montréal dans la première moitié du XXe siècle." *Les cahiers de l'ARMuQ* 12 (avril 1990): 62-74. ISSN 0821-1817.

As critic for *Le Devoir* in Montréal from 1916 to 1944, Pelletier exercised much influence on musical opinion. He was well informed and of strong views, and often engaged in heated polemics with and about his contemporaries.

Romain-Octave Pelletier

564.Laurendeau, Arthur. "Musiciens d'autrefois: Romain-Octave Pelletier." *L'Action Nationale* 35/6 (juin, 1950): 437-51.

A general article that sketches Pelletier's personality, and his place in later 19th century musical life in Québec.

565.Pelletier, Romain. "Octave Pelletier: organiste et pédagogue (1843-1927)." *Qui?* 4/1 (Septembre, 1952): 3-24.

Pelletier's successful career as a Montréal church musician influenced the standards of church music in the city. This sketch of his life is primarily biographical, not musical.

Wilfred Pelletier

566.Huot, Cécile. "Évolution de la vie musicale au Québec sous l'influence de Wilfred Pelletier." PhD dissertation, Université de Toulouse, 1973. viii, 252p.

Huot was the collaborator with Pelletier on his memoirs (no.567). Her dissertation takes the form of a series of elaborations on and corrections of statements contained in those memoirs

567.Pelletier, Wilfred. *Une Symphonie inachevée....* Ottawa: Leméac, 1972. 275p.

Much of Pelletier's autobiography is personal reminiscences about his career, largely in New York, and people he knew. There is, however, also information about his involvement in Québec musical life. See also no.566.

Barbara Pentland

568.Dixon, Gail. "The string quartets of Barbara Pentland." *Canadian University Music Review/Revue de musique des universités canadiennes* 11/2 (1991): 94-121.

The author provides a general outline of the features of each of Pentland's five string quartets, followed by detailed analysis of selected excerpts which together provide insight into the composer's techniques as well as stylistic distinctions among the quartets.

569.Eastman, Sheila and Timothy J. McGee. *Barbara Pentland.* Toronto: University of Toronto Press, 1983. viii, 134p. ISBN 0-8020-5562-1.

Within a biographical framework, much attention is given to the discussion of representative works, with many musical examples. List of works up to 1980 with notes on first performances; discography, bibliography.

570.McGee, Timothy J. "Barbara Pentland in the 1950s: *String Quartet No.2* and *Symphony for Ten Parts.*" *Studies in music from the University of Western Ontario* 9 (1984): 133-152.

The *Quartet* (1953) and the *Symphony* (1957) are taken as representatives of the end and the beginning of differing compositional techniques, notably the addition of timbral considerations as a structural element. Musical examples.

571. Turner, Robert. "Barbara Pentland." *The Canadian Music Journal* 2/4 (Summer 1958): 15-26.

This brief survey of Pentland's music takes note of some distincitve technical features and offers some generalizations on her output as a whole. Musical examples, and a list of works up to 1958.

Gino Quilico (see Louis Quilico)

Lina Pizzolongo Quilico (see Louis Quilico)

Louis Quilico

572. Mercer, Ruby. *The Quilicos, Louis, Gino & Lina: an operatic family.* Oakville, Ontario: Mosaic Press, 1991. 205p. ISBN 0-88962-425-6. (*Les Quilico*, Hervé Juste, trans. [Montréal]: Éditions de l'Homme, 1992. 270p. ISBN 2-7619-1082-6.)

The enthusiastic personal account of the lives and careers of the Quilico family is sometimes marred by incomplete or erroneous information. Many photographs; index.

Imant Raminsh

573. Dyck, Arthur Philip. "The choral music of Imant Karlis Raminsh." DMA dissertation, University of Iowa, 1990. xii, 257f.

A brief biographical section precedes a detailed study of the *Magnificat* (1983). There is an annotated list of choral works arranged alphabetically by title, and a chronological list of complete works up to August, 1990.

John Rea

574. Rea, John. "Sur *Las Meninas*, pour piano." *Les cahiers de l'ARMuQ* 15 (mai 1994): 27-31. ISSN 0821-1817.

The composer sets out the conceptual origin of his piano piece, *Las Meninas*, and its relationship to Schumann, Picasso and Velasquez.

Godfrey Ridout

575. Hatton, Helen. "Interview! A musical conservative." *Le Compositeur Canadien/The Canadian Composer* 93 (September 1974): 4-14.

Ridout discusses his conservative musical views in relation to the popular *avant garde*.

Léo Roy

576. Brisson, Irène. "La Correspondance de Léo Roy." *Les cahiers de l'ARMuQ* 10 (juin 1988): 11-18. ISSN 0821-1817.

A very brief summation of the contents of a collection of letters, photographs, and miscellaneous items in a collection at l'Université Laval. Almost no information is given about the nature or contents of the items themselves.

577. Marcoux, Guy. "Léo Roy vu par un ami." *Les cahiers de l'ARMuQ* 10 (juin 1988): 7-10. ISSN 0821-1817.

A very brief note on Roy by a friend who, in 1988, was working on a biography.

578. Vézina-Demers, Micheline and Claire Grégoire-Reid. *Catalogue des oeuvres musicale du fonds Léo Roy*. Québec: Atelier de musicographie, 1987. x, 143p. ISBN 2-9801120-0-3.

Le Fonds Léo-Roy, at l'Université Laval, consists of more than 350 original works and about 1000 arrangements. This is a listing by category, with three cross-indexes. A short pre-publication note by the authors appeared in *Les cahiers de l'ARMuQ* 10 (juin, 1988): 19-23, but it adds nothing to the information in the catalogue.

Micheline Coulombe Saint-Marcoux

579."An avant-garde composer's insights into her career." *Le
    Compositeur Canadien/The Canadian Composer* 89 (March 1974):
    28-34.

    The composers talks generally about some of her works and
    her musical views. There is a short biographical note and list of
    works up to 1972.

580.Gagné, Mireille. "Hommage à Micheline Coulombe Saint-
    Marcoux." *Les cahiers de l'ARMuQ* 7 (mai 1988): 90-94.

    A short review of the life and work of the composer at the
    time of her death.

581.Lévesque, Carole. "*Transit* de Micheline Coulombe Saint-
    Marcoux: l'aboutissement du cheminement du créateur." *Les
    cahiers de l'ARMuQ* 13 (mai 1991): 78-89. ISSN 0821-1817.

    An outline of the origin, conception and realization of the
    composer's music theatre piece, *Transit*.

    R. Murray Schafer

582.Adams, Stephen. "Murray Schafer's *Patria*: the greatest show on
    earth?" *Journal of Canadian Studies* 23/1 and 2 (Spring/Summer
    1988): 199-207.

    Adams describes Schafer's *Patria III: The Greatest Show* and
    examines the philosophical and symbolic aspects of the work. The
    discussion is extended to include the evolving *Patria* cycle, with
    some reference to other works.

583.------ *Murray Schafer*. Toronto: University of Toronto Press, 1983.
    x, 240p. ISBN 0-8020-5571-0

    A thorough study of Schafer at mid-career. In addition to
    biographical material, there is extensive discussion of his music
    and his writings. List of works, discography, bibliography.

584.Mather, Bruce. "Notes sur 'Requiems for the Party-Girl'." *Les
    Cahiers canadiens de musique/The Canada Music Book* 1
    (Printemps/été 1970): 91-97.

An explication of Schafer's *Requiems for the Party-Girl*, built on the presentation of five ways in which the text is musically illustrated, and a schema of the work in twelve parts.

585.Rea, John. "Richard Wagner and R. Murray Schafer: two revolutionary and religious poets." *Les Cahiers canadiens de musique/The Canada Music Book* 8 (Printemps/été 1974): 37-51.

A running comparison of similarities between the writings of Wagner and Schafer. The article is carefully annotated and frequently critical of perceived weaknesses in the ideas and philosophies of the two composers.

586.Schafer, R. Murray. "Notes for the stage work 'Loving' (1965)." *Les Cahiers canadiens de musique/The Canada Music Book* 8 (Printemps/été, 1974): 9-26.

The text of the article is that of a lecture given in 1965 when Schafer was still working on *Loving*. The completed work, as pointed out in a concluding note, was different from what was discussed in the lecture, but the article provides insights into Schafer's ideas about musical theatre and how he might realize them.

587.------ *Patria and the theatre of confluence.* Indian River, Ont.: Arcana Editions, 1991. 228p. ISBN 1-89512-709-2 (clth), 1-89512-711-4 (pbk).

In a set of essays, the composer discusses his theatrical and environmental works that have appeared under the generic title, *Patria*. The book is intended as a guide to performers and directors and includes details of the works' productions as well as Schafer's larger views of them and their origins. The essays also comprise an issue of *Descant* 22/2 (Summer, 1991).

588.------ *"Patria One: The Characteristics Man." Journal of Canadian Studies* 23/1 and 2 (Spring/Summer, 1988):207-218.

Schafer describes his work and provides information about incidents and ideas that led to its creation. A concluding section outlines his unsatisfactory relationship with the Canadian Opera Company over its presentation of the piece.

589.------ "R. Murray Schafer: a collection." *Open Letter* 4/4-5 (Fall, 1979): pp.7-244.

The entire issue is given over to seven articles by Schafer on his own work, and an extensive bibliography and discography by Stephen Adams. Some of the items appear elsewhere. Much of the material is reproductions of the composer's manuscripts. The libretto of *Loving* is included.

590.------ "The Theatre of confluence (note in advance of action)." *Les Cahiers canadiens de musique/The Canada Music Book* 9 (Automne/hiver, 1974): 33-52.

Written in 1966 while Schafer was working on *Patria*, the essay proposes a theatrical form and presentation that is combinatorial in a way more contrapuntal than synthetic. The author discusses other multi-dimensional works and philosophies and how his own ideas relate to them.

Léopold Simoneau (see Pierette Alarie)

Leo Smith

591.McCarthy, Pearl. *Leo Smith*. Toronto: University of Toronto Press, 1956. ix, 53p.

A personal biographical sketch of the Toronto 'cellist and composer, which includes a list of musical compositions, almost all of which were unpublished.

Maurice Solway

592.Solway, Maurice. *Recollections of a violinist*. Oakville, Ontario: Mosaic Press, 1984. 123p. ISBN 0-88962-234-5/7.

Reminiscences of an important Toronto violinist, chiefly of his studies and career in Toronto, but also about his teacher, Eugène Ysaÿe. The book lacks an index.

Harry Somers

593.Butler, Edward Gregory. "The five piano sonatas of Harry Somers." DMA dissertation, University of Rochester, 1974. viii,146p.

The five *Sonatas* (1945-1957) are each analyzed separately, with a short concluding summary. The study is useful as a general review of the pieces and of Somers' piano style, but the analysis is limited

594.------ "Harry Somers -- the culmination of a pianistic style in the *Third Piano Sonata*." *Studies in music from the University of Western Ontario* 9 (1984): 124-131.

After reviewing Somers' piano works, the author, a pianist and a performer of Somers' music, argues that the *Third Sonata* is his finest keyboard work, and pivotal in his stylistic development. The discussion is couched in general terms and avoids any technical analysis.

595.Cherney, Brian. *Harry Somers*. Toronto: University of Toronto Press, 1975. xii, 185p. ISBN 0-8020-5325-4.

Although much biographical material is included in this study, the emphasis is on discussion and analysis of Somers' music up to 1972, with many musical examples. List of works and discography; detailed synopsis of his opera *Louis Riel*.

596.Enns, Leonard. *The sacred choral music of Harry Somers: an analytical study*. PhD dissertation, Northwestern University, 1982. xii, 243.

The author argues that the sacred choral pieces constitute a small but distinctive group among Somers' work. The five works are each treated to extensive analysis, with a concluding overview. List of works, and very short bibliography.

597.Olnick, Harvey. "Harry Somers." *The Canadian Music Journal* 3/4 (Summer 1959): 3-23.

Something of Somers' personality, his early development, and his attitudes towards music are deftly conveyed, followed by a general survey of his music. Musical examples, and a list of works from 1942 to 1959/60.

598.Schafer, R. Murray. *The Public of the music theatre. Louis Riel: a case study*. Vienna: Universal Edition, 1972. 32p.

The study provides a general cultural and social framework for the production of Somers' opera *Louis Riel* in Toronto (1967), and an analysis of theatre, radio and television productions, including audience response.

599.Somers, Harry. "Harry Somers' letter to Lee Hepner." *Les Cahiers canadiens de musique/The Canada Music Book* 3 (Automne/hiver 1971): 89-97.

In January 1971, Somers wrote a long letter to Lee Hepner (who provides an explanatory introductory note) in which he discusses his approach to composition, his style and technique, and influences on him. See also the letter from Hepner in the same journal 9 Automne/hiver 1974: 11, in which he corrects an editorial feature of the printing of Somers' letter.

600.Zinck, Andrew M. "Music and dramatic structure in the operas of Harry Somers." PhD dissertation, University of Toronto, 1996. iv, 384f.

Proceeding from an examination of the libretti, the author develops a theoretical framework that relates the structures of the drama and Somers' compositional approach in the operas. There is extensive consideration of musical elements with many examples, usually in full score. Comprehensive bibliography and relevant discography.

Teresa Stratas

601.Rasky, Harry. *StrataSphere*. Toronto: Oxford University Press, 1988.114p. ISBN 0-19-540598-6.

Rasky's film about Stratas is the point of departure for a highly personal account of the singer. There is a good deal of biographical material, but the author appears to depend to a great extent on what he has been told. Discography, photographs.

Norman Symonds

602. Schulman, Michael. "Norman Symonds: a third stream composer finally comes of age." *Le Compositeur Canadien/The Canadian Composer* 151 (May 1980): 4-11.

An uncritical but succinctly detailed survey of Symonds' work and career as a jazz, or "third stream" composer.

Charles F. Thiele

603. Mellor, John. *Music in the park: C.F. Thiele, father of Canadian band music.* Waterloo, Ont.: Melco History Series, 1988. [x], 139, [xii]p.

A biography of Thiele, founder of the Waterloo Music Company, that includes much about bands, which Thiele greatly influenced, especially in southern Ontario.

Gordon V. Thompson

604. Thompson, Gordon V. "My first 50 years of music publishing in Canada." *Le Compositeur Canadien/The Canadian Composer* 1 (May, 1965): 14-17, 32-33.

Some anecdotes and a few observations by one of the most successful music publishers in Canada.

David Thomson

605. McCullagh, Harold. *The man who made New Brunswick sing.* St. Stephen, NB: Print'N Press Ltd., 1978. [vi], 97p., photographs 13p. ISBN 0-920732-08-9.

This popular biography of a prominent New Brunswick choral conductor and educator is also useful for glimpses of musical life in the province in the early and mid-20th century.

Gilles Tremblay

606. *Circuit* 6/1 (1995). ISBN 2-7606-2467-6.

This issue of *Circuit* consists mainly of a set of analytical essays by Tremblay, including two on his own works. There is a bibliography by Marie-Thérèse Lefebvre of texts about Tremblay, including notices and reviews in newspapers.

607."Gilles Tremblay: réflexions." *Circuit* 5/1 (1994).

This issue of *Circuit* is devoted to Tremblay. There is an anthology of fifteen texts by him, not about his own music specifically, but about music generally. Biographical chronology with works; a list of articles, interviews, commentaries and broadcasts by him; discography.

Claude Vivier

608.*Circuit* 2/1-2 (1991). ISBN 2-7606-2425-0.

This issue of *Circuit* consists mainly of an anthology of writings by Vivier that include much about specific works. There is an interview with Ligeti about him, and a discography which is followed by commentaries on the recordings

609.Mijnheer, Jaco. "*Shiraz* pour piano de Claude Vivier." *Les cahiers de l'ARMuQ* 13 (mai 1991): 90-105. ISSN 0821-1817.

A brief but detailed exposition of the complex structural devices used in *Shiraz*, which the author finds to be particularly clear examples of Vivier's style. Musical illustrations and facsimiles of structural sketches.

610."Les oeuvres de Claude Vivier." *Canadian University Music Review/Revue de musique des universités canadiennes* 4 (1983): 17-21.

This chronological list of works and a discography were part of memorial tribute to Vivier. There is no information other than date, title and general performance medium (without instrumental details) for each piece.

611.Paquin, Lucie. "Claude Vivier: recueil commenté des sources musicologiques (1960-1985)." MA dissertation, Université de Montréal, 1990. vii, 149f.

Without being a fully biographical study, the introductory material provides a useful review of the main facets of Vivier's musical background, with notes on some of his works. The principal contribution of the dissertation is the listing of about 260 references, arranged chronologically, to Vivier that appeared in journals and newspapers from 1970 to 1985. There are also lists of writings, correspondence, and a list of Vivier's forty-six works with information about publication and recording. No indexes.

612. Rea, John. "Reflets dans l'eau... bénite. Douze images impures: la vie et la musique de Claude Vivier." *Circuit* 1/2 (1991): 71-79.

A personal reflection on Vivier's personality and his music. The author contemplates relationships between the composer and his music. Not analytical.

613. Rivest, Johanne. "La discographie de Claude Vivier." *Canadian University Music Review/Revue de musique des universités canadiennes* 6 (1985): 35-44.

Nine recordings of seven pieces are briefly reviewed, with some background information but little critical comment.

Augustus Stephen Vogt

614. Bridle, Augustus. "Dr. A.S. Vogt." In *Sons of Canada: short studies of characteristic Canadians*, pp.139-147. Toronto: J.M. Dent and Sons Limited, 1916.

Bridle, who was a notable music critic, offers some personal observations on Vogt and chronicles his development of the Toronto Mendelssohn Choir.

John Weinzweig

615. "Dossier , J.J. Weinzweig." *Les Cahiers canadiens de musique/The Canada Music Book* 6 (Printemps/été 1973): 13-79.

Eight short compositions by eight composers are among a set of tributes to Weinzweig on his 60th birthday. Most of the "Dossier" consists of writings by Weinzweig about contemporary composition in Canada.

616.Kasemets, Udo. "John Weinzweig." *The Canadian Music Journal*
4/4 (Summer 1960): 4-18.

A general survey of Weinzweig's music, with some examples,
that suggests something of its technical and aural features. The
language in which the discussion is couched is often evocative but
vague. List of works to 1959.

617.Keillor, Elaine. *John Weinzweig and his music: the radical
romantic of Canada.* Metuchen, N.J.: The Scarecrow Press, 1994.
xv, 317p. Composers of North America, No.15. ISBN 0-8108-
2849-9.

About half of this study is given to short analytical notes on
each of Weinzweig's compositions. The first part is a general
biographical essay. There is a useful list of works, including
incidental music for radio, a bibliography, and a list of serial works
with sets and interval vectors.

618.------ "John Weinzweig's *Wine of Peace.*" *Studies in music from
the University of Western Ontario* 9 (1984): 79-92.

An examination of the serial applications in *Wine of Peace*,
with reference to the composer's development of style up to that
point.

619.Webb, Douglas John. "Serial techniques in John Weinzweig's
divertimentos and concertos (1945-1968)." PhD dissertation,
Eastman School of Music, University of Rochester, 1977. ix, 180f.

Five divertimentos for solo wind instruments and the
concertos for violin, piano and harp are the subjects of this study..
The author sees an evolution towards a more rigorous and more
vertically oriented application of serial technique. The form of
each work is described, and the characteristics and applications of
the rows are examined.

Alfred Whitehead

620.MacRae, C.F. "Alfred Whitehead." *The Canadian Music Journal*
5/3 (Spring 1961): 14-20.

Whitehead's career as organist/composer included periods in Sackville, Sherbrooke, and Montréal, all of which are touched on in this brief biographical note.

Healey Willan

621. Beckwith, John. "Healey Willan." *The Canadian Forum* 52/623 (December 1972): 32-34.

A review of an exhibition about Willan mounted at the National Library in Ottawa and in Toronto. Although brief and descriptive, it includes a number of observations by Beckwith, who had studied with Willan, that give some personal sense of the man and the composer.

622. Bryant, Giles. *Healey Willan catalogue*. Ottawa: National Library of Canada (1972). 174p.

A full catalogue of Willan's musical works arranged by genre. Lists of sound recordings, films. There is an extensive bibliography and a description of archival sources, and useful indexes.

623. Campbell-Yukl, Joylin. "Healey Willan: the independent organ works." DMA dissertation, University of Missouri (Kansas City), 1976. vi, 219p.

The main body of this study is the descriptive analyses of each of the eighteen organ works by Willan not based on liturgical sources, with a summary of style characteristics and a note on registration.

624. Clarke, Frederick. *Healey Willan: life and music*. Toronto: University of Toronto Press, 1983. xii, 300p. ISBN 0-8020-5549-4.

A full account of Willan's life but with little assessment of the particular nature and importance of Willan's life in Canada. Virtually all of Willan's music is discussed, and illustrated with 475 short musical examples.

625.------ "Healey Willan's unfinished *Requiem*." In *Musical Canada: words and music honouring Helmut Kallmann*, pp.203-210. J. Beckwith and F. Hall, eds. Toronto: University of Toronto Press, 1988. ISBN 0-8020-5759-4.

A description of the sketches for an unfinished large-scale requiem on which Willan worked during the period 1914-1918.

626.------ "Healey Willan's quest for a string quartet." *Canadian University Music Review/Revue de musique des universités canadiennes* 2 (1981): 166-76.

An examination of numerous sketches and drafts for a string quartet gives little clue as to why Willan never completed such a work. The author suggests possibly an uneasiness with sonata form, or more likely, a preference for richer sonorities.

627.------ "Two unpublished instrumental works by Healey Willan." *Canadian University Music Review/Revue de musique des universités canadiennes* 1 (1980): 1-7.

Two completed movements from incomplete larger works are examined briefly: a Prelude for organ, and a movement for violin and piano.

628.Hardwick, Peter. "An assessment of the organ miniatures of Healey Willan." *Canadian University Music Review/Revue de musique des universités canadiennes* 1 (1980): 8-21.

A short catalogue of "organ miniatures" is preceded by a general discussion of the works, grouped as "chorale preludes" and "newly composed". The article is a revision of the author's "Healey Willan's organ miniatures", *The Musical Times* (October 1980)

629.Marwick, William E. "The sacred choral music of Healey Willan." PhD dissertation, Michigan State University, 1970. v, 278f.

The biographical introduction is useful, but the analyses of representative works are mechanical and unrevealing. Chronological list of works.

630. McLean, Hugh. "Healey Willan and the Tractarian Movement." *Studies in music from the University of Western Ontario* 8 (1983): 25-36.

An examination of the early influence of the Tractarian (Oxford) Movement on Willan's later musical interests, particularly in plainchant and Anglo-Catholic ritual.

631. Ridout, Godfrey. "Healey Willan." *The Canadian Music Journal* 3/3 (Spring 1959): 4-14.

Ridout was a student and admirer of Willan, and his anecdotal recollections offer some glimpses of the older composer's personality and musical attitudes.

632. Steblin, Rita. "Healey Willan's inscribed copy of John Coulter's *Deirdre of the Sorrows.*" *Canadian University Music Review/Revue de musique des universités canadiennes* 12/1 (1992): 113-22.

The author discovered a copy of the libretto of *Deirdre* with musical annotations by Willan. She examines a biographical detail raised by an inscription, and the association of musical motifs with aspects of the opera.

Native Music

European visitors and explorers from the 17th century onward sometimes remarked on the music of Native Peoples, but serious study of Indian and Eskimo music dates from the late 19th century (Boas, no.641, 642; Stumpf, no.693). The literature on many facets of native music is now extensive, with a great deal of the research having been carried out in recent years. Modern research has tended to differ from earlier work in the degree to which non-Native scholars have attempted to understand the music through criteria that relate to that music and its society, and which do not derive from the quite different techniques and conditions of European music. The titles in this section represent a historical cross-section of research. An excellent overview of scholarship and present standards of study will be found in the *Encyclopedia of music in Canada* (no.10-13) under the entry "Native North Americans in Canada." In addition to the comprehensiveness of the article, there are useful and extensive bibliographies and discographies gathered under six broad groupings. A project that is now in progress is the preparation of an annotated bibliography of written and recorded documentation concerning First Nations' music and dance within Canada. This work originated under the direction of Elaine Keillor (Carleton University, Ottawa) and involves a group of co-authors that include representatives of First Nations.

Although this *Research Guide* has material divided into categories headed "Native Music", "Folk and Ethnic Music", and "Popular Music and Jazz", the categories have sometimes overlapped in actual scholarly practice. Tiersot (no.694) for example, included both native songs and French folksong in his notes; Barbeau, in an article titled "Folk-song" (no.702), includes references to Native music, as does Sargent (no.687). Whidden (no.834) examines country music among Native Peoples. In

Canada, as elsewhere, the rubric "ethnomusicology" has come to include all three of the categories mentioned above. Attention is drawn in this regard to a conference specifically focused on ethnomusicology in Canada that was held in Toronto in 1988. The published proceedings (Witmer, no.794) address some general issues, but primarily they reflect the comprehensive approach of the conference to a broad range of native, folk and popular subjects. To some extent, the conference and its proceedings represent both a point of consolidation and a point of departure for continuing study, not unlike Diamond and Witmer's *Canadian music* (no.101). For a study of ethnomusicology programs in education, see Carlisle, no.842. A conference on Native music held at Brandon University in Manitoba in 1988 provided the basis for an issue devoted to the subject of *The Canadian Journal of Native Studies* 8/2 (1988).

An important group of publications is the Mercury Series, issued by the National Museums of Canada, a number of titles from which are included in this *Guide*. Many of these publications, as well as those from other sources, include or even are primarily collections of music. While printed music has been excluded from earlier sections of this *Guide*, transcriptions of musical repertoires are central to many studies of Native music, hence some such collections are included here. Numerous recordings exist in addition to the archival discs made for study. The CBC Northern Service has produced well over a hundred recordings of Inuit music, and while these were widely distributed within the North American broadcasting community, few have ever been made available commercially.

633. Asch, Michael I. "Social context and the musical analysis of Slavey drum dance songs." *Ethnomusicology* 19/2 (May, 1975): 245-57.

The Drum Dance of the Slavey Indians of the Northwest Territories is examined within its social context, and the relationship of this context to the form of the music itself is considered as an analytical method. There are several charts and musical examples, although the analytical details are presented with little elaboration.

634.Barbeau, Marius. "Buddhist dirges on the north Pacific coast." *Journal of the International Folk Music Council* 14 (January 1962): 16-21.

From a study of about one hundred Native songs of lament from British Columbia and the Yukon, Barbeau theorizes that these funeral songs are related to the dirges of Chinese Buddhists. The idea is based on suggestions of similarities rather than on analytical evidence. Seven Native chants are given as musical examples.

635.------ "Indian songs of the Northwest." *The Canadian Music Journal* 2/1 (Autumn 1957): 16-25.

Eight songs of the Tsimsyan and Dene of north-east British Columbia are transcribed and briefly discussed. An underlying idea is the relationship of this repertoire to music of Asia, particularly of China. See also no.634.

636.------ "Songs of the Northwest." *The Musical Quarterly* 19/1 (January 1933): 101-111.

The article is based on Barbeau's visits to British Columbia in the 1920s and his collection of about three hundred songs. His comments, on eight transcriptions, are not analytical but rather an attempt to convey a sense of the effects of the songs in their social and geographical situations. Two of the transcriptions are also published in no.635.

637.Beaudry, Nicole. "La composition des chants amérindiens: création ou transmission?" *Les cahiers de l'ARMuQ* 14 (mai, 1992): 1-13. ISSN 0821-1817.

The subject of the article is the song of Native People of the Canadian sub-arctic zone, particularly the Dene People. The author finds a contrast between a culture that values originality and one which finds a traditional source in dreams. (The above title appears in the journal index. In the body of the journal the article is "Des rêves et des chants: la création des chants chez les Amérindiens.")

638.------ "*Le Katajjaq*: un jeu inuit traditionnel." *Études Inuit Studies* 2/1 (1978): 35-54.

Not a musical analysis, but a social analysis of the Inuit throat games in terms of both their form and their function.

639.------ "Singing, laughing and playing: three examples from the Inuit, Dene and Yupik traditions." *The Canadian Journal of Native Studies* 8/2 (1988):275-290.

The interrelationships of singing, laughing and playing are examined in three cases: *katajjaq*, *udzi*, and theYupik drum dance. The author raises questions about the nature of humour and play, and particularly their relationships to music.

640.------ "Toward transcription and analysis of Inuit throat-games: macro-structure." *Ethnomusicology* 22/2 (May, 1978): 261-73.

Transcription problems and solutions relating to perception and description are addressed in the transcription processes used for the *katajjaq* (throat games). The process reveals new aspects of textual, pitch and rhythmic performance. See also Charron, no.647.

641.Boas, Franz. "On certain songs and dances of the Kwakiutl of British Columbia." *Journal of American Folk-Lore* 1/1 (April-June 1888): 49-64.

Based on a visit by Boas to British Columbia in 1886-87, the article consists mostly of descriptions of dances which he witnessed and the stories related in the dances and songs. Transcriptions of four songs.

642.------ "Chinook songs." *Journal of American Folk-Lore* 1/3 (October-December 1888): 220-226.

Chinook jargon (as opposed to the Chinook language proper) was a *lingua franca* developed in the Northwest among French, English and Native traders, and used also among Natives of differing languages. At communities in Victoria, Vancouver, and New Westminster, songs arose out of social events. There are texts for thirty-nine of these songs (with a glossary) and music for three of them.

643.Bradley, Ian L. "A bibliography of Indian musical culture in Canada." *The Northian* 12/2 (summer, 1976):4-11. ISSN 0029-3253.

A short but basic bibliography, without annotation, of material up to 1974. Useful for earlier periodical titles.

644.------ "Indian music of the Pacific Northwest: an annotated bibliography of research." *BC Studies* 31 (Autumn, 1976): 12-22.

Although limited to forty entries, the list is useful for the annotations, and for items published in the 19th and early 20th centuries.

645.Bradley, Ian and Patricia Bradley. *A bibliography of Canadian native arts*. Victoria: GLC Publishers, 1977. viii, 109p. ISBN 0-88874-051-4

The greater part of this bibliography is given to Indian and Eskimo arts and crafts, but there are substantial sections on dance and on music. Entries are alphabetical by author. No annotations, no indexes.

646.Broomfield, Howard. "In Doig people's ears." *Canadian University Music Review/Revue de musique des universités canadiennes* 5 (1984): 123-35.

A forty-five minute audio tape, called *In Doig People's Ears*, was derived from about 300 hours of soundscape recording of the Beaver Indian people (Dunne-Za) of the Doig River Reserve in northeastern British Columbia. This article describes nineteen distinct sections of the tape.

647.Charron, Claude. "Toward transcription and analysis of Inuit throat-games: micro-structure." *Ethnomusicology* 22/2 (May, 1978): 245-59.

This study of the phonological data that can be recovered by analysis of the Inuit *katajjaq*. A companion study to Beaudry (no.640).

648.Conlon, Paula Thistle. "Drum-dance songs of the Iglulik Inuit in
the northern Baffin Island area: a study of their structure." PhD
dissertation, Université de Montréal, 1992. xxiii, 232f.; xv, 768f.;
xv, 333f. (4 vol.)

A paradigmatic method for comparative musical analysis is
applied to a repertoire of 315 drum-dance songs. The textual
summary comprises Volume I. Volumes II and III (1-378/379-
768p.) contain the musical and textual transcriptions, without
comment. The fourth Volume includes the paradigmatic charts for
each song.

649.Cringan, Alexander T. "Iroquois folk songs." In *Annual
archaeological report 1902, being part of the appendix to the
report of the Minister of Education, Ontario.* Toronto: L.K.
Cameron, 1903; printed by order of the Legislative Assembly.
pp.137-152. (The *Archaeological report* was issued separately
among the *Sessional Papers* of the Province of Ontario.)

This is the third of Cringan's papers on Native music (see
no.650, 651). The thirty-four songs, transcribed from gramophone
recordings, are from the Tutelo, Delaware and Onondaga Nations.
Each song is accompanied by a short commentary. As with the
earlier transcriptions, there are no texts, and the music is
interpreted by, and made to conform to, the technical
characteristics of late 19th – century European music. All
transcriptions have conventional key and time signatures. Cringan
was a skillled musician, but inexperienced in ethnological studies.
Nevertheless, the transcriptions are not without interest, especially
historically.

650.------ "Iroquois music." In *Archaeological report 1898, being part
of appendix to the report of the Minister of Education, Ontario.*
Toronto: Warwick Bros. and Rutter, 1898; printed by order of the
Legislative Assembly. pp.143-156. (The *Archaeological report*
was issued separately among the *Sessional Papers* of the Province
of Ontario.)

This is the first of Cringan's articles (see no.649, 651) on
Iroquois music. The fifteen songs were sung by the head of the
Seneca Longhouse, who went to Toronto for the purpose of
singing for Cringan. Texts for six of the songs are given
separately.

651.------ "Music of the pagan Iroquois." In *Archaeological report 1899, being part of appendix to the report of the Minister of Education, Ontario.* Toronto: Warwick Bros. and Rutter, 1900; printed by order of the Legislative Assembly. pp.166-190. (The *Archaeological report* was issued separately among the *Sessional Papers* of the Province of Ontario.)

The second of Cringan's studies (see no.649, 650) includes forty-seven songs, without texts, from the Seneca. The transcriptions were made from gramophone recordings.

652.Crossley-Holland, Peter, ed. *Proceedings of the Centennial workshop on ethnomusicology.* [Vancouver]: Government of the Province of British Columbia, 1968. 118p.

Papers and discussions are mostly on non-Canadian subjects, but there are items on the Coast Indians of British Columbia (Roy Carlson; Ida Halpern), and the Eskimos of East Greenland (Poul Rovsing Olsen).

653.Densmore, Frances. *Music of the Indians of British Columbia.* Washington: U.S. Government Printing Office, 1943; Anthropological Paper 27 of the Bureau of American Ethnology, Smithsonian Institution. p.1-99 of Bulletin 136. reprinted New York: Da Capo Press, 1972. 99p., 9 plates. ISBN 0-306-70507-9.

The musical material for this study was gathered in 1926 at Chilliwack, in southern British Columbia, where an industrial camp brought together Indians from widely separated areas of the province. There are 98 song transcriptions, each with a short descriptive and analytical note. There are no texts, and often no free translation.

654.(Diamond) Cavanagh, Beverley. "Annotated bibliography: Eskimo music." *Ethnomusicology* 16/3 (1972): 479-487.

Material relates to music of the Eskimos of Greenland, the Canadian Arctic, and Alaska. Useful not only as a list but also for the annotations.

655.------ "The legato principle in Netsilik Eskimo music." *Studies in music from the University of Western Ontario* 3 (1978): 1-6.

The author examines "legato style" in the performance of drum dance repertoire as a principle that affects many aspects of the music, including rhythm, melody, and text articulation.

656.------ *Music of the Netsilik Eskimo: a study of stability and change.* National Museum of Man Mercury Series (ISSN 0316-1854), Canadian Ethnology Service, Paper no. 82 (ISSN 0316-1862). Ottawa: National Museums of Canada, 1982. 2 vols. xi, 198p.; xvii, 372p.

The traditional styles and genres of the Netsilik Inuit are studied within the context of change which this music has undergone, especially as a result of contact with European and North American music. Volume One deals with the music from the points of view of sound, underlying concepts, and accompanying behaviour. Volume Two contains an edition of 121 Netsilik songs, with music, text, translation and commentary. This is the publication of the author's PhD dissertation of the same title, University of Toronto, 1979. 2 vols. iii, 326p.; xiv, 427p.

657.------ "The performance of hymns in Eastern Woodlands Indian communities." In *Sing out the glad news: hymn tunes in Canada*, pp.45-56. John Beckwith, ed. Toronto: Institute for Canadian Music, 1987.

In reference to Indian groups in Labrador, New Brunswick and Ontario, the suggestion is put forward that religion is to a high degree syncretic in Indian communities, evidence of which is found in the merging of native and Christian musical practices. Some musical examples, and a brief bibliography.

658.------ "The transmission of Algonkian hymns: between orality and literacy." In *Musical Canada: words and music honouring Helmut Kallmann*, pp.3-28. J. Beckwith and F. Hall, eds. Toronto: University of Toronto Press, 1988. ISBN 0-8020-5759-4.

Hymn singing is seen among the Alkonkians to be the result of complex relationships between oral tradition and printed sources (hymn-books). The author concludes that the printed sources of the late 19th and early 20th centuries likely reflect tradition rather than dictate it.

659.Diamond, Beverley, M. Sam Cronk and Franziska von Rosen. *Visions of sound: musical instruments of First Nations communities in northeastern America.* Waterloo, Ont.: Wilfred Laurier University Press, 1994. xviii, 222p. ISBN 0-88920-228-1 (bound); 0-88920-242-7 (pbk.).

The musical instruments that are the subject of this study are not simply described but interpreted in their social, cultural and spiritual contexts. The geographic region is defined roughly by the eastern border of Manitoba and the Atlantic, and by an area just south of the Great Lakes and the St. Lawrence. Many photographs and an extensive bibliography. (There is a projected computer disk, A *Catalogue of musical instruments of First Nations communities in northeastern America,* which will contain over 700 instrument descriptions. Wilfred Laurier University Press, ISBN 0-88920-246-X.)

660.George, Graham. "Songs of the Salish Indians of British Columbia." *Journal of the International Folk Music Council* 14 (January 1962): 22-29.

The author uses transcriptions of fifteen songs recorded by Barbeau in 1912 for an analytical examination of phrase-structure, scale-structure, and interval-structure. Many musical examples.

661.Guédon, Marie-Françoise. "Canadian Indian ethnomusicology: selected bibliography and discography." *Ethnomusicology* 16/3 (1972): 465-78.

Intended only as an interim and incomplete list, this remains an extremely useful bibliography/discography. It includes unpublished material and archival recordings.

662.Hauser, Michael. "Inuit songs from southwest Baffin Island in cross-cultural context." *Études Inuit Studies* 2/1 (1978): 55-83; 2/2 (1978): 71-105. ISSN 0701-1008.

The discovery of a close musical relationship between the Thule district (Greenland) and the southern area of Baffin Island (Canada) is examined as an instance of cultural interchange. The second part of the article consists of transcriptions of 45 Inuit songs, with commentary.

663.Johnston, Thomas F. *Eskimo music by region: a comparative circumpolar study.* Ottawa: National Museums of Canada, 1976. vii, 222p. National Museum of Man Mercury Series (ISSN 0316-1854), Canadian Ethnology Service, Paper no.32.

There are descriptions of musical characteristics in Eskimo areas and sub-areas around the polar region, including Alaska, Siberia, and Greenland as well as Canada.

664.Keillor, Elaine. "Hymn singing among the Dogrib Indians." In *Sing out the glad news: hymn tunes in Canada*, pp.33-43. John Beckwith, ed. Toronto: Institute for Canadian Music, 1987.

The Dogribs, a major group of the Northern Athapaskans, use Protestant hymns sung in Chipewyan in Roman Catholic services, modified by influences of their own musical style. This short examination of the situation explores the social and musical conditions that contributed to this development. Musical examples, and a short bibliography.

665.------ "Indigenous music as a compositional source: parallels and contrasts in Canadian and American music." In *Taking a stand: essays in honour of John Beckwith*, pp.185-218. T. McGee, ed. Toronto: University of Toronto Press, 1995. ISBN 0-8020-0583-7.

The use of musical materials either by quotation or imitation is reviewed first among American composers, then among Canadian. A section on the ways in which this source material is employed contains many perceptive observations on the material itself as well as attitudes towards it. There is an extensive bibliography, and lists of compositions based on Amerinidian or Inuit sources.

666.Kolinski, Mieczyslaw. "An apache rabbit song dance cycle as sung by the Iroquois." *Ethnomusicology* 16/3 (1972): 416-54.

To study the degree of stability in the performance of traditionally rooted music, four versions of a song dance cycle are examined in analytical detail. Three versions were recorded by one informant in 1966, and a fourth in 1967 by another singer.

667.------ "An Iroquois war dance song cycle." *Canadian Association of University Schools of Music Journal* 2/2 (Fall, 1972): 51-64.

The subject of the article is an unidentified recording made at the Six Nations Reserve (Ontario). The article includes a transcription and an extensive analysis of the melodic features of the music, with some remarks on the rhythmic structure.

668. Kolstee, Anton Frederick. *Bella Coola Indian music: a study of the interaction between Northwest Coast Indian musical structures and their functional context.* National Museum of Man Mercury Series (ISSN 0316-1854), Canadian Ethnology Service, Paper n.83 (ISSN 0316-1862). Ottawa: National Museums of Canada, 1982. x, 274p.

A study based on field recordings made by various researchers from 1922 to 1975. A section on the ethnographic context of the music is followed by extensive analysis of structural characteristics, with many examples. Seventy-three transcriptions of ceremonial and non-ceremonial songs are included.

669. ------ "The historical and musical significance of northwest coast Indian *hámáca* songs." *The Canadian Journal of Native Studies* 8/2 (1988):173-182.

The author describes the *hámáca* songs of the Northwest coast, which date from the 19th century, and discusses their ceremonial and historical contexts

670. Kurath, Gertrude. *Dance and song rituals of Six Nations Reserve, Ontario.* National Museum of Canada, Bulletin no.220, folklore Series No.4. Ottawa: Queen's Printer, 1968. xiv, 205p.

Ceremonial events at four Longhouses are the subject of this study. There are descriptions and analyses of songs and dances, discussion of costume, and an attempt to recreate songs and dances by means of choreographic symbols with musical notation. Many photographs, sketches, and diagrams.

671. ------ *Tutelo rituals on Six Nations Reserve, Ontario.* Ann Arbor, Michigan: Society for Ethnomusicology, Special Series no.5, 1981. ix, 119p. ISSN 0270-1766.

The Tutelo were a tribe of southern origin in the USA who moved to Canada after the American revolutionary war. Three great ceremonies are examined, with musical transcriptions and choreographic diagrams. In a concluding section, the author discusses subjects of stylistic significance, both analytical and cultural.

672. Lederman, Anne. "Old Indian and Métis fiddling in Manitoba: origins, structure and question of syncretism." *The Canadian Journal of Native Studies* 8/2 (1988): 205-230.

Fiddle music from Native and Métis communities of western Manitoba, although related to White fiddle traditions, show structural characteristics that have much in common with Native song styles. There are transcriptions of three reels, and seven versions of "Haste to the Wedding."

673. Lee, Dorothy Sara. *Native North American music and oral data. A catalogue of sound recordings 1893-1976.* Bloomington: Indiana University Press, 1979. xvi, 463p.

A guide to about five hundred items in the Indiana University Archives of Traditional Music. Listed alphabetically by individual (collector, editor, performer, etc.) and indexed by culture groups and subject descriptions. Most of the materials relate to the United States, but some Canada-related material can be found through culture group references.

674. Lillos, Brian Martin. "Selective studies in musical analyses of Beaver Indian dreamer songs: a structuralistic approach in ethnomusicology". MMus dissertation, University of British Columbia, 1977. v, 309f.

An extensive introduction on structuralism, and on the background of the Beaver Indians, a group of the Athabascan Indians of the Peace River district of British Columbia. Study based on forty-five dreamer songs.

675. *List of Canadian music inspired by the music, poetry, art and folklore of Native Peoples.* Toronto: Canadian Music Centre, 1980. 22p.

Forty-five musical compositions of all kinds related to Native Peoples in subject or musical materials; listed with performance requirements .

676.Lutz, Maija M. *The effects of acculturation on the Eskimo music of Cumberland Peninsula.* National Museum of Man Mercury Series (ISSN 0316-1854). Canadian Ethnology Service, Paper no.41 (ISSN 0316-1862). Ottawa: National Museums of Canada, 1978. xiii, 168p., recording.

The material written by Franz Boas on the Eskimos, published 1884-1907, serves as the reference point for a proposed investigation into the extent of acculturation in the Cumberland Sound area as exhibited in music. Despite the author's fieldwork in the area, much of the study refers to secondary material and becomes a useful review of research on Eskimo culture and the history of exploration. There are no analyses or musical examples, but the recording which is part of the publication consists of twelve contemporary performances of songs, all of them mentioned in the text.

677.------ *Musical traditions of the Labrador coast Inuit.* National Museum of Man Mercury Series (ISSN 0316-1854). Canadian Ethnology Service, Paper no.79 (ISSN 0316-1862). Ottawa: National Museums of Canada, 1982. vi, 89p.

In the 200 years since the establishment of their first permanent settlement in Labrador, Moravian missionaries have had a strong influence on Inuit Labrador culture. As a result, borrowed ideas have become integral to Inuit music in Labrador. In this article, earlier commentaries are reviewed, and current trends are surveyed.

678.Mishler, Craig Wallace and Céline Veillet. "Musique inuit du Québec arctique: contribution à une méthode d'analyse en anthropologie de la musique." *Les cahiers de l'ARMuQ* 3 (juin 1984): 58-81.

The article outlines a procedure for considering a body of music beyond simple musical analysis but as an integrated aspect of a community. A section deals specifically with *katajjait*, a kind of musical game.

679.Monpetit, Carmen and Céline Veillet. "Recherches en ethnomusicologie: les *katajjait* chez les Inuit du Nouveau-Québec." *Études Inuit Studies* 1/1 (1977): 154-64.

An exposition of numerous points regarding the context and structure of the musical throat games (*katajjait*) leads to a hypothesis that the games relate to the sound and certain activities of the Canada Goose.

680. Nattiez, Jean-Jacques. "Comparisons within a culture: the example of the *katajjaq* of the Inuit." In *Cross-Cultural Perspectives on Music*, pp.134-140. Robert Falck and Timothy Rice, eds. Toronto: University of Toronto Press, 1982. ISBN 0-8020-5510-9.

An analytical grid is proposed that can be used to deal with differences in information for the same musical genre in various groups, using "throat-games" as the object of comparison.

681. ------ "Some aspects of Inuit vocal games." *Ethnomusicology* 27/3 (September, 1983): 457-75.

The "vocal games" or "throat games" -- *katajjaq* -- of the Inuit are the subject of various studies. In this article, aspects of the *katajjaq* are reviewed in the light of recent research, with some comment on the research itself. Charts, musical examples, and a short discography.

682. Ogg, Arden C. "Four Cree lovesongs: the interaction of text and music." *The Canadian Journal of Native Studies* 8/2 (1988):231-250.

Four recent (1980s) songs from Saskatchewan -- two in English, two in Cree -- are examined for relationships of text and musical structure. Each song is given in transcription, with a short commentary.

683. Pelinski, Ramón Adolfo. *La musique des Inuit du Caribou: cinq perspectives méthodologiques*. Montréal: Presses de l'Université de Montréal, 1981. 231p. ISBN 2-7606-0513-2.

Material is based on research at Rankin Inlet and Eskimo Point in 1974, 1975 and 1976. Five chapters represent five approaches to study: ethnographic; semiotic, in the utilization of musicological terminology in an intercultural context; interval study; computer-based melodic study; structural.

684.Pelinski, Ramón Adolfo, Luke Suluk, and Lucy Amarook. *Inuit songs from Eskimo Point*. National Museum of Man Mercury Series, Canadian Ethnology Service Paper no.60 (ISSN 0316-1862). Ottawa: National Museums of Canada, 1979. xvi, 122p., phonodisc.

This collection of forty-one songs derives from recordings made in 1977. Texts are in English and Inuktitut. There is no discussion or analysis of the material.

685.Roberts, Helen H. and D. Jenness. *Songs of the Copper Eskimos. Report of the Canadian Arctic Expedition 1913-18*, vol. XIV. Ottawa: The King's Printer, 1925. 506p.

Most of this pioneering study consists of 137 song transcriptions with analytical notes and charts, but there is also introductory material and a short section on tonal preferences in the songs.

686.Roberts, Helen H. and Morris Swadesh. *Songs of the Nootka Indians of Western Vancouver Island. Transactions of the American Philosophical Society*, New Series, vol. 45, part 3. Philadelphia: The American Philosophical Society, 1955. pp.199-327.

All but three of the ninety-nine Nootka songs that comprise the musical material of this volume were recorded by Edward Sapir in 1910 and 1913-14. The commentary includes essays on the structure and melodic content of the songs, and on linguistic and ethnological aspects of the Nootka.

687.Sargent, Margaret. "Folk and primitive music in Canada." *Journal of the International Folk Music Council* 4 (1952): 65-68.

Despite its brevity, this article provides a measure of the interest in Canada at mid-century in the study of both Native music and folkmusic, with optimistic enthusiasm for current activities. There is a short list of Canadian and American publications.

688.Sargent, Margaret. "Seven songs from Lorette." *Journal of American Folklore* 63/248 (April-June, 1950): 175-180.

Seven songs from among fifty-seven collected in 1911 by
Marius Barbeau from an elderly respondent are transcribed, with
brief remarks. Lorette was a Huron village just north of Québec
City.

689. Smith, Nicholas N. "St. Francis Indian dances." *Ethnomusicology*
6/1 (January, 1962): 15-18.

A feature of a 300th anniversary celebration in 1960 at the
village of St. Francis, Québec, was a performance of dances by the
Wabanaki Indians. The noteworthy aspect was that religious
authorities had forbidden such dancing since 1925. The short
descriptions of the dances provide examples both of persistence
and acculturation in a tradition.

690. Smith, Gordon E. "Lee Cremo: narratives about a Micmac
fiddler." In *Canadian music: issues of hegemony and identity*,
pp.541-556. Beverley Diamond and Robert Witmer, eds. Toronto:
Canadian Scholars' Press, 1994. ISBN 1-55130-031-1.

The social and cultural links between Cremo, a Cape Breton
fiddler, and both Native and non-Native life are examined through
interviews with Cremo and with those who know him.

691. *Sound of the drum: a resource guide.* [Sam Cronk, ed.]. Brantford,
Ont.: Woodland Cultural Centre, 1990. 103p. ISBN 0-919725-
233-3.

This is an informative and useful collection of interviews
about music with individuals from various First Nations
communities in Canada.

692. Stuart, Wendy Bross. "Gambling music of the coast Salish
Indians". MMus dissertation, University of British Columbia,
1972. v, 114f.

The presentation, with musical examples and information
about the collecting, and the basic analytical detail, of 194 of the
songs used in slahal, a gambling game.

693. Stumpf, Carl. "Lieder der Bellakula-Indianer." *Vierteljahrschrift
für Musikwissenschaft* 2 (1886): 405-426 reprinted in *The Garland*

library of readings in ethnomusicology, K.K. Shelemay, ed. vol.7, pp.45-62. New York, 1990.

In addition to background discussion, there are nine songs with original texts, with analytical remarks for each song. This study results froma meeting by Stumpf and Franz Boas with a group of Native singers who visited Germany in 1885.

694.Tiersot, Julien. "La musique chez les peuples indigènes de l'Amérique du Nord (États-Unis et Canada)." *Notes d'ethnographie musicale*. Paris: Librairie Fischbacher, 1905. 93p. Extrait du recueil de la Société internationale de musique, année XI, Liv. 2.

The notes were made by Tiersot on a trip to North America, which in Canada was confined to the areas of Québec City and Montréal. There are some observations on French folksong, and some transcriptions of native songs heard by the author. A bibliography of approximately 175 titles is interesting primarily for 19th-century references.

695.von Rosen, Franziska. "'Thunder, that's our ancestors drumming': music as experienced by a Micmac elder." In *Canadian music: issues of hegemony and identity*, pp.557-579. Eds. Beverley Diamond and Robert Witmer. Toronto: Canadian Scholars' Press, 1994. ISBN 1-55130-031-1.

Mostly through interview and quotation, the author relates something of the experiences and music of Micmac fiddler and story-teller in New Brunswick, Michael Francis.

696.Whidden, Lynn. "An ethnomusicological study of the traditional songs of the Chisasibi (James Bay) Cree." PhD dissertation, Université de Montréal, 1986. viii, 264f.

Using a group of ninety songs, the author analyses text and music, and attempts to locate these hunting songs in their original context, a context that now exists largely in memory as a result of external influences on Cree society. Transcriptions of music and texts.

697.Witmer, Robert. *The musical life of the Blood Indians*. National Museum of Man Mercury Series (ISSN 0316-1854), Canadian

Ethnology Service paper no.86 (ISSN 0316-1862). Ottawa: National Museums of Canada, 1982. ix, 185p.

This description of the musical life of the Blood Indians, of southwestern Alberta, derives from field work done in 1968. Among the topics discussed are the historical and social aspects of music, musical acculturation, and performance practices. There is no transcribed repertoire.

698.------ "Recent change in the musical culture of the Blood Indians of Alberta, Canada." *Yearbook for Inter-American Musical Research* 9 (1973): 64-94.

This article examines the impact of white influence on the musical culture of the Blood Indians, including the social and musical characteristics of Indian practitioners of white music.

Folk and Ethnic Music

Some of the remarks at the beginning of the section "Native Music" apply equally here, including the importance of the 1988 conference on ethnomusicology in Canada. Attention should also be drawn to Diamond and Witmer, *Canadian music: issues of hegemony and identity* (no.101), which contains several articles on a variety of pertinent subjects. Research into various aspects of folk and ethnic music in Canada is notably represented in several periodical publications. The *Canadian Folk Music Journal* (1973-) is published annually by the Canadian Society for Musical Traditions/la Société canadienne pour les traditions musicales (before 1989, the Canadian Folk Music Society/la Société canadienne de musique folklorique.) The quarterly *Bulletin* (1966-) of the same Society contains articles, reviews and notices. Particularly useful for abstracts, publication notices and general information is *Folklore* (1976/77-), the Bulletin of the Folklore Studies Association of Canada/Bulletin de l'association canadienne pour les études de folklore. The Journal of this Association is *Canadian Folklore Canadien* (1979-), which includes a wide range of topics, among which music figures only intermittently.

Among non-Canadian journals, the *Journal of American Folklore* has often included material relating to Canada, and has published several Canadian issues, some with musical material: 32/123 (1919), 33/129 (1920), 53/208-209 (1940), 63/248 (1950), and 67/263 (1954). Also of note are the publications of the International Folk Music Council: the *Journal* (1949-1968), the *Yearbook* (1969- ; since 1981 *Yearbook for traditional music*); and the *Bulletin* which deals chiefly with business matters but also contains reports on national activities.

699.Barbeau, Marius "La complainte de Cadieux, coureur de bois (ca.1709)." *Journal of American Folklore* 67/no.264 (April-June, 1954): 163-183.

Barbeau examines the origins of the *complainte*, the legends attached to it, and its musical and textual variants.

700.------ *En roulant ma boule.* Ottawa: Musée national de l'Homme, Musées nationaux du Canada, 1982. (Deuxième partie du *Répertoire de la chanson folklorique française au Canada.*) xxvi, 753p. ISBN 0-660-90267-2.

A collection of 277 songs associated with traditional activities such as dancing, playing games, and working, including voyageur songs. Melody and text, sometimes with a short commentary.

701.------ "The Ermatinger collection of Voyageur songs (ca.1830)." *Journal of American Folklore* 67/no.264 (April-June, 1954): 147-161.

Eleven songs of the Voyageurs from the collection made by Edward Ermatinger, an employee of the Hudson's Bay Company (1818-1826). Barbeau provides a background to the songs as well as some analytical comments. One of the earliest collections to include music and texts.

702.------ "Folk-song." In *Music in Canada*, pp.32-54. Ernest MacMillan, ed. Toronto: University of Toronto Press, 1955.

Barbeau provides an overview of folksong collecting, then deals specifically with repertoire of the Indians of the Pacific northwest, and of the White Man. There is a number of musical examples. While informative, much of the interest of the essay is in the personal nature of the account.

703.------ "French and Indian motifs in our music." In *Yearbook of the arts in Canada 1928-1929*, pp.125-132. Bertram Brooker, ed. Toronto: MacMillan Company of Canada, 1929.

Not an article but a review of various realizations in concerts of folk music. Barbeau has some particularly harsh comments on the second (1928) of the Canadian Pacific Railway's celebrated Québec festivals.

704.------ "French-Canadian folk-songs." *Musical Quarterly* 29/1 (January 1943): 122-137.

In this summary article based on many years of folksong collecting in Québec, Barbeau presents his views on repertory origins and genre types.

705.------ *Jongleur songs of old Quebec.* New Brunswick, N.J.: Rutgers University Press, 1962. xxi, 202p.

Forty-two songs prepared for use by singers rather than by scholars, but with a short commentary on each song, with notes on references and sources.

706.------ *Le roi boit.* Ottawa: Musée canadien des civilisations, Musées nationaux du Canada, 1987. (Troisième partie du *Répertoire de la chanson folklorique française au Canada*) xxviii, 623p. ISBN 0-660-90280-X.

A collection of 220 songs, mostly associated with festive occasions. There is usually only the briefest of commentaries on the songs.

707.------ *Romancero du Canada.* Toronto: Macmillan Co. of Canada, 1937. 254p.

Fifty songs are presented (melody and text), with an extended commentary for each and a catalogue of known versions in collections in Canada and abroad.

708.------ *Le rossignol y chante.* Ottawa: Musée national de l'Homme, Musées nationaux du Canada, 1979. (Première partie du *Répertoire de la chanson folklorique française du Canada* 485p. (first published Ottawa: Musée National du Canada, 1962.) ISBN 0-660-00140-3.

Approximately 150 songs are presented with melody and text, and sometimes a brief commentary. The material is derived from collections made in 1916, 1918 and 1922.

709.------ *"Trois beaux canards." Les Archives de Folklore* 2 (1974): 97-138.

Ninety-two Canadian versions of the song *Trois beaux canards* are cited, with a note on textual variants, and the source of each version.

710.Béland, Madeleine. *Chansons de voyageurs, coureurs de bois et forestiers.* Québec: Les Presses de l'Université Laval, 1982. x, 432p. ISBN 2-7637-6942-X.

In a lengthy introductory section (pp.2-130) the subjects and texts of the songs are examined comprehensively. The anthology consists of 90 songs with music, text and brief annotation.

711.Berg, Wesley. *From Russia with music: a study of the Mennonite choral singing tradition in Canada.* Winnipeg: Hyperion Press, 1985. 152p. ISBN 0-920534-08-2.

Waves of Russian Mennonite immigration to Canada, first in the 1870s and again in the 1920s, established characteristic musical practices, especially choral singing, that have had far-reaching influence on musical life even outside the Mennonite community. The social and musical background to the immigration, and the development of the tradition in Canada are closely examined up to about 1960. Bibliographical references are contained in the end-notes and not listed separately.

712.Brassard, François. "French-Canadian folk music studies: a survey." *Ethnomusicology* 16/3 (1972): 351-59.

A brief but comprehensive overview of the collecting of folk music in French Canada. There is a short but useful bibliography. Companion essay to Fowke, no.728.

713.Brednich, Rolf Wilh. "Erziehung durch Gesang. Zur Funktion von Zeitungsliedern bei den Hutterern." *Jahrbuch für Volksliedforschung* 27/28 (1982/83): 109-33. ISSN 0075-2789.

With reference to two specific songs, the author examines songs in the social and religious context of a Hutterite community in Saskatchewan.

714.Carpenter, Carole Henderson. *Many voices: a study of folklore activities in Canada and their role in Canadian culture.* National Museum of Man Mercury Series (ISSN 0316-1854), Canadian Centre for Folk Culture Studies paper no.86 (ISSN 0316-1897). Ottawa: National Museums of Canada, 1979. x, 484p.

Music is not treated as a separate category, but the subject appears frequently within the text of this survey and assessment of Canadian folklore study. Similarly, the bibliography of major Canadian folklore works, which is organized under seven general categories, does not have a music section, but it is nonetheless useful for the many music titles that are listed. Includes bibliographical material on Native Peoples.

715.Carrier, Maurice and Monique Vachon. *Chansons politiques du Québec 1765-1833.* vol. 1. *Chansons politiques du Québec 1834-1858.* vol. 2. Ottawa: Les Éditions Leméac, 1977, 1979. 363, 450p. ISBN 0-7761-5253-7/0-7761-5264-5 (vol. 1); 0-7761-5263-7/0-7761-5273-4 (vol. 2)

This large collection of songs which reflect the volatile political period following the advent of the British regime, includes much historical material that provides a context for the songs. The commentary about identity and independence rings sympathetically with present-day political events in Québec.

716.Casey, George J., Neil V. Rosenberg and Wilfred W. Wareham. "Repertoire categorization and performer-audience relationships: some Newfoundland folksong examples." *Ethnomusicology* 16/3 (1972): 397-403.

An examination of the importance of locality in Newfoundland folksong and its performance, as evidenced in two communities, one of Irish, the other of English background.

717.*Catalogue of LP's, cassettes, and books.* Calgary: The Canadian Society for Musical Traditions, 1990/1991/1993.

An on-going set of catalogues for the mail-order service of the CSMT. Useful not merely for ordering recordings but also for the annotations that accompany each item. Recordings are arranged by categories (geographic, children, multicultural, etc.) and indexed by performer and by song title.

718. Cohen, Judith R. "Judeo-Spanish songs in the Sephardic communities of Montréal and Toronto: survival, function and change." PhD dissertation, Université de Montréal, 1989. 267, lxxxvp.

While the central concern of the study is the repertoire itself of Judeo-Spanish songs existing in Canada and seen within the longer global tradition of Sephardic Jews, there is a good deal of discussion about the establishment of Sephardic communities in Montréal and Toronto since the 1950s. About 300 songs were collected from these two communities.

719. Cox, Gordon Sidney Allister. *Folk music in a Newfoundland outport.* National Museum of Man Mercury Series (ISSN 0316-1854), Canadian Centre for Folk Cultural Studies, Paper no.32. Ottawa: National Museums of Canada, 1980. xiv, 220p.

A contextual study of musical life in two close communities in the south-east part of Newfoundland in 1975 and 1976. "Folk music" is construed in a broad meaning to include hymns and carols. Bibliography and discography of material referred to in text.

720. Creighton, Helen. "Canada's maritime provinces -- an ethnomusicological survey (personal observations and reflections)." *Ethnomusicology* 16/3 (1972): 404-14.

A few personal recollections that sometimes provide anecdotal background to Maritimes collecting. Bibliography/discography.

721. ------ *La fleur du rosier.* Sydney, N.S.: University College of Cape Breton Press, 1988. xiii, 262p. ISBN 0-920336-19-1 (cloth); 0-920336-21-3 (pbk.).

A collection of 123 Acadien songs, which includes many songs collected in the later 1940s in the south-west of Nova Scotia, as well as in other regions of Acadie. Introductory material, notes and song texts in French and English.

722.------ *Folksongs from southern New Brunswick.* Ottawa: National Museum of Man, National Museums of Canada, 1971. x, 238p. four phonodisks.

A remarkable feature of the 118 songs in this anthology is that most of them were obtained in the 1950s from one singer, who had learned them as a child. All the songs are in the British tradition. Short note to each song.

723.------ *Songs and ballads from Nova Scotia.* Toronto: J.M. Dent & Sons, 1932. reprinted New York: Dover Publications, 1966. xxii, 334p.

This collection of 150 songs with English texts is preceded by a picturesque account of Creighton's introduction to folksong collecting. For each song there is a brief commentary, usually about its provenance and variants.

724.Creighton, Helen and Doreen H. Senior. *Traditional songs from Nova Scotia.* Toronto: McGraw-Hill Ryerson Ltd., 1987. xvi, 284p. ISBN 0-07-549510-4.

This extensive collection of songs consists primarily of melodies and texts, with sometimes a brief note on the background to or variants of a song.

725.de Surmont, Jean-Nicolas. "Les conditions de production et de circulation de l'oeuvre de *La Bonne Chanson* de Charles-Émile Gadbois." *Les Cahiers de l'ARMuQ* 16 (1995): 65-78. ISSN 0821-1817.

Derived from a movement that originated in France in 1907, the Canadian idea of "La Bonne Chanson" originated with Abbé C-É. Gadbois in 1937. The aim was to promote the singing of good songs, within a context that included religion as well as culture and language.

726.d'Harcourt, Marguerite and Raoul d'Harcourt. *Chansons folkloriques française au Canada: leur langue musicale.* Québec:

Presses Universitaires Laval, 1956; Paris: Presses Universitaires de France, 1956. xii, 449p.

Based on material recorded 1916-1918 by Barbeau and Massicotte, this collection of 186 songs is preceded by an essay on the style of the songs, with particular attention to modal characteristics. There is a short note on each song that may deal with musical characteristics, background, or variants.

727. Fife, Austin E. and Francesca Redden. "The pseudo-Indian folksongs of the Anglo-American and French-Canadian." *Journal of American Folklore* 67 (1954): 239-51, 379-394.

The article is based on a study of Anglo-American folksongs, especially of Utah, Idaho and California, in which Native Americans figure both favourably and unfavourably. The authors were intrigued by their observation that French-Canadian folksongs that refer to Native Peoples reflect the same patterns as American songs, and they include a few references to them, with music and text for two songs.

728. Fowke, Edith. "Anglo-Canadian folksong: a survey." *Ethnomusicology* 16/3 (1972): 335-50.

Within the limits of a short essay, Fowke provides a good deal of detail and mentions many songs of particular interest. There is a good bibliography and a discography of recordings of traditional singers. A companion essay to Brassard, no.712.

729. ------ "History of English ballads research in Ontario." In *Ballades et chansons folkloriques*, Actes de la 18e session de la Commission pour l'étude de la poésie de tradition orale, pp.3-7. Conrad Laforte, ed. Québec: CÉLAT, Université Laval, 1989. ISBN 2-920576-29-1.

Less a history than some personal reminiscences, this short essay deals mostly with Fowke's early collecting experience.

730. ------ "Labor and industrial protest songs in Canada." *Journal of American Folklore* 82/323 (January-March 1969): 34-50.

While there are many work-related songs, songs that arise out of discontent with organized, unionized or industrial work appear to be relatively rare in Canada. There are some, however, dating from a sealers' strike in 1902, and Fowke surveys them and provides numerous texts, although no music.

731.------ *Lumbering songs from the northern woods.* Transcriptions by Norman Cazden. Austin: University of Texas Press for the American Folklore Society, c1970; reprinted Toronto: NC Press Ltd., 1985. xxiii, 232p. ISBN 0-920053-51-3 (bound); 0-920053-80-7 (pbk.).

Sixty-five lumbering songs from Ontario and western Québec. Short note on each song giving background, provenance and related tunes. In an analytical note, Cazden strongly opposes the use of conventional modal analysis of the songs.

732.------ "'Old favourites': a selective index." *Canadian Folk Music Journal* 7 (1979): 29-56.

The *Family Herald and Weekly Star*, a rural newspaper published in Montréal, published a column called "Old Favourites" from 1895 to 1968. At York University (Toronto), Fowke indexed more than 30,000 titles of poems that appeared, of which she estimates about 15 per cent were songs. From these she has culled this list of popular texts that she thinks were collected in Canada and that appeared in the newspaper.

733.Fowke, Edith and Carole Henderson Carpenter. *A bibliography of Canadian folklore in English.* Toronto: University of Toronto Press, 1981. xx, 272p. ISBN 0-8020-2394-0.

Only items that originated in English or that have been translated are included. The arrangement is by general categories, including dissertations, recordings and films. The section "Folk music and dance" (pp.62-100), contains 637 titles, with additional cross-references.

734.[Fowke, Edith and Barbara Cass-Beggs.] "A reference list on Canadian folk music." *Canadian Folk Music Journal* 11 (1983): 43-60.

This is a revision of lists published in the *Canadian Folk Music Journal* 1 (1973): 45-56; and 6 (1978): 41-56. The material is arranged in sections: Indian and Eskimo, Franco-Canadien,

Anglo-Canadian, and Other Language Groups. There is a list of recordings, but the listing of compositions based on folk music, that appeared in the 1973 and 1978 lists, has been dropped. Selective, without any attempt at completeness, but a good survey. The authors, who compiled the original list in 1966 which is the basis of subsequent lists, are not mentioned in the revisions.

735. Gagné, Marc and Monique Poulin. *Chantons la chanson*. Québec: Les Presses de l'Université Laval, 1985. xvi, 398p. ISBN 2-7637-7025-8.

The forty-three songs and eleven reels and gigues that comprise this anthology come from the Beauce region of Québec. For each musical transcription there is a commentary, and a photograph and biographical note for the informant. The song texts are given in a phonetic version as well as in standard transliteration.

736. Gallaugher, Annemarie. "Trinbago north: calypso culture in Toronto." In *Canadian music: issues of hegemony and identity*, pp.359-382. Eds. Beverley Diamond and Robert Witmer. Toronto: Canadian Scholars' Press, 1994. ISBN 1-55130-031-1.

The large number of Toronto residents with origins in the Caribbean are the focus of this study, and in particular the music closely identified with them. The author discusses calypso music as a "migrating" music, its relationship to the Caribbean community, and attitudes towards it outside the community. The time period covered is from 1967, the date of the first annual Toronto Caribana festival, to the 1990s.

737. Garrison, Virginia Hope. "Traditional and non-traditional teaching and learning practices in folk music: an ethnographic field study of Cape Breton fiddling." PhD dissertation, University of Wisconsin-Madison, 1985. xiv, 370f.

The transmission process for Cape Breton fiddling has become increasingly institutionalized. This study, based on research carried out 1979-1985, includes a review of past and related literature on the subject, and an assessment of the current situation and its significance for education and folkmusic transmission. Extensive bibliography.

738.Gauthier, Dominique. *Chansons de Shippagan*. Transcription musicale de Roger Matton. Québec: Les Presses de l'Université Laval, 1975. xxviii, 178p. (*Les Archives de Folklore* 16). ISBN 0-7746-6730-3.

The Shippagan region is located on the extreme north-east point of New Brunswick. This collection of 70 songs from the area includes a short introductory essay on stylistic points, a table of modes and ambitus, and a very brief note for each piece.

739.Gillis, Frank and Alan P. Merriam, compilers. *Ethnomusicology and folk music: an international bibliography of dissertations and theses*. Middletown, Conn.: Wesleyan University Press, 1966. viii, 148p.

United States universities are the primary sources for titles, but a number of foreign universities are also included. Entries are by author, with an index of subjects. A useful list but limited simply by the fact that most university-based research on Canadian topics has been carried out since publication.

740.Glofcheskie, John Michael. *Folk music of Canada's oldest Polish community/La musique traditionnelle de la plus ancienne communauté polonaise du Canada*. Ottawa: National Museum of Man, Mercury Series (ISSN 0316-1854), 1980. Canadian Centre for Folk Culture Studies, Paper no.33. viii, 89p.

A study of the repertoire of a community in Renfrew County, Ontario, that was settled by Poles in the early 1860s. Commentary in French and English.

741.Haywood, Charles. *A bibliography of North American folklore and folksong*. 2nd revised edition. New York: Dover Publications, 1961. 2 vols. xxx, 748; ix, 749-1301p.

This is a corrected republication of the 1951 edition, with a new index supplement. The "Canada" section (pp.422-428) contains few music entries, none later than the 1930s.

742.Henderson, Carole and Neil V. Rosenberg. "The MacEdward Leach Collection of Canadian folklore." *Canadian Folk Music Society Newsletter* 5 (1970):1-10.

In 1970 Memorial University of Newfoundland received the loan of materials from the University of Pennsylvania, consisting of Canadian material in a bequest made by MacEdward Leach. A general description of the contents is given, including its shortcomings, but there are no details about the material, nor is there a catalogue. Text in French and English.

743.Henry, Frances. "Black music in the Maritimes." *Canadian Folk Music Journal* 3 (1975): 11-21.

There appears to be neither survival nor development of a folksong tradition among the Black population of Nova Scotia, something that this paper attempts to explain. Four examples of religious songs are included.

744.Hickerson, Joseph C., compiler. "A list of folklore and folk music archives and related collections in the United States and Canada." *Journal of American Folklore Supplement* (May, 1972):17-23.

Collections are listed by State and Province. There are few Canadian entries.

745.Ives, Edward D. *Folksongs of New Brunswick.* Fredericton, N.B.: Goose Lane Editions, 1989. 194p. ISBN 0-86492-104-7.

The fifty-two songs of the collection are organized by the singers, all of whom had been woodsmen, who performed them for Ives. The comments tend to be personal recollections by the author of the singers and the circumstances of the recording.

746.------ *Larry Gorman: the man who made the songs.* Fredericton, N.B.: Goose Lane Editions (originally published Bloomington: Indiana University Press, 1964; reprinted New York: Arno Press, 1977). xvii, 225p. ISBN 0-86492-152-7.

This biography of Gorman, a prolific songwriter and a lumberman who was born on Prince Edward Island in 1846, includes the tunes for twenty-six of his popular songs, and the texts for more than seventy. Fully documented with notes on archival sources and bibliography.

747. Ives, Edward D. and Bacil Kirtley. "Bibliography of New England-Maritimes folklore." *Northeast Folklore* 1/2 (summer, 1958): 19-31; 2/2 (summer, 1959): 19-24.

A broad view of "folklore" includes Indian subjects. The bibliographies in the two issues are not continuous, but are both organized by subject. Musical items are relatively few.

748. Karpeles, Maud. *Folk songs from Newfoundland.* London: Faber and Faber, 1971. 340p. ISBN 0-571-09297-7.

There are 89 songs in the anthology, often with variants, collected in 1929-30. The short notes on each song include references in other collections.

749. Klymasz, Robert B. "'Sounds you never before heard': Ukrainian country music in Western Canada." *Ethnomusicology* 16/3 (1972): 372-80.

A study of 514 musical items on forty-two long-playing record albums. It appears that the decline of traditional Ukrainian folksong in western Canada has been both arrested and modified by urban commercial influences.

750. ------*The Ukrainian folk ballad in Canada.* New York: AMS Press, 1989. 332p. ISBN 0-404-197475-3. Musical transcriptions by Kenneth Peacock.

The fifty-six ballads (narrative accounts of real or legendary events) were recorded in western Canada in the mid-1960s. They attest to the lingering popularity of the traditional ballad, modified by the new social influences of life in Canada.

751. Labbé, Gabriel. *Les pionniers du disque folklorique québécois 1920-1950.* Montréal: Éditions de l'Aurore, 1977. 216p. ISBN 0-88532-122-7.

A list of instrumentalists and singers of Québec who recorded traditional folk music. There is a biographical note on each musician, followed by a discography.

752. Laforte, Conrad, ed. *Ballades et chansons folkloriques.* Actes de la 18e session de la Commission pour l'étude de la poésie de

tradition orale. Québec: CÉLAT, Université Laval, 1989. viii, 389p. ISBN 2-920576-29-1.

A number of the essays in this report have Canadian subject matter. The historical essays and summaries of research are indexed separately in this *Guide*.

753. Laforte, Conrad. *Le Catalogue de la chanson folklorique française*. Québec: Les Presses de l'Université Laval, 1958. xxix, 397p.

A small limited edition, which was a preliminary version of no.754.

754. ------ *Le Catalogue de la chanson folklorique française.* new edition.

I. *Chansons en laisse*. Québec: Les Presses de l'Université Laval, 1977. cxi, 561p. *Les Archives de Folklore*, 18. ISBN 9-7746-6824-5. (an *errata*, and an appendix "Tableau des laisses" appear at the end of Vol. IV)

II. *Chansons strophiques*. Québec: Les Presses de l'Université Laval, 1981. xiv, 841p. *Les Archives de Folklore*, 20. ISBN 2-7637-6917-9.

III. *Chansons en forme de dialogue*. Québec: Les Presses de l'Université Laval, 1982. xv, 144p. *Les Archives de Folklore*, 21. ISBN 2-7637-6883-0

IV. *Chansons énumératives*. Québec: Les Presses de l'Université Laval, 1979. xiv, 295p. *Les Archives de Folklore*, 19. ISBN 2-7637-6883-0.

V. *Chansons brèves (Les enfantines)*. Québec: Les Presses de l'Université Laval, 1987. xxx, 1017p. *Les Archives de Folklore*, 22. ISBN 2-7637-7125-4.

VI. *Chansons sur des timbres*. Québec: Les Presses de l'Université Laval, 1983. xvii, 649p. *Les Archives de Folklore*, 23. ISBN 2-7637-7000-2.

This monumental work attempts to catalogue some 80,000 variants of French folksongs from Europe and North America, organized according to a system set out in *Poétiques* (no.756). For each song, the references are grouped by country. Although many songs have European references, there is an extraordinary number that relate to Canada.

755.------ *La chanson folklorique et les écrivains du XIXe siècle (en France et au Québec).* Montréal: Éditions Hurtubise (Les Cahiers du Québec), 1973. 154p.

About half the book is an examination of the various relationships between popular song and literature -- the writing of texts in popular style, and reference to or use of original or imitative songs in literature. The remainder discusses the relationship to Canada of the setting up in France in 1852 of le Comité de la langue, de l'histoire et des arts de la France, which had as one of its objects the study of *la chanson populaire*. There is an extensive bibliography, including lists of manuscripts and published collections of French-Canadian folksongs.

756.------ *Poétiques de la chanson traditionnelle française.* Québec: Les Presses de l'Université Laval, 1976. ix, 162p. (*Les Archives de folklore*, 17.) ISBN 0-7746-6661-7. 2nd edition, 1993. 205p. (*Les Archives de folklore*, 26.) ISBN 2-7637-7320-6.

Although it deals with the texts of French folksong, it is primarily an introduction to the *Catalogue* (no.754) and provides a system of classification for that catalogue. The second edition takes into account the experience gained from the publishing of the catalogue. Extensive bibliography, including archival sources, and indexes.

757.------ *Survivances médiévales dans la chanson folklorique: poétique de la chanson en laisse.* Québec: Les Presses de l'Université Laval, 1981. viii, 300p. ISBN 2-7637-6928-4.

An exhaustive investigation of the forms of the texts of the *chansons en laisse*, the first of Laforte's six categories of folksong. Indexes, and an extensive bibliography of collections, sources and printed materials.

758. Laforte, Conrad and Carmen Roberge. *Chansons folkloriques à sujet religieux.* Québec: Les Presses de l'Université Laval, 1988. xii, 388p. ISBN 2-7637-7155-6.

An anthology of 83 folksongs with religious subjects, each with melody, text and brief annotation. The collection has an introduction (p.1-78) which deals with the narrative categories and poetic structures. Some of the songs are European in origin, but most come from French Canada.

759. Leach, MacEdward. *Folk ballads and songs of the lower Labrador coasts.* Ottawa: National Museum of Canada, 1965. viii, 332p. Bulletin no.201, Anthropological Series no.68.

A short essay on "The Musical Style" is provided by Bruno Nettl, who made the musical transcriptions. There are 138 songs, all with English texts, with a commentary on each song that deals mostly with the text and with variants or related versions.

760. Magee, Eleanor and Margaret Fancy. *Catalogue of Canadian folk music in the Mary Mellish Archibald Library and other special collections.* Sackville: Ralph Pickard Bell Library, Mount Allison University, 1974. iv, 88p.

Although limited to the holdings of the University, those holdings are extensive and this still makes a useful checklist of song collections, monographs, periodicals, and recordings. Cross-indexed by author/subject/title, and by song title.

761. Manny, Louise and James Reginald Wilson. *Songs of Miramichi.* Fredericton, N.B.: Brunswick Press, 1968 (reprinted 1970, 1976). 330p. ISBN 0-88790-022-4.

An introduction provides a history of the Miramichi region in northeastern New Brunswick and a short commentary on the tunes. Each of the 101 songs has a short annotation that might include information on the origin, significance or variants of the tune or text.

762. Martens, Helen. "The music of some religious minorities in Canada." *Ethnomusicology* 16/3 (1972): 360-71.

A résumé of musical life in communities of Mennonites, Hutterites and Doukhobors.

763.McCook, James. "Some notes on musical instruments among the pioneers of the Canadian West." *The Canadian Music Journal* 2/2 (Winter 1958): 21-24.

The author recounts some musical incidents about the movement of settlers across the West from the 1860s but gives no documentation for any of the information.

764.McCormick, Chris. "Maritime folk song as popular culture: an applied study in discourse and social relations." *Canadian University Music Review/Revue de musique des universités canadiennes* 5 (1984): 60-86.

The author takes the view that folk-song, notably that from the Maritime provinces, is romanticized out of context and this in turn romanticizes Maritime life, to create a fictionalized account of both the songs and real life. The article shows how the songs may be re-situated culturally to reveal new understanding of the body of folk-songs and the society that produces them.

765.McIntyre, Paul. *Black Pentecostal music in Windsor*. National Museum of Man Mercury Series (ISSN 0316-1854). Canadian Centre for Folk Cultural Studies, Paper no.15 (ISSN 0316-1897). Ottawa: National Museums of Canada, 1976. 124p.

Music, religion and social condition are inseparable elements in examining the music at Mount Zion Church in Windsor (Ontario). The study is entirely descriptive and provides narrative accounts of the music and the services in which it is used.

766.McKay, Ian. *The quest of the folk: antimodernism and cultural selection in twentieth-century Nova Scotia*. Montreal and Kingston: McGill-Queen's University Press, 1994. xvii, 371p. ISBN 0-7735-1179-2 (cloth); 0-7735-1248-9 (paper).

The author's thesis is that urban investigators constructed the idea of the "Folk" as an antithesis to modern industrial life in the city. While the subject is folklore in general, music is included in the examination, and there is a substantial chapter devoted to

Helen Creighton, who is seen to be a major figure in the fashioning of the idea of folk culture in Nova Scotia.

767. Mercer, Paul. *Newfoundland songs and ballads in print, 1842-1974: a title and first-line index*. St. John's: Memorial University of Newfoundland, 1979. xv, 343p. ISBN 0-88901-038-2.

In an introduction, the author reviews the history of studying and publishing Newfoundland songs. The main text consists of an alphabetical listing of song titles. The list of books, pamphlets and articles on which the title list is based is itself extensive and very useful.

768. ------ "A supplementary bibliography on Newfoundland music." *Canadian Folk Music Journal* 2 (1974): 52-56.

The list is presented as a supplement to no.734, and is derived from the working bibliography for no.767.

769. Peacock, Kenneth. "Establishing perimeters for ethnomusicological field research in Canada: on-going projects and future possibilities at the Canadian Centre for Folk Culture Studies." *Ethnomusicology* 16/3 (1972): 329-34.

In this short essay, Peacock outlines the difficulties of developing field research in a country that was, especially at the time of writing, striving to be a bilingual and multicultural federation.

770. ------ "Folk and aboriginal music." In *Aspects of music in Canada*, pp.62-89. A. Walter,ed. Toronto. University of Toronto Press, 1969. ISBN 8020-1536-0.

This brief narrative survey is treated under four main headings: Aboriginal music, French folk music, English folk music, and ethnic folk music. The essay conveys much of the activity of collecting and study, as well as the astonishing diversity of musical life in Canada.

771. ------ *Songs of the Newfoundland outports*. Bulletin no.197, Anthropological Series no.65. Ottawa: National Museum of Canada, 1965. 3vols. xxv, 1035p.

The songs were gathered by Peacock in the period 1951-1961. In addition to the tune and text for each song there is often a short note on the origin, structure or significance of the piece. The songs are arranged under topics (lumbering, murder, love adventures, etc.) and indexed by title.

772. Pelinski, Ramón. "The music of Canada's ethnic minorities." *Les Cahiers canadiens de musique / The Canada Music Book* 10 (Printemps/été 1975): 59-86.

The Canadian census for 1971 registered forty-one official ethnic groups. The author, in a broad survey, outlines the musical contributions of these groups and something about current research on the subject. Native, French and British groups are not taken into account.

773. Perron, Marie-Louise. "État de la recherche sur la chanson folklorique en Saskatchewan." In *Ballades et chansons folkloriques*, Actes de la 18e session de la Commission pour l'étude de la poésie de tradition orale, pp.29-44. Conrad Laforte, ed. Québec: CÉLAT, Université Laval, 1989. ISBN 2-920576-29-1.

A short report on research undertaken on French folksong in Saskatchewan, and on materials deposited in the Saskatchewan archives. Short bibliography.

774. Pichette, Jean-Pierre. "La chanson folklorique en Ontario français." In *Ballades et chansons folkloriques*, Actes de la 18e session de la Commission pour l'étude de la poésie de tradition orale, pp.17-28. Conrad Laforte, ed. Québec: CÉLAT, Université Laval, 1989. ISBN 2-920576-29-1.

An outline of the history of the French speaking community of Ontario, and the interest in folksong study that began in 1949.

775. Posen, I. Sheldon. *For singing and dancing and all sorts of fun.* Toronto: Deneau, 1988. xvii, 144p. ISBN 0-88879-178-X.

A study of the Ottawa valley song, *The Chapeau Boys*, which is also a study of the song tradition that the author found in 1977 in the village of Chapeau. There is consideration of the historical, geographical and social background of the song, and its place in the village community of the 1970s.

776. Proctor, George A. "Fiddle music as a manifestation of Canadian regionalism." In *Regionalism and national identity*, pp.127-133. Reginald Berry and James Acheson, eds. Christchurch, New Zealand: Association for Canadian Studies in Australia and New Zealand, 1985. ISBN 0-473-00385-6.

Fiddle music is considered to display marked regional differences. Briefly outlined are distinctions found in the fiddle music of Cape Breton, Newfoundland, the Maritimes, Ontario, the Western Provinces, and Québec.

777. ------ "Old-time fiddling in Ontario." In *National Museum of Canada Bulletin No. 190, Contributions to Anthropology, 1960, Part II*, pp.173-208. Ottawa: Queen's Printer, 1963.

The study is based on field research carried out in 1960 in three regions of anglo-Ontario. There are observations of different styles and their characteristics, and some notes on the fiddlers. There are twelve complete musical examples.

778. Qureshi, Regula. "Ethnomusicological research among Canadian communities of Arab and East Indian origin." *Ethnomusicology* 16/3 (1972): 381-96.

There is some basic information about music in Arab and East Indian communities, chiefly in Alberta, and a note on research priorities in the relatively new area of study of minority non-european communities. There is a short bibliography and a list of community and religious organizations at the time of publication.

779. Rahn, Jay. "Canadian folk music holdings at Columbia University." *Canadian Folk Music Journal* 5 (1977): 46-49.

This brief catalogues outlines the holdings of about 1000 items, including music of the Inuit and First Nations, held at the Center for Studies in Ethnomusicology at Columbia University, New York.

780. Robbins, James. "North America: Canada." In *Ethnomusicology: historical and regional studies*, pp.63-76. Helen Myers, ed. New

York, W.W. Norton & Co., 1993. ISBN 0-393-03378-3. London, The Macmillan Press, 1993. ISBN 0-333-57632-2.

Despite its brevity, this survey of folk, ethnic and native studies is comprehensive and remarkably thorough in its citation of works and activities. Useful bibliography arranged chronologically from 1609 to 1989.

781.Roberge, Carmen. "Historique des recherches sur la chanson folklorique au Québec." In *Ballades et chansons folkloriques*, Actes de la 18e session de la Commission pour l'étude de la poésie de tradition orale, pp.9-16. Conrad Laforte, ed. Québec: CÉLAT, Université Laval, 1989. ISBN 2-920576-29-1.

A brief sketch of the interest in the study of French-Canadian folksong, from the 19th century, built around references to the principal collectors and researchers.

782.Rosenberg, Neil V. "Folksong in Newfoundland: a research history." In *Ballades et chansons folkloriques*, Actes de la 18e session de la Commission pour l'étude de la poésie de tradition orale, pp.45-52. Conrad Laforte, ed. Québec: CÉLAT, Université Laval, 1989. ISBN 2-920576-29-1.

A short review of folksong study in Newfoundland, especially with reference to Gerald S. Doyle, whose interest began in the 1920s.

783.------ "A preliminary bibliography of Canadian old time instrumental music books." *Canadian Folk Music Journal* 8 (1980): 20-22.

Although there are only about thirty titles, this preliminary list gathers together commercial publications from the 1940s to the 1970s of "old time" fiddle and accordion music.

784.Roy, Carmen. *La littérature orale en Gaspésie*. Ottawa: Ministre du Nord canadien et des Ressources nationales, 1955. v, 389p. (Bulletin no.134; no.36 de la Série Anthropologique).

This study surveys a wide variety of subjects transmitted orally, including such things as medical lore, the supernatural, stories, as well as folksong. There are transcriptions of twenty-three songs, and indexes by title, by refrain and by subject of 1233 songs.

785. Sargent, Margaret. "Folk and primitive music in Canada." *Journal of the International Folk Music Council* 4 (1952): 65-68.

The brevity of the historical summary and the short note on the work of the National Museum are chiefly interesting as indicators of how limited ethnomusicological study was in Canada before 1950. Very brief bibliography.

786. Satory, Stephen. "Táncház in Toronto: a transplanted tradition." *Canadian University Music Review/Revue de musique des universités canadiennes* 8 (1987): 45-61.

Táncház, or "dance-house" tradition of improvised dancing was developed in the Toronto Hungarian community in a choreographed version in the 1980s. The objective study of the dance style and the relationship to the maintenance of Hungarian identity are discussed.

787. Song, Bang-song. *The Korean-Canadian folk song: an ethnomusicological study.* National Museum of Man Mercury Series. Canadian Centre for Folk Culture Studies, Paper no.10. Ottawa: National Museums of Canada, 1974. xiii, 225p.

Twenty-one songs and nine instrumental pieces, recorded in the Toronto area in 1973, are the basis for an examination of the state of Korean music among immigrants who live within the cultural environment of a European majority. In addition to analysis and discussion about the music, there is cultural background to the Korean community.

788. Steiner, Margaret. "Regionalism, revival, and the reformation of community at the Miramichi Folksong Festival." *Lore and Language* 12/1-2 (1994): 241-252. Papers from the 22nd International Ballad Conference. Lock, UK: Hisarlik Press, 1994. ISBN 1-874312-17-6.

The regional identity of communities in the Miramichi area of New Brunswick is inextricably connected with ballads and folksongs. This phenomenon is examined in relation to the local

Folksong Festival, with a consideration of the influence of collector Louise Manny.

789. Taft, Michael. "A bibliography for folklore studies in Nova Scotia." In *Three Atlantic Bibliographies*, pp.106-205. Halifax: Saint Mary's University, 1975. Occasional Papers in Anthropology, No.1.

A broadly based list of readings on folklore and related topics, with about 100 titles on music. Entries are arranged by author and indexed by subject.

790. ------ *A regional discography of Newfoundland and Labrador 1904-1972*. St. John's, Newfoundland: Folklore and Language Archive, Memorial University of Newfoundland, 1975. xxx, 102p.

The introduction provides a history of recording by Newfoundlanders and the record business in Newfoundland, with mention of the "acculturation" that often shows up in recordings of local songs by local musicians. There are two lists, one of recordings by Newfoundlanders, the other of Newfoundland songs recorded by outsiders. Entries are by performer, and indexed by song title.

791. Ullmann, Christiane. "German folksongs of Lunenburg County, N.S." *German-Canadian Yearbook* 5 (1979): 143-53.

The survival of a few songs in one of Canada's earliest German settlements is examined, with music and text for six songs.

792. Webb, Jeff A. "Cultural intervention: Helen Creighton's folksong broadcasts, 1938-1939." *Canadian Folklore Canadien* 14/2 (1992): 159-170.

Creighton produced a CBC folksong program in 1938-39. The author finds that the choice of music and its manner of presentation, however creditable in many ways, reflected an elitist attitude to folksong and, incidentally, to education, and that there were negative as well as positive implications in the broadcasts.

793. Whitcomb, Ed. *Canadian fiddle music, vol I.* Ottawa: Ed Whitcomb, 1990. 228p. ISBN 0-9694667-0-6.

    A collection of music, but there is a short introduction on fiddling and very brief notes on a large number of fiddlers.

794. Witmer, Robert. ed. *Ethnomusicology in Canada.* Toronto: Institute for Canadian Music, 1990. xiv, 413p. CanMus Documents, 5. ISBN 0-7727-8556-2.

    Proceedings of a conference held in Toronto in May, 1988. The text of this report ranges from brief abstracts of papers read at the conference to fully developed articles (there are sixty-four items), and transcripts of twenty-one discussion sessions and two panels. Virtually every aspect of ethnomusicological studies in Canada is touched upon, including methods and approaches, ethnicity and identity, native traditions, fiddling, dance, popular music, jazz, and a section on Latin American and Caribbean cultures. There is a cumulative bibliography of "publications cited."

795. Wrazen, Louise. "The *Góralski* of the Polish Highlanders: old world musical traditions from a new world perspective." PhD dissertation, University of Toronto, 1988. iv, 329f.

    The *góralski*, a dance/music performance event, is the focus of a study of the effect of immigration on the event itself, and of the significance of music within the immigration process. The study draws on Polish communities in Toronto and Chicago, and observes the shift from spontaneous traditional performance to rehearsed and staged presentations.

796. Young, Russell Scott. *Vieilles chansons de Nouvelle France.* Québec: Les Presses de l'Université Laval, 1956. 129p. (*Les Archives de Folklore* 7).

    Fifty songs are presented from among some 400 recorded in 1953-54 in the region around Québec City. A short note in an appendix deals with problems of rhythmic transcription. Other than to note the details of the singer who was the source of each song, there are no notes or analyses for the repertoire.

Popular Music and Jazz

The critical and historical study of jazz in Canada is relatively recent, as is the study of popular music everywhere. Nevertheless, if the list is relatively short, there is evidence of a good deal of activity, albeit directed primarily to music in Toronto and Montréal. Einarson's study (no.804)) of Winnipeg rock bands is exceptional. For the study of popular music, the work of John Shepherd should be noted at the School for Studies in Art and Culture, Carleton University (Ottawa). A jazz magazine, *Coda*, has been published since 1958.

Included in this section are items about individual musicians whose careers have been devoted to popular music and jazz, such as Guy Lombardo (no.801), Mart Kenney (no.815), or Oscar Peterson (no.817, 825).

As in the two preceding sections, there is sometimes a crossing over of popular music with other types. Mary Travers, known as La Bolduc, achieved great popularity in French Canada with her own songs, although both she and her music have virtually been absorbed into the folk mystique. Folk and country music are treated together by Rosenberg (no.829), as are Native and country music by Whidden (no.834).

797.Adria, Marco. *Music of our times: eight Canadian singer-songwriters*. Toronto: James Lorimer & Company, 1990. 158p. ISBN 1-55028-317-0; 1-55028-315-4 (pbk.)

This set of eight short studies of popular singer-songwriters provides some biographical information and general comments on their music. The style is non-technical and always admiring. There is a useful bibliography for each musician. The subjects are Gordon Lightfoot, Leonard Cohen, Neil Young, Joni Mitchell, Bruce Cockburn, Murray McLauchlan, Jane Siberry, and k.d. lang.

798.Baudot, Alain. *La chanson québécoise, documentation sélective.* Toronto: Glendon College, York University, 1980. 45f.

Although prepared as a general reference list for a convention of the *American Association of Teachers of French*, this modest work remains useful for its selective bibliography, discography, and audio-visual list. Most of the material is arranged by artist, with much of the bibliographic reference drawn from magazines and newspapers.

799.Bell, Leslie. "Popular music." In *Music in Canada*, pp.208-215. Ernest MacMillan, ed. Toronto: University of Toronto Press, 1955.

The author mentions a few composers, performers and pieces that achieved "popular" status, but there is scant appraisal, or even genuine acknowledgment, of the place or extent of popular music, either historically or at the mid-20th century.

800.Benoit, Réal. *La Bolduc. Biographie de Mme Bolduc, chanteuse populaire canadienne.* Montréal: Éditions de l'homme, 1959. 125p.

The first biography of the popular Québec singer of the 1930s. The book traces her life and career in a popular narrative style.

801.Cline, Beverly Fink. *The Lombardo story.* Don Mills, Ontario: Musson Book Company, 1979. 158p. ISBN 0-7737-0042-0.

Although much of the material centres on Guy Lombardo, this is mainly the story of his band, the Royal Canadians, and his collaborating brothers. Included are lists of songs written by Carmen Lombardo and by Guy Lombardo, and a short discography of recordings available at the time of publication.

802.Cormier, Normand, Ghislaine Houle, Suzanne Lauzier and Yvette Trépanier. *La chanson au Québec 1965-1975.* Montréal: Gouvernement du Québec, Ministère des Affaires Culturelles, 1975. xiii, 219p. (Bibliographies québécoises, no.3).

A bibliography of 2049 items, of which sixty-two are books and the rest are articles drawn from newspapers and magazines. The arrangement is by author, with indexes of titles and of subjects. "La chanson" refers to the popular song of the day.

803."Country music -- a special section." *Le Compositeur Canadien/The Canadian Composer* 85 (November 1973): 18-37.

This section on country music consists of five short articles built around major performers, and the commercial problems of developing the style in Canada.

804.Einarson, John. *Shakin' all over: the Winnipeg sixties rock scene.* Winnipeg: the author, 1987. xvi, 166p. ISBN 0-9693018-0-4.

The title is that of a 1965 hit by the Guess Who, the most famous of many bands that originated and played in Winnipeg in the 1960s. In chronicling the success of the bands and individual musicians in Winnipeg in the decade 1960-70, the author provides a local history of live popular music in the city. Many photographs, list of bands with personnel, discography.

805.Fetherling, Doug. *Some day soon.* Kingston, Ont.: Quarry Press, 1991. 176p. ISBN 1-55082-000-1.

Five essays are devoted to five singer-songwriters who came to prominence in the 1960s: Gordon Lightfoot, Leonard Cohen, Joni Mitchell, Robbie Robertson, Neil Young. In the author's view, they each represented a Canadian style despite their varied musical personalities. Selected bibliographies for each musician.

806.Gilmore, John. *Swinging in paradise: the story of jazz in Montréal.* Montréal: Véhicule Press, 1988. 322p. ISBN 0-919890-87-3.

After a survey of activity through the 1920s and 1930s, this study concentrates on the period from the 1940s to the 1970s. Bands and individual musicians are discussed in some detail, but the Montréal's jazz history is always viewed within a social and cultural environment.

807.------ *Who's who of jazz in Montréal: ragtime to 1970.* Montréal: Véhicule Press, 1989. 318p. ISBN 0-919890-92-X.

Individuals who figured in Montréal jazz up to 1970 are the subjects of this biographical dictionary, but information about them frequently extends into the 1980s. Entries are arranged alphabetically; no index.

808. Giroux, Robert, ed. *En avant la chanson.* Montréal: Éditions Triptyque, 1993. 249p. ISBN 2-89031-176-7.

A collection of thirteen essays on popular music, seven of which relate directly to Québec and one to Ontario. Among the subjects treated are publication of Québec songs, the recording industry, and the role of women in the recording and performance industry. There are extensive bibliographies for most of the articles.

809. Goddard, Peter and Philip Kamin, eds. *Shakin' all over: the rock'n'roll years in Canada.* Toronto: McGraw-Hill Ryerson, 1989. ISBN 0-07-549773-5.

This highly commercial publication, directed to a popular audience, is nevertheless a source of considerable information about popular music in Canada, especially in the 1970s and 1980s. Thirteen performers and people in the business each contribute an essay, and there are many short notes on performers who had very localized or short-lived success. Material is mostly about anglophone Canada, with one essay on Québec.

810. Graham, June. "From the Happy Gang to Guernsey." *Le Compositeur Canadien/The Canadian Composer* 44 (November 1969): 4-9.

The article provides some information on Robert Farnon's training and early work in Canada before moving to Britain, and notes some of his composition, both serious and popular.

811. Grant, Barry K. "'Across the Great Divide': imitation and inflection in Canadian rock music." *Journal of Canadian Studies* 21/1 (Spring 1986): 116-127.

In developing an aesthetic framework for Canadian rock music, the author argues that Canadian musicians subverted those

American conventions that the music industry demanded as the price for Canadian entry into the United States market.

812. Harry, Isobel. "Reggae inna Canada." *Le Compositeur Canadien/ The Canadian Composer* 152 (June 1980): 4-17.

This report on the growth of the Jamaican popular music, reggae, in Canada and particularly in Toronto, is accompanied by five short notes on performers who settled in Toronto.

813. "Interview: the roots and reasons for Quebec's music." *Le Compositeur Canadien/The Canadian Composer* 92 (June 1974): 10-19.

The interview is entirely direct quotation from Gilles Vigneault, who talks about his own style, but most extensively about the relationship of his work to, and the place of the chansonnier, in Québec culture, particularly in the context of Québec nationalism.

814. Jackson, Rick. *Encyclopedia of Canadian rock, pop and folk music.* Kingston, Ont.: Quarry Press, 1994. 319p. ISBN 1-55082-107-5(bound), ISBN 1-55082-098-2 (paperback).

An alphabetical list of groups and individuals who were popular from the 1950s onward. Each entry includes a short biographical/historical note and selective discography. There is no index to locate individuals who are listed only under bands, and there are very few Francophones in the list.

815. Kenney, Mart. *Mart Kenney and his Western Gentlemen.* Saskatoon: Western Producer Prairie Books, 1981. xi, 177p. ISBN 0-88833-072-3.

An autobiography by one of the most successful bandleaders from the 1930s through the 1970s. It mostly chronicles the activities of Kenney's bands, and includes lists of musicians who played with him.

816. Lamothe, Maurice. *La chanson populaire ontaroise 1970-1990: ses produits, sa pratique.* Montréal: Éditions Triptyque, 1994/Ottawa: Le Nordir, Université d'Ottawa, 1994. 391p. ISBN 2-89031-183-X (Triptyque); 2-921365-29-4 (Nordir).

The development of popular music in the French-speaking community of Ontario is examined as an element in the consolidation of identity, especially against the increasing nationalism of Québec. The complex social and economic relationship of performers with Québec is also discussed. There is an extensive bibliography, especially of journal and newspaper items, arranged by performer.

817. Lees, Gene. *Oscar Peterson: the will to swing*. Toronto: Lester & Orpen Dennys, 1988. vii, 294p. ISBN 0-88619-127-0 (bound), 0-88619-129-7 (pbk).

A biography of Peterson that concentrates on the events of his career. The author's personal account is based on experience and on many interviews. In addition to musical matters, the author makes many references to racial incidents that involved Peterson as well as other musicians.

818. Litchfield, Jack. *The Canadian jazz discography 1916-1980*. Toronto: University of Toronto Press, 1982. 945p. ISBN 0-8020-2448-3.

This represents an attempt to list every record -- including piano rolls and motion pictures -- made by a Canadian jazz artist up to 1980. Listings are alphabetical by musician, with full details for each of their recordings. Indexes by tune titles and for musicians.

819. Lonergan, David. *La Bolduc: la vie de Mary Travers (1894-1941)*. Bic, Qué.: Issac-Dion Éditeur, 1992. 215p. ISBN 2-9802497-1-8.

This biography of the popular Québec singer includes a complete discography, a selective but useful bibliography, and many photographs.

820. McNamara, Helen and Jack Lomas. *The Bands Canadians danced to*. Toronto: Griffin Press, 1973. vii, 118p. ISBN 0-88760-063-8.

This lively survey of popular dance bands, from the 1920s to the 1960s, consists of individual notes on all the important bands, with a great many photographs

821.Miller, Mark. *Boogie, Pete & the Senator. Canadian musicians in jazz: the eighties.* Toronto: Nightwood Editions, 1987. 312p. ISBN 0-88971-112-7.

In some ways a continuation of *Jazz in Canada* (no.823), this survey of jazz activity in Canada after 1980 is built around forty musicians, ranging from the long-established to relative newcomers. As with the earlier book, much of the material is drawn from interviews with the subjects and from the author's experience. No discographies.

822.------ *Cool blues: Charlie Parker in Canada, 1953.* London, Ont.: Nightwood Editions, 1989. 115p. ISBN 0-88971-119-4.

In 1953 Parker spent three nights at the Jazz Workshop in Montréal, and one night in Toronto at a concert that became legendary. In both places he had extraordinary impact. This study is as much about the developing jazz community in each city as about Parker.

823.------ *Jazz in Canada: fourteen lives.* Toronto: University of Toronto Press, 1982. [x], 245p. ISBN 0-8020-2476-9

Miller covers the period from about 1929 to 1980 in an introduction and ten essays on fourteen musicians whom he considers to be among the most important -- not always the most famous. Much of the information comes from interviews with the subjects and their associates. Discographies. See also no.821.

824.------ "The new jazz: a national survey." *Le Compositeur Canadien/The Canadian Composer* 170 (April, 1982): 24-31.

In a review of the 1981 "'Ear It Live International Festival of Improvised Music and Jazz," the author surveys the styles and distinctions of many performers of free and improvised music. There is a short discography of this specialized repertory.

825.Palmer, Richard. *Oscar Peterson.* Tunbridge Wells: Spellmount Ltd., 1984; New York: Hippocrene Books, 1984. 93p. ISBN 0-946771-45-6 (UK), 0-87052-011-3 (USA).

There is little personal biographical information, the material being confined mostly to an account of Peterson's professional career. Selective discography.

826.Rice, Timothy and Tammy Gutnik. "What's Canadian about Canadian popular music?: the case of Bruce Cockburn." In *Taking a stand: essays in honour of John Beckwith*, pp.238-256. Ed. T. McGee. Toronto: University of Toronto Press, 1995. ISBN 0-8020-0583-7.

This survey of Cockburn's career examines his evolving musical style, which is seen to be personal and original. The commentary reveals much about his relationship to Canadian society and politics and his objective to be "Canadian." There are also pertinent observations on Canadian popular artists who adopted American modes of writing and performing.

827."Ron Collier: a serious approach to jazz." *Le Compositeur Canadien/The Canadian Composer* 18 (May 1967): 4-5, 44-45.

A short biographical résumé, and some views by Collier on jazz composition.

828.Rosenberg, Neil V. "Ethnicity and class: Black country musicians in the Maritimes." *Journal of Canadian Studies* 23/1-2 (Spring/Summer 1988): 138-156. Reprinted in *Canadian music: issues of hegemony and identity*, pp.417-446. Beverley Diamond and Robert Witmer, eds. Toronto: Canadian Scholars' Press, 1994. ISBN 1-55130-031-1.

Popular musicians of African descent have long been residents of the Maritime provinces. This article considers such elements as history, social and racial discrimination, influence of the minstrel tradition, and the complex relationship to American country music. The notes to the article are a good source of related bibliographical items.

829.------ "'Folk' and 'country' music in the Canadian Maritimes: a regional model." *The Journal of Country Music* 5 (1974): 76-83. reprinted in *Country music in the Maritimes: two studies*. St. John's: Memorial University of Newfoundland, Department of Folklore Reprint Series, No.2 (1976; 1980): 1-11.

If commercial country music has its origins in folk music, it seems equally clear that country music has developed regional characteristics that are influenced by local folk culture. This relationship is examined in respect to the eastern Canadian provinces, with some reference to other regional country musics.

830. Sellick, Lester B. *Canada's Don Messer.* Kentville, N.S.: Kentville Publishing Co., 1969. vi, 170p.

This account, based on interviews and personal acquaintance, traces Messer's career as fiddler and band leader over some thirty-five years. Particular attention is given to the cancellation in 1969 of his popular CBC television show.

831. Smith, Bill. "A concise history of hot music in a cold climate." *Le Compositeur Canadien/The Canadian Composer* 102 (June 1975): 28-33.

This survey of the development of jazz in Canada, particularly in Toronto, in the 1940s and 1950s is too brief to be informative beyond the useful mention of a number of important musicians and performance locations.

832. Tremblay-Matte, Cécile. *La chanson écrite au féminin: de Madeleine de Verchères à Mitsou, 1730-1990.* Montréal: Éditions Trois, 1990. 391p. ISBN 2-920887-16-5.

The author traces the changing styles and evolving place of women in French-language popular song in Canada, both from point of view of composition as well as performance. Individuals are treated briefly within the narrative, and there is an appendix of their songs and recordings.

833. ------ "Les chansonnières au Québec, 1960-76." *Les cahiers de l'ARMuQ* 12 (avril 1990): 18-47. ISSN 0821-1817.

An outline of popular Québec female singers, with lists of songs by composer, discography, bibliography. This article is taken from chapter 5 of no.832.

834. Whidden, Lynn. "'How can you dance to Beethoven?': Native People and country music." *Canadian University Music*

Review/Revue de musique des universités canadiennes 5 (1984): 87-103.

In order to consider the pervasive popularity of country music in native society, during 1980-82 the author observed several native groups, mainly Cree and Sioux, in Manitoba. Some suggestions are advanced to explain this popularity, and to place the repertoire in a cultural context.

835. Wright, Robert A. "'Dream, comfort, memory, despair': Canadian popular musicians and the dilemma of nationalism, 1968-1972." *Journal of Canadian Studies* 22/4 (Winter, 1978-88): 27-43. Reprinted in *Canadian music: issues of hegemony and identity*, pp.283-301. Eds. Beverley Diamond and Robert Witmer. Toronto: Canadian Scholars' Press, 1994. ISBN 1-55130-031-1.

The author argues that, despite a coolness to the idea of Canadian nationalism on the part of some major performers, there was nevertheless a maturing of English-Canadian popular music just after the centennial of Confederation in 1967. An important influence was, ironically, American folk-protest music and the involvement of Canadians in it.

836. Yorke, Ritchie. *Axes, chops & hot licks: the Canadian rock music scene*. Edmonton: M.G. Hurtig Ltd., 1971. xii, 224p. ISBN 0-88830-052-2.

In 1970, a regulation came into effect that required Canadian radio stations to programme Canadian works as at least thirty per cent of their broadcast content between 6 AM and midnight. The author sees this as the beginning of vastly increased activity in Canadian popular music. The book is built on a series of short essays about bands and individual musicians, based on interviews and the author's experience. The style is brash, but there is a fine sense of the mood of the time, and a good deal of information about the recording and promotion of popular music in Canada.

Education

Music has a significant place in Canadian educational research. Most study, however, has been pedagogical in focus, and while the material of the study may be Canadian, the results are not primarily local in their applications. For this reason, the following list does not include such pedagogical items. The titles given here represent work that is historical or speculative in intention, and which contributes to the broader sense of music in Canada. The definitive historical survey is Green and Vogan (no.852).

In the *Introduction*, mention was made of bibliographic projects that list theses (p.xi), a category in which a very large number of pedagogical studies appear. The John Adaskin Project, which is a project to develop educational repertoire, is discussed in the introduction to *Bibliographies and Lists* (p.13), and the reader is referred to those remarks. The Canadian Music Education Research Centre, at the Faculty of Music, University of Toronto, has a continuing collection of theses in music education which are by no means confined to Canadian subject or origin, but the collection does contain many studies related to Canada, and includes titles of pedagogical interest that are omitted from the following list.

The principal journal is this field is the *Canadian Music Educator/Le musicien éducateur au Canada* (1959-), which is directed to school educators. A similar journal directed to private teachers outside the school systems is *Music News* (1990-), which continues the earlier *Newsletter* of the Canadian Federation of Music Teachers' Associations. *Recherche en éducation musicale au Québec* (1982-) is published annually by l'Université Laval; a summary of contents by volume, 1-13, appears in volume 14 (January 1996).

837.Adaskin, Harry. "Music and the University." *Royal Architectural Institute of Canada Journal* 32/9 (September, 1955): 349-51. (reprinted in *The Canadian Music Journal* 1/1 (Autumn 1956): 30-37.)

A personal and very general reflection by a notable performer and teacher on the need to educate audiences. No philosophical position is advanced, nor is there any analysis of the current situation regarding universities and music.

838.Bartel, Lee R. and Patricia Martin Shand. "Canadian music in the school curriculum: illusion or reality?" In *Taking a stand: essays in honour of John Beckwith*, pp.125-145. Ed. T. McGee. Toronto: University of Toronto Press, 1995. ISBN 0-8020-0583-7.

The authors review various projects since the 1960s to promote Canadian music in schools. They then report on an analysis of provincial music curricula published 1980-90 to determine the extent of Canadian repertoire and content in educational policy. Many tables, and a bibliography of music curriculum documents.

839.Bell, Leslie. "The failure of music appreciation." *The Canadian Music Journal* 2/3 (Spring 1958): 20-27.

The author examines the music appreciation courses in Ontario elementary and secondary schools in the mid-1950s and finds them wanting in their emphasis on facts over listening, and limiting in the projection of a narrow, conventional and often prosaic view of music. For the period, Bell's opinions cound be considered radical.

840.Bellingham, Bruce A. "Canadian higher education in music: a view from a distance." *Canadian Association of University Schools of Music Journal* 6 (Spring, 1976): 81-96.

A somewhat superficial survey of university music programs, and their staff and student distributions by specialization. Nevertheless, it does provide a résumé of the situation just at the point that preceded a period of great expansion and development.

841.Bouchard, Claire. "L'enseignement musical au Saguenay-Lac-Saint-Jean: premier mouvement." *Les cahiers de l'ARMuQ* 14 (mai 1992): 28-41. ISSN 0821-1817.

The author traces the development in musical training in the district of Saguenay-Lac-Saint-Jean, from the arrival of religious communities in 1864 to the reform of Québec education in the 1960s.

842.Carlisle, Roxane C. "The current ethnomusicology curriculum in Canadian universities." *Ethnomusicology* 16/3 (September, 1972): 488-98.

This survey, now greatly out of date, serves only to show how little attention was given to ethnomusicology in Canadian universities in 1972. Many of the courses mentioned are, moreover, on Canadian music history, not specifically ethnomusicological.

843.*Conference on music in the schools of the Atlantic Provinces.* Sackville, N.B.: Mount Allison University, 1960 (mimeographed). 42f.

Exploratory in nature, the conference considered current situations in teaching and training as well as future possibilities. Much of the discussion is general or philosophical in nature, but there is also a comprehensive view of school music in the Atlantic provinces at the end of the 1950s

844.*Contemporary music and audiences/La musique contemporaire (sic) et le public.* conference report. Canadian Music Council, 1969. 77p.

Ten short addresses and synopses of three panel discussion about the problems of educating and engaging audiences in the presentation of new music.

845.Cooke, Richard W. "Competition festivals." In *Music in Canada*, pp.198-207. Ernest MacMillan, ed. Toronto: University of Toronto Press, 1955.

This essay is mostly interesting for its unquestioning support of the competitive festival in Canada and the satisfaction with close association with Great Britain. There is some information on the origins of the movement, both in Britain and in Canada.

846."Courses in composition and Canadian composers." *Le Compositeur Canadien/The Canadian Composer* 4 (December, 1965) 20-1, 31, 42, 46; 5 (January, 1966) 20-21; 6 (February, 1966) 38-39; 7 (March, 1966) 6-7, 41; 8 (April, 1966) 6.

The magazine asked seventy-two schools in Canada for information about courses in composition and the place of Canadian compositions in the curriculum. The twenty-eight responses are reprinted. Many of the replies are very brief, the responses as a whole projecting a rather bleak picture of Canadian-related music education in the 1960s.

847.Davey, Earl. "The development of music curricula at the University of Toronto, 1918-68." MA dissertation, University of Toronto, Ontario Institute for Studies in Education (1977). v, 151f.

Davey examines the evolution from an English model to a modern music school in the North American style of a Faculty that served as a reference point for the development of most other university music schools in Canada. He notes especially the changes that followed from the introduction of the School Music programme in 1946 and the reorganization of the General course in 1952.

848.------ "The development of music programmes in English-language universities in Central and Eastern Canada, 1960 to 1969." PhD dissertation, University of Toronto, Ontario Institute for Studies in Education, 1983. 317f.

In 1960, the major enrolments in Canadian university music schools was at Acadia, Mount Allison, McGill, Toronto and Western Ontario universities. This remained the case in 1969, but by then enrolment had increased six-fold, and it was a decade of unprecedented expansion elsewhere. The author provides a short historical background, and analyses of programmes and changes in requirements and staffing over the decade.

849.*L'enseignement de la musique au Québec à l'heure du rapport parent.* Québec: Les Presses de l'université Laval, 1965. 103f.

This is essentially a policy paper and set of recommendations formulated by a group of members of the Faculty of Music, l'Université Laval, at a time when education was undergoing extensive examination and change in Québec.

850. Fenwick, G. Roy. *The function of music in education: incorporating a history of school music in Ontario.* Toronto: W.J. Gage, 1951. v, 89p.

Much of the book is about general principles of music education. Despite the title, there is little historical information. There is some interest in the fact that there is discussion about education in Ontario in the period 1935-50, based on the author's experience as Director of Music for the Ontario Department of Education.

851. ------ "Music in the schools." In *Music in Canada*, pp.146-157. Ernest MacMillan, ed. Toronto: University of Toronto Press, 1955.

Only the most cursory examination of music in public school systems across the country is possible in so short an essay, which in any case gives the most attention to Ontario.

852. Green, J. Paul and Nancy F. Vogan. *Music education in Canada: a historical account.* Toronto: University of Toronto Press, 1991. xvi, 30 plates, 534p. ISBN 0-8020-5891-4.

This comprehensive survey of musical education at all levels is organized around regions and set out in three large sections: on patterns developed in the 19th and early 20th centuries; developments during the 1920s and 1930s; developments after 1945. Despite the complexity of the topic, there is a remarkable amount of detailed information, not only about educational systems but also about related organizations. Extensive annotations; bibliography.

853. Grégoire-Reid, Claire. "Les Manuels canadiens de théorie musicale publiés au Québec entre 1811 et 1911." *Les cahiers de l'ARMuQ* 10 (juin 1988): 58-73. ISSN 0821-1817.

A comparative survey of twenty-four music manuals published in Québec. Little detailed information is given about the contents, but sufficient to obtain some idea of the materials in each item. List of titles by date.

854. Haig, Alastair P. "Henry Frost, pioneer (1816-1851)." *The Canadian Music Journal* 2/2 (Winter 1958): 35-40.

Frost was a school teacher in York County, near Toronto, who produced a set of twelve manuals for instruction in musical rudiments. There is very little information given about Frost or his manuals, but a few samples of the material are reproduced.

855. Haughton, Harry. "Music as social and cultural reproduction: a sociological analysis of educational processes in Ontario schools." *Canadian University Music Review/Revue de musique des universités canadiennes* 5 (1984): 38-59.

Using the results of research in the Ontario school system, the author argues that the music curriculum projects and is determined by certain established social and cultural norms. The rigidity of official regulations inhibits the kind of musical instruction that is given, and ignores the possibilities in the varied backgrounds of many students.

856. *The John Adaskin Project.* Report on the policy conference. Toronto: Canadian Music Centre, 1967. 145p.

A record of addresses and discussion about methods and philosophies relating to the teaching of music in elementary and secondary schools.

857. Jones, Gaynor G. "'Exam wars' and the Toronto territorial connection." *Canadian University Music Review/Revue de musique des universités canadiennes* 11/2 (1991): 51-67.

When the University of Trinity College, Toronto, offered *in absentia* MusBac degrees in London in the 1880s, a fierce controversy broke out between rival parties in England and Canada that involved some of the most important musicians in both countries. This article presents the details of the controversy and its musical, commercial and even political undertones.

858. Jorgensen, Estelle R. "Selected indexes of the academic and professional preparation of music supervisors in Canada." *Journal*

of Research in Music Education 28 (1980): 92-102. Reprinted in *A cross-section of research in music education*. Stephen H. Barnes, ed. Washington, D.C.: University Press of America, 1982. Pp. 128-45.

The information is based on a national questionnaire circulated in January, 1977, which had a 43.2% response. Statistical analysis is used to develop a profile of music supervisors, which revealed a large degree of homogeneity across Canada, but also a frequent discrepancy between theory and practice of what was required of supervisors.

859. Kemp, Walter H. *To listen and to teach*. A report on the professional circumstances, activities and taste of the private music teacher in Ontario: commissioned by the Ontario Registered Music Teachers' Association, Toronto, 1976. 66f.

Primarily statistical in its investigation and report, this study provides a profile of the background, training, teaching approaches, and tastes of private music teachers in Ontario.

860. Lambert, R.S. "Music in school broadcasting." In *Music in Canada*, pp.153-157. Ernest MacMillan, ed. Toronto: University of Toronto Press, 1955.

In spite of the brevity of the essay, there is some sense of the organization and content of a widely heard system of radio broadcasts directed to Canadian elementary schools in the 1940s and 1950s.

861. MacMillan, Sir Ernest. "Music in Canadian universities." *The Canadian Music Journal* 2/3 (Spring 1958): 3-11.

At a time when professional music training in Canadian universities was still relatively rare, MacMillan argues that only in the universities can the standards and seriousness of study be accomplished to the degree then needed in the country.

862. Mazzoleni, Ettore. "Music teaching in Canada." Music Teachers National Association *Proceedings* 40 (1946): 94-100.

A very general statement about the chief conservatory and university schools then (1940s) operating, with nothing about philosophies, methods or curricula.

863. Morey, Carl. "Musical education in nineteenth-century Toronto." In *Taking a stand: essays in honour of John Beckwith*, pp.113-124. T. McGee, ed. Toronto: University of Toronto Press, 1995. ISBN 0-8020-0583-7.

A review of the foundations of all aspects of musical training that were established in Toronto during the 19th century, both privately and in public and specialized schools.

864. Morgan, Kit. "Lloyd Burritt: electronic music." *Le Compositeur Canadien/The Canadian Composer* 55 (December 1970): 4-9.

There is some information on Burritt's activities as a composer, but much of the interest is in Burritt's discussion of his use of electronic music in his elementary school teaching in Vancouver.

865 *Music education and the Canadians of tomorrow*. conference report, Canadian Music Council, 1968. 75p.

Fifteen short addresses that survey music education regionally throughout Canada, along with reports from Denmark and Sweden.

866. Payzant, Geoffrey. "The competitive music festivals." *The Canadian Music Journal* 4/3 (Spring 1960): 35-46.

Competitive music festivals annually engaged hundreds of thousands of young musicians, but by the late 1950s serious doubts were being voiced about their real usefulness. Payzant examines the situation from several points of view, mainly sympathetically, but primarily to help generate thoughtful discussion.

867. Peaker, Charles. "Canadian competitive musical festivals." Music Teachers National Association *Proceedings* 40 (1946): 113-117.

A positive review of the festival movement at what was probably its peak of popularity in the 1930s and 1940s.

868. *The Pros and cons of the festival movement in Canada.* conference report, Canadian Music Council, 1965 (irregular pagination; reproduced typescript).

A synopsis of discussions and panels reflecting various points of view about the competitive music festival. Includes addresses by Boyd Neel and Richard Johnston.

869. Rouleau, Jocelyne, ed. *Who teaches what in the arts/Qui enseigne quoi en arts.* Ottawa: Canadian Conference of the Arts, for the Department of Communications, 1989. iii, 328p. ISBN 0-920007-26-0.

A directory of post-secondary institutions with programs in the arts, with basic information about admission criteria, duration, etc. Index enables user to isolate music (and other) programs. Information in French or English as appropriate to the institution.

870. Trowsdale, George Campbell. "A history of public school music in Ontario." EdD dissertation, University of Toronto, 1962. 2 vols. xviii, 566f.

This is an exhaustive study of methods and policies in public education from 1846 to 1960 in elementary schools. As well as curricular matters, the training and certification of teachers is also examined. The extensive bibliography is especially useful for periodical items. There is a list of archival and unpublished material.

871. ------ "Music and performing arts institutions in public education: the Toronto experience, 1962-1969." *Canadian Association of University Schools of Music Journal* 7 (1977): 106-57.

The attempt to establish a high school of music, or of the performing arts, in Toronto during the late 1960s brought into conflict opposing philosophies of public education and training in the arts. While some sectors were supportive, others were hostile. This analysis traces carefully all aspects of what was ultimately an unsuccessful project, with extensive documentation of the many reports and opinions.

872. ------ "Vocal Music in the Common Schools of Upper Canada." *Journal of Research in Music Education* 18/4 (1970): 340-54.

After an account of the place of music in the schools of Upper Canada (Ontario) in the early part of the 19th century, the author examines the development of vocal music instruction under the aegis of Egerton Ryerson, who was appointed the first Chief Superintendent of education in the Province in 1844.

873. Trudeau, Nicole. "L'éducation musicale à l'école québécoise et à l'école française: ce que nous en rélèvent les programmes." *Les cahiers de l'ARMuQ* 6 (septembre 1985): 28-37. ISSN 0821-1817.

The preparation of teachers, as well as the general content of public music teaching, is discussed through a comparison of French and Québec systems of education. Nothing is said of the possible influence of other Canadian or of American models on the Québec systems.

874. Vogan, Nancy Fraser. "The history of public school music in the Province of New Brunswick, 1872-1939." PhD diss., Eastman School of Music, University of Rochester, 1979. x, 323f.

The focus is on the cities of Moncton, Fredericton and Saint John. In 1872, free non-sectarian schools were established; in 1939 a new programme of studies was issued that included music. The thesis examines the development of music in the educational systems between these two events. There are extensive quotations from reports and other documents, and many facsimiles of reports, programmes and instructional materials. The bibliography includes a useful list of theses and unpublished studies.

875. ------ "Music instruction in Nova Scotia before 1914." In *Musical Canada: words and music honouring Helmut Kallmann*, pp.71-78. J. Beckwith and F. Hall, eds. Toronto: University of Toronto Press, 1988. ISBN 0-8020-5759-4.

A survey of musical training, both private and public, throughout Nova Scotia from the 18th century to the early 20th century.

876. Walter, Arnold. "Education in music." In *Music in Canada*, pp.133-145. Ernest MacMillan, ed. Toronto: University of Toronto Press, 1955.

A vaguely philosophical essay that mentions several Canadian situations, viewed within a larger context, but not informative.

877.------ "The growth of music education." In *Aspects of music in Canada*, pp.247-287. A. Walter,ed. Toronto. University of Toronto Press, 1969. ISBN 8020-1536-0.

While the essay provides some information and a general overview of musical education, the author rambles over much quasi-philosophical material, with an occasional statement based on error. To be read with caution.

Media

The Canadian Broadcasting Corporation/Radio Canada, and the National Film Board are arguably the most widely influential musical bodies in Canada. The CBC originated in 1932, and the NFB was set up in 1939. If activities for both organizations have diminished in the 1990s, it remains the case that each has commissioned hundreds of original works, if not thousands, for concerts, broadcast dramas, and films. The CBC moreover has been the principal disseminator of music through broadcasting throughout the country. It is surprising that neither organization has been subject to careful study from a musical point of view, with the result that despite the richness of the field, there are few titles that relate to it.

Recording has had an erratic history, the earlier part of which is chronicled by Moogk (no.883). A number of small commercial studios have issued recordings, but there is no fully dependable source of information about them, although *Canadiana* (no.36) has listed sound recordings since 1970. The Canadian Broadcasting Corporation and the Canadian Music Centre both have fairly extensive catalogues of recordings. The CBC catalogue can be obtained at: CBC Records, PO Box 500, Station A, Toronto, Ont., M5W 1E6. The CMC can be contacted online at: http://www.ffa.ucalgary.ca/cmc/.

1. Radio and Recording

878.Beaudet, Jean-Marie. "Broadcasting in Canada." Music Teachers National Association *Proceedings* 40 (1946): 107-112.

A sketch of the broadcasting system (Canadian Broadcasting Corporation), and examples of some CBC programming.

879.Beckwith, John. "Recordings." In *Music in Canada*, pp.158-166. Ernest MacMillan, ed. Toronto: University of Toronto Press, 1955.

This review, although brief, of the activity of Canadians in recordings contains much information, chiefly about individual artists who have recorded, but also about new (1950s) projects to develop an indigenous recording industry.

880.Bell, Leslie. "An experiment in network broadcasting." *The Canadian Music Journal* 5/2 (Winter, 1961): 13-19.

In April 1960 the Canadian Broadcasting Corporation initiated an 18-month period of network FM radio broadcasting. This article reviews some of the advantages and difficulties of the system, and the response to the CBC's plan.

881.Drolet, Roger. "Société sonore et marchandisation de la culture: l'enregistrement musical au Québec." MA dissertation, Université Laval, 1986. v, 175f.

This consideration of the production and consumption of recorded popular music is sometimes speculative but perceptive. There is a survey of one day of broadcasting at two Montréal radio stations, and the discussion engages the idea of the market versus the symbolic value of the music and the recording of it, particularly in reference to Québec within the context of Canada, and Canada within North America.

882.Kellogg, Patricia. "Sounds in the wilderness: fifty years of CBC commissions." In *Musical Canada: words and music honouring Helmut Kallmann*, pp.239-261. J. Beckwith and F. Hall, eds. Toronto: University of Toronto Press, 1988. ISBN 0-8020-5759-4.

The Canadian Broadcasting Corporation compiled a catalogue (unpublished) of works commissioned for radio from 1939 to 1986. This provides the basis for the present article, which documents the evolution of CBC commissioning -- policies, influences, results.

883.Moogk, Edward B. *Roll back the years: history of Canadian recorded sound and its legacy.* Ottawa: National Library of Canada, 1975. reprinted 1980. xii, 444p. ISBN 0-660-01382-7. In French as *En remontant les années: l'histoire et l'héritage de l'enregistrement sonore au Canada, des débuts à 1930.* Ottawa: Bibliothèque nationale du Canada,1975.

The history of sound recording in Canada is traced up to 1930. About half the book is devoted to discographies of Canadian-related recordings (artists, composers, etc.). A phonodisc that was included with the original issue was not part of the reprinting.

884.*Music and Media.* conference report, Canadian Music Council, 1967. 66p.

Twelve short addresses, and brief synopses of panel discussions, but not well-focused; the contributors clearly lack experience with the still relatively new medium of television.

885.Roberts, John. "Communications media." In *Aspects of music in Canada*, pp.167-246. A. Walter,ed. Toronto. University of Toronto Press, 1969. ISBN 8020-1536-0.

Most of the essay is given to a year-by-year account of highlights in radio programming by the Canadian Broadcasting Corporation, from 1945 to 1966. CBC television is also discussed, as is recording. Private broadcasting is also mentioned.

886.Robertson, Alex. *Canadian Compo numericals.* Pointe Claire, Qué.: mimeographed, 1978. v, 82p.

The Compo Company, of Montréal, issued popular music recordings on various labels. This compilation, listed by label and by number, includes issues from 1929 to 1942. No indexes.

887.*Sound recordings and the federal government/Le gouvernement fédéral et l'enregistrement sonore*. Ottawa: Minister of Supply and Services Canada, 1990. 26/26p. ISBN 0-662-57346-3.

   A guide to the Sound Recording Development Program, set up in 1986, to assist the production and marketing of Canadian musical products. Primarily a list of offices and addresses.

888.Waddington, Geoffrey. "Music and radio." In *Music in Canada*, pp.126-132. Ernest MacMillan, ed. Toronto: University of Toronto Press, 1955.

   The author, who was Musical Director of the Canadian Broadcasting Corporation, makes some important points about the origins of broadcasting in Canada, and presents briefly the main involvement of the CBC in music performance broadcasting in the 1950s.

889.Winters, Kenneth. "Towards the 'one justifiable end': six discs." In *Musical Canada: words and music honouring Helmut Kallmann*, pp.286-297. J. Beckwith and F. Hall, eds. Toronto: University of Toronto Press, 1988. ISBN 0-8020-5759-4.

   In an unusual essay, Winters contemplates the problems of acceptance of contemporary music by Canadians. The basis of his reflections is six recordings, from which he ranges over questions of composition, composers, performers, and recording itself.

2. Television and Film

890.Applebaum, Louis. "Film music." In *Music in Canada*, pp.167-176. Ernest MacMillan, ed. Toronto: University of Toronto Press, 1955.

   After a brief background to the development of documentary film making, the essay concentrates on activity at the National Film Board, since there was little film music written in Canada except for the Board. Part of the essay is given to a description of the process of developing and recording a film score.

891.------ "The paradox and puzzle of music on Canadian television." *Le Compositeur Canadien/The Canadian Composer* 137 (January, 1979): 18-23, 44-45.

The author examines from a personal perspective the paucity of serious music broadcasting on television and raises some questions about what form such broadcasting might take.

892.Spurgeon, C. Paul. *Musical scores, film and video media and the Canadian composer: facts to consider/Réflections sur la composition de musique pour le cinéma et la vidéo.* [Toronto]: Composers, Authors and Publishers Association of Canada, Limited [1982]. 14/14p.

A short guide by a legal staff member of CAPAC on questions of copyright, fees, contracts, etc. for agreements between composers and producers of films and videos.

Commerce

The first of the following three sections contains items that touch mostly on legal aspects of music in Canada, such as questions of contract and performance rights (see also Spurgeon, no.892). The literature on such subjects is not extensive outside technical considerations of such complex matters as copyright, but the items given here provide some access to practical matters that affect the business of music. The remaining two sections on publishing and instruments are more in keeping with the historical view that informs most of this *Guide*. A related item on instruments will be found in Cselenyi (no.98).

1. General

893. "CAPAC's first quarter century: pioneer years." *Le Compositeur Canadien/The Canadian Composer* 105 (November 1975): 24-33.

The article covers the period 1925-1950 when there was much activity to establish performance rights legislation and related questions of copyright. The is also a "financial footnote" that gives basic fees and income figures for the years 1968-74. CAPAC was a performing rights organization (Composers, Authors and Publishers Association of Canada).

894. MacMillan, Keith. "Of music, money and better mousetraps: the performing rights agencies of Canada." In *Célébration*, pp.108-116. G. Ridout and T. Kenins, eds. Toronto: Canadian Music Centre/Centre de musique canadienne, 1984. ISBN 0-9690836-5-3.

This rather chatty account of performing rights organizations provides some background, but primarily it describes then current activities of CAPAC and BMI/P.R.O. Canada, including their relationships to the Canadian Music Centre. Performance, recording, publication, and promotion are all briefly treated.

895.Sanderson, Paul. *Musicians and the law in Canada*. [Scarborough, Ont.]: Carswell, 1992. 2nd. revised edition. xli, 507p. ISBN 0-459-56780-2.

The author attempts to review all aspects of Canadian common law that touch on the business matters that relate to musicians and music, as of March 1, 1992. Subjects are divided and subdivided so as to provide access to particular situations. In the appendices are sample forms and checklists. Although intended as a guide for professional musicians, the book provides a digest in non-technical language of Canadian common law as it relates to the music business. Extensive bibliography.

896.*A selective bibliography of Canadian and international readings in arts administration and cultural development*. [Toronto], Canadian Conference of the Arts, 1974. 24 leaves.

A list of English-language material compiled for use in the Programme in Arts Administration at York University (Toronto). Although very little is directly concerned with music, the list is useful for general subjects such as administration, funding and policy development. About half the titles are Canadian.

897.*SOCAN facts: a guide for composers, authors and music publishers*. [Don Mills, Ont.]: Society of Composers, Authors and Music Publishers of Canada, 1980. 12p.

A layman's guide to performing rights in Canada, in non-technical language; very basic information on such questions as copyright, royalties, membership in the Society.

2. Publishing

898.Calderisi Bryce, Maria. "John Lovell (1810-93) Montreal Music Printer and Publisher." In *Musical Canada: words and music honouring Helmut Kallmann*, pp.79-96. J. Beckwith and F. Hall, eds. Toronto: University of Toronto Press, 1988. ISBN 0-8020-5759-4.

There is a résumé of the life and activities of the enterprising Lovell, with lists of the known and reported imprints by him. The lists comprise "sheet music" and "books and pamphlets", the latter being mostly publications of music.

899.------ *Music publishing in the Canadas, 1800-1867/L'édition musicale au Canada, 1800-1867*. Ottawa: National Library of Canada, 1981. 128/124p. ISBN 0-660-50454-5.

A highly informative history of music publishing in Canada, which touches on engraving and copyright as well as publication, is followed by lists of various kinds of publications that contained music and a checklist of A.&S. Nordheimer plate numbers. Bibliography and index. French and English versions bound together.

900.------ "La politique et l'édition musicale avant 1867." *Les cahiers de l'ARMuQ* 6 (septembre 1985): 2-13.

John Neilson and Napoléon Aubin were politically-minded newspaper publishers at a time of political upheaval in Canada in the early 19th century. They were also important in the new trade of music publishing. Illustrations.

901."Canadian Music Sales promotes Canadian compositions." *Le Compositeur Canadien/The Canadian Composer* 9 (May, 1966): 16-17, 42-43.

A very general survey of the activity of the publisher, Canadian Music Sales, which was established in 1932.

902."Frederick Harris Music lists largest inventory." *Le Compositeur Canadien/The Canadian Composer* 7 (March 1966): 16-17, 42-43,44, 46.

An outline of the history of the business that Frederick Harris founded in England in 1910, and the Canadian company that he opened in 1912.

903.Galaise, Sophie. "Chronique de l'édition de musique contemporaine québécoise (1945-1992)." *Les cahiers de l'ARMuQ* 15 (mai, 1994): 18-26. ISSN 0821-1817.

A list, with short annotations, of publishers and other organizations in Québec that issue classical contemporary music, not pop music.

904.Gilpin, Wayne. *Sunset on the St. Lawrence: a history of the Frederick Harris Music Co., Limited 1904-1984*. Oakville, Ont.: The Frederick Harris Music Co., Limited, 1984. [v], 136p. ISBN 0-88797-147-4 (bound)/0-88797-266-8 (pbk.).

This is very much an "in-house" history that recounts the successes and lists a great many of the publications of the company. Disputes over copyright are discussed, and there is some biographical material about Harris. No index.

3. Instruments

905.Bégin, Carmelle. *Opus: the making of musical instruments in Canada*. Hull, Qué.: Canadian Museum of Civilization, 1992. 148p. ISBN 0-660-14006-3. In French as *Opus, la facture instrumentale au Canada*.

Over 100 modern instruments of all kinds are the subject of this book. There are notes on the instruments and their makers, and many photographs. A selected bibliography by Kevin James lists many items about instrument makers in Canada in the period 1971-1991.

906. Conquer, Thérèse. "Hubert Bédard: À la recherche des sons d'antan." *Les Cahiers canadiens de musique/The Canada Music Book* 8 (Printemps/été 1974): 53-60.

The Ottawa-born Bédard (d.1989) was an important restorer and builder of harpsichords and clavichords, chiefly in France.

907. Dufourcq, Norbert. "Au Canada: Beckerath et Casavant." *L'Orgue* 102 (1962): 38-44.

A review of recent organs, with specifications, in Montréal, Québec City, and Saint-Hyacinthe, including the first Casavant tracker organ.

908. Dufourcq, Norbert and Antoine Bouchard. "Quelques instruments canadiens." *L'Orgue* 118 (1966): 80-86.

A review of recent (1960s) organs, with specifications, in Québec.

909. Huot, Cécile. "Rosario Bayeur, luthier, 1875-1944." *Les Cahiers canadien de musique/The Canada Music Book* 9 (Automne/hiver 1974): 53-64.

Bayeur was a cabinet-maker by trade who developed a skill as a violin maker in the 1920s. His reputation was established after winning sixth prize in a contest in Paris in 1921.

910. *Instrument makers*. Burnaby B.C.: The Burnaby Art Gallery, 1974. n.p.

This catalogue of an exhibition at the Burnaby Art Gallery of instruments by British Columbia makers includes a number of photographs, and a list of the instruments in the display. Most of the instruments are modern versions of historical instruments.

911.Kallmann, Helmut. *Canadian-built 19th century musical instruments: a checklist.* 2nd edition, revised. Edmonton: Edmonton Public Library, 1966. [6f.]

Brief and incomplete, this list has interest as a first attempt to establish a list of surviving musical instruments built in Canada before 1900.

912.Kelly, Wayne. *Downright upright: a history of the Canadian piano industry.* Toronto: Natural Heritage/Natural History Inc., 1991. 160p. ISBN 0-920474-60-8.

Historical information is provided for most of the major manufacturers, with notes on all known brand- and stencil-name Canadian pianos. Where known, serial numbers are given.

913.Lichtenwanger, William, comp. *A survey of musical instrument collections in the United States and Canada.* Ann Arbor: Music Library Association, 1974. xi, 137p. ISBN 0-914954-00-8(bound)/0-914954-01-6(pbk.).

The number of Canadian entries is small but nonetheless useful in its inclusion of collections that might be overlooked.

914.Steed, Graham. "The rebuilding of Christ Church Cathedral organ, Victoria, British Columbia." *The Canadian Music Journal* 2/4 (Summer 1958): 27-33.

A short description of the rebuilding of the organ in 1957 is preceded by a review of earlier organs in Victoria, with specifications of instruments built in 1862 and 1872.

Periodicals

The entry "Periodicals" in the *Encyclopedia of music in Canada* (no.10-13) lists about 550 titles of music periodicals and periodicals that included significant musical coverage, from the colonial period up to the 1990s, and provides the best overview of musical journals in Canada. Its listing, however, is alphabetical by title, and consequently gives no indication of specialization, or of concentration of publishing in place or time. One of the abiding characteristics of Canadian music journals has been brevity of publication life, especially those journals directed to the profession and which include material of some technical level. While in the 1990s there are numerous musical publications (see McMorrow no.918), in a research guide such as this one there seems to be limited value in listing them without also considering important periodicals of the past. The number of entries in the *EMC*·indicates the difficulty and the magnitude of such a task. The list below, therefore, is short, and confined to bibliographies of periodicals, but it should allow a researcher to trace titles of journals both active and defunct.

Locating copies of periodicals is sometimes difficult since many survive only in a very limited number of copies, widely dispersed among libraries. The *Union list* (no.917) should be helpful in locating copies. Attention is also drawn to the CIHM/ICMH project (no.915), which, in the mid-1990s, is still in a stage of development but which will make available microform copies of 19th century periodicals.

Locating material in early publications can be achieved only through bibliographical location of an article title, since no comprehensive indexes exist. Material in major periodicals of recent and current publication is indexed in *Canadian index*

(no.33) and *Canadian periodical index* (no.34). Several Canadian
periodicals are also included in *The Music index* (Detroit:
Information Service, 1950-66; Information Coordinators, 1967-86;
Harmonie Park Press, 1988-); and in *RILM abstracts of music
literature* (Répertoire international de littérature musicale)(1967-)
For two specialized indexes, see Keillor, no.56, 57.

915.*Catalogue   of   periodicals   in   CIHM's   microfiche
    collection/Catalogue des périodiques dans la collection de
    microfiches de l'ICMH*. Ottawa: Canadian Institute for Historical
    Microreproductions/Institut   canadien   de   microreproductions
    historiques, 1994. [iv], 84p.

The CIHM/ICMH project will make available in microform
all Canadian periodicals published in the period 1800-1900. This
interim catalogue of items completed up to 1994 lists titles
alphabetically, with no cross-indexing. See also no.31.

916.Kallmann, Helmut. "A century of musical periodicals in Canada."
    The Canadian Music Journal 1/1 (Autumn 1956): 37-43; 1/2
    (Winter 1957): 25-36.

A narrative survey of musical periodicals published in Canada
from the mid-19th century up to 1955 is followed by a check-list
of seventy-five titles. Dates of publication are given, and libraries
that include a title in their holdings.

917.Lewis, Larry C., ed. *Union list of music periodicals in Canadian
    libraries/Inventaire des publications en série sur la musique dans
    les bibliotèques canadiennes*. 2nd. edition. Ottawa: Canadian
    Association of Music Libraries, 1981. [vi], 293p. ISBN 0-
    9690583-0-6.

This second edition is a revision of an earlier publication of
1964 and a 1967 supplement. Periodicals are listed by title without
further indexing or cross-reference. There are 1783 titles which
were held in 45 participating libraries. While the list is one of
periodicals of all national origins, it is virtually the only source for
locating Canadian music periodicals.

918.McMorrow, Kathleen. "Music periodicals in Canada." *Fontes Artis Musicae* 34/4 (1987) 250-54.

An annotated list, with commentary, of journals, newsletters, house organs, etc., currently (1987) issued in Canada.

Archives and Collections

Two issues of *Fontes Artis Musicae* (the journal of the International Association of Music Libraries) have been devoted largely to Canadian collections and bibliography: 34/4 (1987), and 41/1 (1994). The 1987 issue is particularly interesting for its twenty-two articles, most of them brief, that provide an excellent broad survey of libraries and specialized activity across Canada. The 1994 issue consists of six specialized articles, four of which are relevant to Canadian studies and are indexed individually in this present *Research Guide*.

The first issue of *Les cahiers de l'ARMuQ* (avril 1983) (the journal of the Association pour l'avancement de la recherche en musique du Québec) is comprised of several reports on the collections of the National Library of Canada, les Archives du Québec, and la Bibliothèque nationale du Québec. Provincial government archives often contain music-related items, and various university libraries also have specialized archival collections, but there is no comprehensive guide to their musical contents. Several items listed below provide information on numerous archives throughout the country.

Attention is directed to an earlier reference to on-line access to the Canadian Association of Music Libraries, p.3. The reader should also refer to the sections *Catalogues and Directories* and *Bibliographies and Lists*.

919. *Directory of Canadian archives/Annuaire des dépôts d'archives canadiens*. Bureau of Canadian Archivists, Bureau canadien des archivistes, Association of Canadian Archivists, Association des archivistes du Québec. n.d. 130p. ISBN 0-9690797-1-0.

An up-dating of the 1977 publication *Directory of Canadian records and manuscript repositories.* Addresses and brief notes on national, provincial, and local archives, both public and private. Indexes of repositories by geographical location, and by subject.

920.Barriault, Jeannine. "Les Archives musicales au Canada." *Fontes Artis Musicae* 41/1 (1994): 32-39.

Archival collections outside the National Library are surveyed, with no intention of completeness but as an indication of other resources. There is a short list of guides to archival collections in Canada.

921.Barriault, Jeannine and Stéphane Jean. *Catalogue of the archival fonds and collections of the Music Division/Catalogue des fonds et collections d'archives de la Division de la musique.* Ottawa: National Library of Canada, Music Division, 1994. xiv, 109/xiv, 115p. ISBN 0-660-59086-7.

At the time of publication, the Music Division of the National Library housed 229 fonds and three collections. The items are listed alphabetically, with short descriptive notes. There is an index of names. This is the largest documentary collection relating to Canadian music, both historical and contemporary.

922.*Directory of music resources in the Pacific Northwest,* compiled by the Pacific Northwest Chapter of the Music Library Association. Nov. 1985. vi, 136p.

A list of twenty-two archives, museums and collections in British Columbia that have some musical materials.

923.Bolduc, Anicette. "Catalogue collectif des archives musicales au Québec." *Les cahiers de l'ARMuQ* 9 (mai 1988): 1-127. ISSN 0821-1817.

The catalogue describes about 300 collections of musical items in sixty-one archives in the Province of Québec. There is a brief note on each collection, including reference to a catalogue or article in the literature. The list is by collection, with an index by archive and an index of names.

924. Grégoire-Reid, Claire and Micheline Vézina-Demers. "Exposition au monastère des Ursulines de Québec." *Les cahiers de l'ARMuQ* 8 (mai 1987): 80-85. ISSN 0821-1817.

The Ursulines were the first in Canada to provide musical instruction and to influence musical development. This short catalogue lists about fifty items -- books, printed music, manuscripts -- mostly dating from the 19th century, that represent the extensive archives of the order.

925. *Guide des fonds d'archives musicales du Service des archives de l'Université de Montréal.* Montréal: Université de Montréal, Service des archives, 1988. ii, 33p. ISBN 2-89119-069-6.

There is a description of six fonds housed at the Université de Montréal: Guillaume-Couture; Pierre-Paul; de la Commission diocésaine de musique sacrée de l'Archevêché de Montréal; Léopold-Christin; Serge-Garant; la Faculté de musique. In an introductory section, mention is made of other musical collections in the city of Montréal.

926. Lefebvre, Marie-Thérèse. "Inventaire partiel de la collection Villeneuve de la Faculté de musique de l'Université de Montréal." *Les cahiers de l'ARMuQ* 8 (mai 1987): 51-79. ISSN 0821-1817.

The extensive private collection of Arthur Villeneuve, a provincial civil servant, contains periodicals, books, printed music and manuscripts. This list of titles is confined to items published in Canada or whose authors are Canadian, mostly with a connection to Québec. The material covers the period approximately 1800-1950.

927. *Music resources in Canadian collections/Ressources musicales des bibliothèques canadiennes.* Ottawa: National Library of Canada, 1980. vi, 103p./vi, 108p. ISBN 0-660-50451-0.

A directory of libraries with substantial musical material (not necessarily Canadian) in their collections. There is statistical information, brief descriptions of the collections, addresses, and general information for public, university and other institutional libraries. Printed, manuscript, recorded and filmed sources are surveyed. Although many details are now out of date, nevertheless the publication is valuable as a comprehensive guide to collections and services. In English and French versions, bound together.

928. Poirier, Lucien. "Le fonds musical Dessane de l'Université Laval: compte rendu et état de travaux d'inventaire et de préparation du catalogue des oeuvres musicales entrepris au lendemain de son acquisition." *Les cahiers de l'ARMuQ* 6 (septembre 1985): 22-27. ISSN 0821-1817.

A note on the preparation of a catalogue of the Antoine Dessane collection. Dessane was a prominent 19th-century musician in Québec city.

Indexes

1. Title

2. Authors and Editors

3. Subject